In the Hamptons

ALSO BY DAN RATTINER

Ballet Parking

Dan's Shorts

Who's Here: The Heart of the Hamptons

It's All His Fault (illustrator)

It's All Her Fault (illustrator)

Attack of the Space Creatures

The Eat All You Want and Still Lose Weight Cookbook

Loose Change in the New World

Albert Einstein's Summer Vacation

What to Do When Gravity Fails

In the Hamptons

MY FIFTY YEARS *with* FARMERS, FISHERMEN,

ARTISTS, BILLIONAIRES, *and* CELEBRITIES

DAN RATTINER

THREE RIVERS PRESS
NEW YORK

Published in the United States by Three Rivers Press,
an imprint of the Crown Publishing Group,
a division of Random House, Inc., New York.
www.crownpublishing.com
www.threeriverspress.com

Three Rivers Press and the Tugboat design are registered
trademarks of Random House, Inc.

Originally published in hardcover in the United States by
Crown Publishers, an imprint of the Crown Publishing Group,
a division of Random House, Inc., New York, in 2008.

Library of Congress Cataloging-in-Publication Data
Rattiner, Dan.
    In the Hamptons: my fifty years with farmers, fishermen,
  artists, billionaires, and celebrities / Dan Rattiner.
    1. Rattiner, Dan. 2. Journalists—United States—Biography.
  3. Hamptons (N.Y.)—Social life and customs. I. Title.
  PN4874.R29A3   2008
  974.7'25043092—dc22
  [B]   2008009125

ISBN 978-0-307-38296-2

Printed in the United States of America

Map on pages xvi–xvii by Kelly Merritt and Barbara Sturman

DESIGN BY BARBARA STURMAN

10 9 8 7 6 5 4 3 2 1

First Paperback Edition

To Christine,

who made this book possible

CONTENTS

Foreword by Edward Albee / xi

At the Print Shop / 1

Merton Tyndall / 12

Babette Tweed / 19

Jackson Pollock / 33

Howie Carroll Jr. / 40

Balcomb Greene / 51

Esther and Sarah (and the Rolling Stones) / 59

Russ Corser / 69

John Steinbeck / 76

The Flesh Eaters / 90

Frank Mundus / 97

Uncle Ed / 107

The Ladies Village Improvement Society / 117

Richard Nixon / 124

Saving the Montauk Lighthouse / 130

Bob Kennelly / 143

Lieutenant James Kealy / 152

Willem de Kooning / 165

Frank Tuma Jr. / 173

Cecil Hoge Jr. / 185

Jim Jensen / 195

Speed King / 203

Nonie Self / 221

Ken Scanlon / 234

Bobby Van / 242

Stuyvesant Wainwright II / 258

Saving the Bull's Head Inn / 270

Robert David Lion Gardiner / 281

George Plimpton / 292

Billy Joel / 308

Spalding Gray / 323

Bill Clinton / 332

ACKNOWLEDGMENTS / 345

FOREWORD

D AN Rattiner has lived in "the Hamptons" even longer than I have. It's forty-four years for me now, although on the ocean in Montauk, which many of us who live there do not consider to be a part of the Hamptons. Montauk, as Dan succinctly points out, is of an independent turn of mind, and while the "McMansions" are starting to turn up here and there, Montauk manages to retain much of what endeared it to Dan and me so long ago.

While Dan's book evokes the changes that have threatened what those of us who have been here a long while love and treasure about the Hamptons, it is, in the main, a long love poem to the area and the extraordinary people who have occupied it and, more often than not, helped to preserve its character.

Dan is, front and center, a journalist—and a damn good one—and this book, a journal of a place and its people, is wonderful reading. In its pages I've learned a lot I didn't know and met a lot of people I wish I had.

If I write here that I cannot imagine a chronicle more inclusive and revealing, fascinating and objective, yet for the greater

part affectionate, I am not piling it on too thick. This book is
damn good work.

SOME addenda.
    I wish I had known Dan while he was writing his piece
on Nixon's stays at Gurney's Inn in Montauk. My house, looking down on the beach, is not far from that spot and, one day,
I was looking over my gradual cliff and I saw an extraordinary
sight: There was a man in a suit and tie and shoes walking the
beach among the sunbathers, shaking hands with those who
were willing to have their hands shook. Five paces behind him
were two other men, similarly dressed but with their right arms
extended and covered with beach towels. It is so clear to me
now: There was Nixon and there were his bodyguards with
guns. The mind boggles: What if I'd been gifted with insight
into the future and what if I'd been, by nature, a killer. Just
think what I could have saved the country, from my perch on
my cliff!

    I have one quarrel with Dan's pungent writing about the
disaster that was Sag Harbor in the 1960s, and it concerns his
appraisal of John Steinbeck who was, I must state here, a close
friend of mine, though we disagreed politically very frequently.

    In his quoting of John's letter outlining his theoretical in-
vention of more efficient killing weapons for the Vietnam War,
Dan fails to understand the deep and awful humor that moti-
vated the suggestions. John wouldn't have hurt a fly, and I read
in his advice the subtext "Well, I disapprove of this brutal and
wrongheaded war, *but*, if you want to do it in a really effective
brutal and wrongheaded way . . ."

Sorry, Dan; I can't let you have that one the way you saw it. Friendship can blind us, though, and while I doubt it, you may be right.

A minor quarrel, I guess, with a book I feel anyone who wants to fully understand the Hamptons must read.

—EDWARD ALBEE
New York City, 2007

In the Hamptons

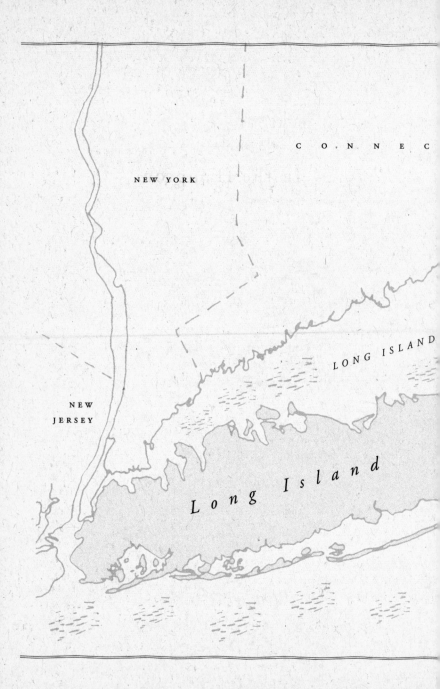

NEW YORK

C O N N E C

NEW JERSEY

LONG ISLAND

Long Island

RHODE
ISLAND

TICUT

BLOCK ISLAND SOUND

SOUND

Montauk

Sag Harbor

Amagansett

East Hampton

Bridgehampton

Southampton

Shinnecock

Westhampton Beach

ATLANTIC OCEAN

N

At the Print Shop

A T 4:00 A.M. on a warm summer night in 1960, filthy with sweat and black printer's ink, I wandered out the front door of the *Suffolk County News* in Sayville, Long Island, in search of a place to lie down. There wasn't any. Overhead, the streetlights in front of the stores glowed. A hot wind rustled the leaves of the oak trees. All was quiet.

Where could I lie down? My car was right there, parked in front of the print shop, but I couldn't stretch out fully in that. Behind me, inside the building I had just come out of, were several dark front rooms—an editorial office, a business office, an advertising office, a lobby and counter—but none had a couch or even a comfortable chair. Behind those rooms was the big open space that housed the print shop. Fluorescent lights lit the room at that hour. Men bustled around. No place to lie down there either. I'd have to look elsewhere.

I liked Sayville. It is, and was then, a small town halfway between Manhattan and Montauk quite similar to the one where I had grown up in New Jersey. Record stores and dress shops, a Woolworth's and a men's shop, even three ice cream

parlors lined the main street. But at 4:00 A.M. they were all closed. Even the "all-night diner" was closed. There was just nobody around.

I had seen a park in back of Main Street and so I wandered down an alley along the side of the little *Suffolk County News* building toward it. It was a city block in size, and there were rows and rows of oak trees, bordering a gravel path that meandered down one side of the park and up the other. It was also dimly lit, by just four streetlights at the corners. Perhaps I could find a spot off somewhere in the dark where a tree provided some shadows. Or maybe there was a park bench. I looked for one. But there wasn't one. And so I retreated to a dark patch under a tree, sat down on the ground, noticed I was sitting on acorns that were quite hard, brushed them away with my hand and then lay down on the grass, got myself comfortable, and began to drift off to sleep.

HERE is how my little weekly newspaper in Montauk was prepared for printing in 1960: It was almost exactly as Gutenberg printed things some five hundred years earlier. There were iron frames, much like picture frames, that had interior dimensions exactly the size of the newspaper page. You laid these frames on a stone counter, and into them you loosely assembled thousands and thousands of little pieces of lead type, each one a backward letter of the alphabet, or a backward word or series of words. The largest pieces, the headlines, were made of individual blocks of wood, each bearing one raised letter, made of a piece of zinc glued on the top. When the frames got filled up with all these letters in just the order you wanted them, you locked them in place by inserting an iron key into a slot and twisting clockwise a quarter of a turn. The frames ratcheted inward as you turned the key. The letters were thus pressed tightly against one another.

Then you got a piece of steel about the size and shape of a cookie sheet and slid it between the counter and the frame. With this in place to keep the little letters from falling out if they were not in quite as tight as they should be, you'd pick the whole thing up and walk it to the pressroom, where you'd slide it onto a shelf inside a twelve-foot-long flatbed press. Then you'd slide out the cookie sheet, lock the frame onto the press, bring over all the other frames in this manner, put ink into a trough, and press a button to turn the press on.

In the early days of printing, you wouldn't press a button. You'd turn a crank. And the gears and the levers and the rollers of the press would move. In a three-step operation, a rubber roller would slide over a trough with ink in it, get inked, and then roll across the frames, wetting the letters. After that, a piece of paper would slide down gently onto the frames, and the clean rollers would roll the paper hard against the frames, transferring the ink from the letters to the paper. When the operation was over, a lever would peel the paper off the frames and there would be all the words, all black and shiny. You'd set the paper down to dry briefly, a metal folder lever would fold it, and there it would be, one page of a newspaper.

At midnight, Mike the Pressman had loaded fifteen frames onto the press. My newspaper that night was sixteen pages. Now there was just this last frame on the counter. And I saw, even backwards, that there was a wrong letter in a word. We'd have to fix it.

Near the counter were two Linotype machines the size of refrigerators. Men sat at them, facing keyboards, and they'd type a line. Eight feet up, at the top of the Linotype, tiny doors in tiny boxes would open, and with the keyboard controlling which doors would open by means of wheels and cables, little pieces of brass would come sliding noisily down a metal chute and assemble themselves in a row on a stand, miraculously arranging themselves to spell out words. The operator would press another button, and a perfect amount of hot silvery lead, bubbling until that moment in an open pot boiling above a gas flame, would pour into the brass pieces, covering them. When the lead cooled, it would have hardened into a line, one line, a unique sequence of letters and words extending exactly one column width wide. You could pick it up and carry it over to the frame and replace the one with the wrong letter. And your mistake was fixed.

And because of my mistake that is now what had to happen. Bob Sr. typed the line with the correction—the regular Linotype operator had gone home hours earlier when his shift ended—and I gave the line to Mike. Using a flat tool, Mike flicked out the old line with the mistake—it made a pinging sound as it bounced across the floor—and he slipped in the new one.

Once again he locked the frame, but this time he did not go for the cookie sheet. He'd carry the frame over to the press without it.

"What are you doing?" I asked. I stared at him, a worried look on my face. At the press, Bob Jr., Bob Sr.'s son, waiting for the frame, stared at him. At the Linotype machine Bob Sr. looked over to see what Mike was doing. He was about to try defying gravity.

"I do this all the time," he said. But I'd never seen it.

The Bobs and I stood stock-still. "Watch this," Mike said as with one hand under one side of the frame and the other hand under the other side he unsteadily lifted it up. He took three steps toward the press, and then the stuff inside the frame exploded, spraying thousands of bits of type everywhere in the room, onto the walls and the floor, into other pieces of machinery. Nobody moved for a while.

Then Mike said, "We'll have to do this one again."

Growing up in New Jersey, I had worked on the school paper at Millburn High School. And I had been out to the print shop in Irvington when we put it together and had smelled the hot lead, and heard the chatter of the Linotype and the thump-thump of the flatbed, and savored the pungent smell of black printer's ink. As my journalism teacher had said at the time, I had gotten "ink under my nails."

In my last year of high school, I got a job as a "stringer" covering high school sporting events for the *Newark Evening News*. A sports editor took all us stringers, about ten in all, on a tour through the dusty, dirty six-story office and printing plant building in that blue-collar city. After the tour, we returned to the city room, where the editor sat us on stools and stood in front of us, pacing around.

"Now here's what we need. Details. The score. Names of high scorers. The highlights. A brief description of the ebb and flow. You are to leave the game when it is over, the football game, the basketball game, or whatever, and you are to go to a pay phone and take out a nickel and call us immediately. We'll take the story right over the phone.

"Here is what we *don't* want. I had this happen once. The phone rang and I picked it up. On the other end, I could hear a crowd of people, cheering. And then this breathless voice. All excited. '*We won! We won! We won!*' And then he hung up. That's what we don't want."

A T 7:00 A.M., rested, I returned to the print shop. The flatbed press was just finishing churning out my six thousand newspapers at the rate of one a second—the rate of a heartbeat—and the last of them were being bundled up with string, stacked up on handcarts, and pushed out across the sidewalk to my convertible, which was still parked on Main Street. It was dawn. The bundles made a big pile in my car. There were some in the passenger seat, a big mound in the backseat, the rest in the trunk.

I started the car and headed out toward an entrance to Sunrise Highway, heading east into the dawn. I leaned forward and turned on WINS, the rock-and-roll station, and with the music thumping at a volume as loud as I could get it, I listened once again to "Shake, Rattle and Roll" as I banged the side of my car with the flat of my hand to keep time.

I glided out onto the highway. My T-shirt was streaked with ink and sweat. Ink was in my eyes and ears. In my hair. Under my nails. And then I passed the Bellport exit of Sunrise Highway and came upon the place where the limbs of the trees arch over the passing lanes of the road. I stood up in my car—a filthy Roman chariot driver—and, keeping one hand on the wheel, stretched the other up toward the foliage trying to touch it, failed, but then whooped with joy.

Two hours later, in the fishing and resort town of Montauk, I would begin to deliver the papers bundle by bundle and handful by handful to the tops of cigarette machines in restaurants, to the counters by cash registers in souvenir stores, to the little tables in motel lobbies by the padded chairs, and so forth and so on until everything was delivered. Then, with the sun lowering toward the horizon, I'd drive to the beach, hot and filled with joy, and I would leap out of my car, run down the sand toward the ocean cheering at the top of my lungs, and dive in. People in town would now be reading what I wrote. I was in love.

FOUR years earlier, on a Sunday morning in June of 1956, my father had driven our family to the eastern tip of Long Island from Millburn. We were told this would be, like it or not, our new home. I'd never been here before. I was sixteen years old. Out the window of the car, I watched the city and its suburbs fall away behind us to be replaced by miles and miles of potato and duck farms. Finally, as we approached the end of this five-hour trip, we arrived in the Hamptons, where I saw the most beautiful white beaches imaginable, cliffs and forests, harbors and wetlands, wooden windmills and old New England colonial downtowns. We passed through the sleepy little villages of Westhampton, Hampton Bays, Southampton, Bridgehampton, East Hampton, and Amagansett. Every village was quiet as a mouse on that Sunday afternoon. The stores were closed. A few early-afternoon church services were just letting out. And then, past Amagansett, as we drove down a hill to a flat, sandy peninsula called Napeague, the temperature abruptly dropped five degrees and there was a sudden, biting smell of salt sea air. Out the window, along both sides of the road, there was now mist and fog, and beyond it, the sea. Ten minutes later, we burst into sunshine in this windy, Wild West motel and fishing village called Montauk. There were people on horseback—Dad told me there were two cattle ranches just outside of town— and in that downtown about twenty brand-new motels, one built in a Hawaiian motif with waterfalls and swimming pools, another in an Indian motif with a totem pole. They bore names such as East Deck, the Ronjo, White Sands, the Oceanside. There were crowds of people on vacation walking around, there were little sailboats on a pond, there were lifeguard stands and fishermen's trucks and souvenir stores. And presiding over it all, in a field, a six-story abandoned office building. I had never seen anything like this.

From downtown Montauk, my father continued on, indicating a drugstore at the far end of town, and then continuing on six miles to the very tip of the peninsula, to a classic lighthouse right on the point. I was in love with this place.

Of course, even at sixteen, I knew the reason my father brought us here from a more ordinary and conventional life in suburbia. My father had become unhappy working as a salesman for a national cosmetics company. One day he came home from one of his long trips to tell us he had met a customer at a drugstore in a coastal town in Massachusetts, and the customer, a family man, had taken him deep-sea fishing in his fishing boat. Dad thought, I could do this too. Have a boat by the shore. Go fishing. Own a store. Indeed, he had a degree in pharmacy, which he had gotten years before at the Brooklyn College of Pharmacy. So it was possible. But what would he do for money? We were not rich. And where could it be? Perhaps he could find a drugstore—not in New Jersey, but in the state of New York, where he was licensed—that was for sale, successful, but so remote or unusual that the owner could not find a buyer and would be at a certain level of desperation. Perhaps he'd sell it to Dad for no money down, but half the profits until it was paid off. Dad got a stack of trade magazines and began to search the classifieds and after a while found just such a store in Montauk, New York, wherever that was, which was called White's Drug Store, that really only did a decent business during the three summer months of the year. And so that's where we moved, and that's where we stayed. I've lived in Montauk and, later, in the Hamptons just adjacent for fifty years.

Why write this book? Well, the story of how the Hamptons and Montauk transformed itself from a sleepy backwater into the glittering world-class summer resort it is today has never been properly told. In this place, at the age of twenty, I founded what many believe to be the first free newspaper in America. And I'm still working at it today.

Here is how we prepared *Dan's Papers* for printing last week. On Tuesday night, our production manager, Nicole, one among fifty-five people who work here at this newspaper, clicked a mouse. There's no hot lead, no wooden blocks of type, no black printer's ink anywhere here in our offices. The click of the mouse sent billions of electronic bits streaming south to Voorhees, New Jersey. The next day, two moving vans, weighted down with about a hundred tons of the newspaper, arrived in Bridgehampton, where the drivers and some helpers plopped about sixty thousand copies of this free 200-page full-color weekly newspaper onto the platform in front of the garage in the back of our offices. So much for the Gutenberg process. And so much for sleeping on the ground in a park.

In any case, every day, every single day here in the Hamptons, stuff happens. And when you run a newspaper, you get to hear about it and see it. Every little bit of it.

This book is about the people who, intentionally or not, led or followed along through the fifty-year transformation of this place. I know these people and what they did. And so I present them here as best as I can through the filter that is *Dan's Papers,* in rough chronological order, the billionaires, the fishermen, the farmers, politicians, movie stars, bankers, artists, presidents, WASPs, rebels, rock stars, and town characters. (Many of the names and identifying characteristics have been changed to protect their privacy.) I hope you enjoy reading about them as much as I have enjoyed writing about them.

East Hampton, April 2008

(Courtesy of Dan Rattiner)

Merton Tyndall

ERE in the fabulous Hamptons, the largest and most prominent Starbucks in any of our old New England villages is on Main Street in Bridgehampton. It is in the most formidable building in town, a large three-story brick affair. You go inside, order a decaf cappuccino grande, wet with one Equal, and note that this Starbucks looks exactly like every other Starbucks in every other city and town in the United States, except for one thing. Behind the bar there is the entrance to a massive money vault. This was once, indeed, a bank.

I remember the first time I was in it, and my first encounter with the legendary man who presided over the bank, Merton Tyndall. It was in 1964, and he had been president for almost fifty years by that time. I was very, very nervous to be seeing him. A clerk had led me back to his office. To do so, you went around the tellers' windows, through a door, past a secretary, and then through another door into a dark, mahogany-paneled room with a huge wooden desk. Behind it was perhaps the most important man on the eastern end of Long Island at the time. Mr. Tyndall was white haired, heavyset, and avuncu-

lar. He spoke slowly and carefully, but politely. He seemed almost kindly.

"So you are at Harvard?" Mr. Tyndall asked, peering over his glasses at me.

"Graduate school," I said.

"Your father told me you were coming. So what can I do for you?"

"Well, this is very embarrassing to me, but it seems I need to borrow a thousand dollars."

"Why is that?"

"To tell you the truth, I don't exactly understand it. Four years ago, I started my little newspaper in Montauk. It's called the *Montauk Pioneer* and it comes out in the summertime when the tourists are here. I brought you a copy. Have a look. It was originally eight pages long. Then the next summer it was six-teen pages long. Then last year twenty-four pages long. Last year, I also started a newspaper in the Hamptons, which I've called *Dan's Papers*."

"I've seen it. *Dan's Papers* is an odd name."

"Yes. I know. But people like it. And last year that was twenty-four pages too. So now I'm paying my way through grad school with these newspapers. Last fall I went around to see the store owners for this upcoming year and they bought even *more* advertising. I'm going to have to publish thirty-six pages a week in *both* papers."

"And now you need to borrow a thousand dollars." He smiled.

"Yes. But I'll pay it back. Here. Look at all the orders I have. But for the first time I can't afford to pay the printer without this thousand dollars."

"You are being ruined by your own success."

"Sort of. But then the money will come in, and I'll pay you back, which should be in July, and then I'll make even more than I did last year. I really don't understand it."

"That's how it goes," he said.

"You'd think that the more business I did, the *less* amount of money I'd have to borrow."

"That's why banks are in business."

"So you'll do this?"

"If you say you'll pay it back, I think you'll pay it back." He leaned forward. "I judge you to be a man of your word."

I was twenty-four. Merton Tyndall took a checkbook out of his desk drawer and right there in the president's office made out a check to me for $1,000. He handed it to me. And I thanked him and left.

Back in the main lobby of the bank, I went to a teller's window and opened an account with it. Then I left the bank and went out to the street. Out front was the car I had driven there in, a sand-colored 1957 Ford Fairlane convertible with gold trim that my father had bought for me after that first summer. He had been so proud of me.

I had the top down. The sun was shining. It was early May.

Sitting here on a standard-issue Starbucks sofa, forty-four years later, I note that I am just about where I stood when I opened that account. The bank, Bridgehampton National Bank, is gone, having vacated the premises eleven years ago for a new main office at the other end of town ten times the size of this building. It took more than a year to complete. From a window in my offices, a two-story building across the street and several hundred yards east of the new Bridgehampton National Bank, I watched as it went up. It was four stories tall, almost the size of the Bridgehampton School, with columns out front and a big cupola with a working clock tower up on the roof.

I received an invitation for the opening-day ceremonies of the new bank building. Merton Tyndall was long gone. The new bank president was Thomas Tobin, a man whom I found to be very formal and by the numbers. He was somebody who kept you at arm's length. He also had almost no sense of humor, none that I could find anyway. But the bank, in total deposits, was now fifty times the size of what it had been before. I replied to the invitation.

"Dear Mr. Tobin," I wrote. "I would be delighted to attend

the grand-opening-day party and ceremony at your new bank. I think it is a wonderful building, but I have a request. Up until now, from the second floor of our offices down the road, we've been able to watch the sun set over the potato fields and the shopping center beyond. Would it be possible to move the bank perhaps just two hundred feet to the north so we could once again enjoy that view?"

I got no answer.

I DID indeed pay back that $1,000 that Merton Tyndall had lent me. But the following spring I was back asking for $2,000. The papers had grown once again. And Merton Tyndall expressed delight and wonder at that fact as I showed him the numbers. I paid that back in July too.

"This is what America is all about," he said as he wrote me that second check.

In 1966, in May, I was putting the newspapers together once again, this time with the help of $5,000 from the pen of Mr. Tyndall. And then one day he called me.

"I'm sorry to call you about this," he said. "But I wondered if you could find the time to stop by the bank. Tomorrow, perhaps."

"Is anything wrong?" I asked.

"Nothing we can't fix," he said.

They ushered me into his office the next day around 10:00 A.M.

Merton Tyndall smiled. "You know, I have always lent you this money and you have always paid it back," he said.

"Yes?"

"Well, it seems I have to get something in writing. There is a banking regulations board called the FDIC. And they came by. And they said I had to ask you to come in to sign a note."

"A note?"

"A promissory note. A paper that says you will pay this back. Damned if I know. I told them you *always* pay it back. Your word is good. But they said no, ask him to come in and sign this note. So, I have to."

Merton Tyndall looked out the window for a moment. Out that window, you could see where the paving of Lumber Lane and the Sag Harbor Turnpike came together at a sharp angle. Beyond it was the property of the Bull's Head Inn, a big foursquare mansion that had been built around 1840. And I noticed that just exactly adjacent to this window there was a black-and-white photograph framed on the wall, of precisely this view, but from about 1910. There was an early automobile, a team of horses and a cart, and a woman in a big dress with a bustle. As for the streets, they were mud.

"I sign here?" I asked, looking at the paper he had on his desk.

He looked back. "That's the spot."

I signed. "That's quite a photograph," I said.

"I never get tired of looking at it. I started working here in 1912, as a clerk. The next year, they paved the roads. About five years later, I got promoted to vice president and they gave me a desk. In one of the drawers was this photograph. I called the man who had had the desk, and he said he had left it for me. A present. It was taken the year I started here."

M ERTON Tyndall died in 1978. I went to his funeral service at the Bridgehampton Presbyterian Church just
across the street and down the road from the old bank. It is a
magnificent white-shingle structure, with a tall steeple and a
porte cochere, where years earlier local parishioners could drive
their families up in their carriages and park for a moment,
sheltered from the weather, so the ladies and their children
could get out and walk into the church without getting their
fine Sunday clothes wet from the rain. Today, Starbucks may
be in the most formidable building in downtown Bridgehampton, but the Presbyterian church is the tallest and most grace-
ful. It was the proper place for a funeral oration in memory of
Merton Tyndall.

I sat in the back and cried. They were bitter tears. I would
have thought the whole town would have turned out and
packed the place, but there were just a few dozen people.

Merton Tyndall was ninety years old when he passed away.
He had been a wonderful, kindly man, but he had been retired from the bank for more than a decade. And now life had
moved on. It does that.

Babette Tweed

THE single most expensive real estate transaction in the Hamptons in 2006 was the sale of the former Andy Warhol estate on the ocean beach east of Ditch Plains in Montauk. It went for just under $30 million. In various magazines there were pictures of it. One from the air shows the whole property, a compound with five small beach houses surrounding a big lawn and facing out to the Atlantic. Another photograph shows the view from the beach on the east side of the property. Again, you can see the beach houses. I know this view. But when I last saw it, it was twenty-five minutes past midnight, I was alone, dressed in black, soaking wet, and trying to sneak on the property without being seen.

ON a Saturday morning in the second week of July 1961, at breakfast, my father asked if I was free to work in the store that day.

"I know you are finished delivering the paper," he said. I did deliveries on Friday. "Terry Sigler is sick. And I could use a hand."

Around two in the afternoon, a tall, elderly man with a silver walking stick and a three-piece suit came into the store. I was putting stickers on bathing suits at the time and I was struck by his appearance: formal, perfectly erect, totally humorless. I was even more struck by whom he came in with. She was small, dark haired, and stunning in a very little-girl sort of way. She looked fifteen. But she was probably eighteen. I thought she was one of the most beautiful girls I had ever seen.

I didn't wait on them. They went to the main counter, and the older man bought something. He took out a small purse and he paid for it. Then they started back out, coming down the side aisle where the bathing suits were. She walked one step behind him. And our eyes met.

"Hi," I whispered.

"Hi," she said. Then they were gone.

I was frantic. I talked to the salesperson who had waited on them. She had no idea who they were. I asked another salesperson who had seen them come in. She had no idea either. Finally, I went to the prescription room and asked my father. And he knew.

"That is Harrison Tweed," he said. "A very rich man. Has a beachfront house. One of the old Association homes along the ocean designed by Stanford White. I think he's a New York lawyer."

"And her?"

"That's his daughter, Babette."

I was smitten. By late in the afternoon, I had gotten her phone number. It was in the phone book. Harrison Tweed III. And after three aborted attempts, I got up the courage to call her.

"Is Babette there?"

"Who's calling?" It was a deep, female voice. Not a Babette voice.

"Dan Rattiner."

"One moment."

There was no shouted cry of "Babette!" No other comment, just the phone being set gently down. And then, after a while, Babette came to the phone.

"Hello."

"Hi, Babette. I met you earlier today in the drugstore. My name is Dan. I was the clerk in the bathing suits?"

"Oh, hi."

I suggested a date that evening, but she said she was busy. I suggested the next evening. But she was busy that evening too.

"Why don't you come over here?" she asked. "We're going back to the city tomorrow, but we'll still be here at lunchtime."

"Are you sure that would be all right?"

"Oh, sure. And we're playing croquet."

I could not sleep that night. But the next morning, about a quarter to twelve, I got in my convertible, put the top down, and followed the directions to her house. I went down Ditch Plains Road, headed east toward the lighthouse parallel to the beach, and then past two wooden posts that flanked the road. One of them had a small PRIVATE, KEEP OUT sign on it. The paving ended here. But you could see what was ahead. Along the beach were seven magnificent Victorian mansions, each three stories tall, each with stone chimneys, gingerbread under the eaves, and, on the ground floor, wraparound porches. They were set some distance apart from one another. The Tweeds'

THE TWEED MANSION, 1948.
(Courtesy of the Montauk Library)

was the farthest one in. "You'll see a sign for Momeyer," Babette had said. "That's the one just before ours."

I had wondered, when my father first told me their last name, if Mr. Tweed was, perhaps, the famous and corrupt Boss Tweed from New York City's Tammany Hall. He was, indeed, an old man. But he wasn't that old. Boss Tweed, as I recall, had ruled New York City in the 1860s. He could be, perhaps, a grandson or a great-grandson.

"I have no idea," my father said when I asked him.

I had never been down this dirt road before. It was two ruts, bumpy, and slow, and bramble bushes brushed up against the sides of the car. I passed Momeyer. I had chosen, for the occasion of lunch and croquet, a white pullover sports shirt, white shorts, and Keds tennis sneakers. I had combed my hair. And I had a plan. Probably a bad one, looked at from this per-

spective all these years later, but a plan nevertheless. I would ig-
nore Babette. I would, instead, charm her father. And her
mother and brothers and sisters, if she had any. And that way I
would get to Babette.

The gravel crunched under the car and soon I reached the
place where, right after the Momeyers' driveway, a fork of the
road went off to the right, which would be the driveway to
the Tweed residence. I took it. And shortly I came up the rise of
a hill to where I could park at a small turnaround along the side
of the house. From there, a flight of stairs went up to the front
porch. Babette had heard the car and she was out on the porch
to greet me. She waved. My heart leaped. I was looking up at
white teeth, a sailor suit all starched, creased, and pressed, a
little white hat.

"Hi."

We went inside together. Babette introduced me all around.
There was a mother, quite lovely, who looked me up and down,
and Mr. Tweed, sitting in a rocking chair, telling some sort of
story to a middle-aged man sitting facing him. They both
stood up and we shook hands. And then I was steered away to
meet the dog. A black Lab, older, wagging his tail and pushing
up against me looking for a pat. The thing I most noticed, besides Babette, was that there was no food. There was, however,
a wooden bar cart on wheels in the living room, with a bucket
of ice, glasses, mixers, and open liquor bottles. All three of the
adults had drinks in their hands with ice in them. Babette invited me outside to help her set up the croquet wickets.

It was, after all that, actually quite a splendid lunch. Early
on, Mr. Tweed told me about the house. He told me there had

been a group of seven families from Manhattan who had become tired of the summer social scene in Newport and wanted to start a summer colony of their own at Montauk. It was the 1880s. They had hired Stanford White to design them their homes. There was also a dining hall and kitchen building. Everyone ate together. But the dining hall soon burned down.

"Would you like to see what remains of it?" he asked.

"Sure," I said.

We were still waiting for the lunch to appear at that point. Mr. Tweed and his friend—the Colonel—got up, and Mr. Tweed, after telling his wife that we would be back in just a few minutes, took us out onto the porch and down a rocky path that led through some beach grass to a stone foundation.

"Here it is," he said.

Nobody spoke for a moment. A foggy mist was rolling in, and you could hear the ocean roar far off. It was odd, but though these houses were all beachfront, as was this foundation, all the structures were set back a considerable distance from the sea. It was quite a hike through the dunes to get to the ocean, which was only barely visible from the houses. Strange.

"It burned down in 1904," Mr. Tweed continued. "And it was never rebuilt. The following year, the daughter of one of the homeowners fell from a carriage and was seriously injured and died. She might have lived if they had been near medical help. But they were a day away. So much for roughing it. As a result of this, the members of the Association, as it was called, abandoned the colony. And the houses were then sold separately. Of course, each had its own kitchen put in."

I dreamt of Babette all week. I can still see her standing in that living room. You had to shade your eyes. It was dark and gloomy there, the walls filled with shelves of books, the floor a deep oak. And yet, the sun flooded in somehow. So it was magical, airy and dusty. What a place for a beautiful young woman.

I had asked Babette at one point during the early afternoon if she would go out with me the next weekend, on Saturday night, and she said she would see. She wasn't even sure they were coming. I should call Saturday. So I did.

"Hello?" she answered the phone.

"You're here," I said.

"Yes."

"Is tonight okay?"

"Sure. Where do you want to go?"

There was no movie theater in town. Just the Surf and Sand Inn, the Manor Hotel, and the Blue Marlin. Everybody hung out. And then usually wandered down to the ocean to a bonfire.

"How about the Surf and Sand?"

She asked me to pick her up at eight. And I said I would be there.

A green pullover. No. I looked in the mirror. Took it off. I had a white V-neck sweater, a preppy thing. That would be better. I put on chino pants. And the sneakers. I only had the sneakers. And then the phone rang. And it was Babette, sobbing.

"Dan?"

In the background, I could hear people shouting at one another.

"Yes."

"I can't go out with you tonight," she said.

I looked at the clock. It was seven thirty. Outside toward town, the sun was setting.

"Is there a problem?"

More sobbing. "I can't go out with you ever again," she said. And then she started to cry. "I have to go."

And she hung up. I stared at the phone. What a development. And then, suddenly, it rang again. I snatched it up. Again I heard shouting in the background, and in the foreground, more sobbing. Then it stopped. And there was a very soft but deliberate whisper.

"Meet me on the beach in the front of the house at midnight," Babette said. And then she hung up again.

I held the dead phone to my ear for the longest time. I couldn't move. Then, finally, I set it down. My heart was beating a mile a minute. And I stared at myself in the mirror. No. A white sweater and chinos would not do. I had four hours to work on this, and I would look for black.

EVERYBODY watched television. We had three channels. My sister went off to bed at ten. My mother and father at eleven.

"You coming up?" my dad asked from the stairs.

"I'm going to be up for a while," I said. "The *Late Late Show* is coming on. I'll see what movie is on."

"You okay?"

"Just restless. I might go out."

I had spent a long time making a plan on getting to Babette. I could not drive directly up to her house, obviously.

And there really seemed no way to go up that private road and come down toward the beach anywhere else in the Association home area. There was the Momeyer house before the Tweeds'. And heaven knew what was after the Tweeds'. So I'd have to park at the beach and walk down to her either from the east or the west. I considered the east. Ditch Plains. Lots of small houses and even a few motels. Also, it would be about half a mile. Somebody would see me. And the west? There was a dirt road that led down from Montauk Highway right alongside the most southerly pasture of the Indian Field Ranch. Nobody would be there that time of night. This road ended at a woods, at the overgrown entrance to an estate we kids knew of as the Churches'. The Churches, whoever they were, were almost never there. And you could walk through a path in the woods and come out on the beach, which was something I had done once. Down at the beach, you could turn right and cross in front of the Churches', something I never had done, and then you would be at the Association homes, the nearest of which would be Babette's. No contest. What a night I had ahead of me.

I drove slowly out our driveway and down South Fairview Avenue toward Ditch Plains. It was eleven thirty. No sense rushing this. Plenty of time. Except I really didn't know how long it would take me to walk down the beach to her. What if there were big boulders and rocks?

At eleven forty, I bumped down the dirt road—absolutely nobody there, just as I had thought—and parked my car where the road ended, rolling it one car length into the brush. Nobody would ever see it there.

I climbed out. I was wearing a black T-shirt, a dark brown

bathing suit, and my sneakers. And that was it. Babette, I knew, would have the blankets. Probably would sneak them out to the porch and throw them over the railing, then pick them up on the way out there.

The path was partially obstructed with brush. But I was a man on a mission, a wild man, and I easily pushed through. And then I was out on the beach. A starry, dark night. No moon.

I turned right. And I slowly picked my way along the beach, at the water's edge. It's public property at the water's edge. I knew that. A state law. If you can get out to the water's edge, which I had just done, you could walk all the way down the beach and nobody could stop you. The beach was for the people. All of them.

I had walked for about fifty yards, arriving at the spot where I could make out the shadows of the beach cottages of the Church estate, when I heard dogs barking. I pressed on. And now, suddenly, they appeared on the beach in front of me. Three German shepherds, baring their teeth, standing in a line, wagging their tails and growling. I shall not pass.

I shall pass. I tried talking to them. This is a public beach, I told them. They growled louder. One of them took a step toward me, then a step back. He was daring me.

I will go around them, I thought. And I stepped backward about ten yards—see, I'm leaving—and then I waded straight out into the ocean, or started to wade out into the ocean, the cold shocking me as a wave hit me, and I hadn't even turned to the west when I heard them. They too were standing in the ocean, haunch high, all three of them, splashing around. I couldn't believe it. They would swim!

MR. AND MRS. HARRISON TWEED III ON THE STEPS OF
THE TWEED MANSION, CIRCA 1935.
(Courtesy of the Montauk Library)

All I could think about was Babette. She'd be lying there, un-
doubtedly, in a two-piece bathing suit, stretched out on a towel,
waiting, staring up at the stars. I *had* to find a way. I feinted as
if I was moving back, then stopped and started to swim west, to
make a big arc out into the ocean to get around them. And they
let out such a racket of barking and growling that I stopped
swimming and again started back. I would die if I did this.

As I once again swam back, I looked toward the shore to
see if they were coming. They weren't. They had returned to
shore in front of the house and were just holding their ground,
but what I did see, in that starlight, was the scene of those
beach houses that has stuck with me all these years, and which
I had seen in the real estate brochures. In the brochures, they
were painted and spiffed up. In real life, for me, they were vacant and forlorn. With mad dogs.

There has got to be a way, I thought. But there wasn't a way. I tried to think of something, anything, that would get me around them. Perhaps I should go around the back of the house. No. That wouldn't work. Perhaps I should swim even farther out. But I was not a strong swimmer.

I gave up. Wet and exhausted, I finally went back up the path to the car, climbed in, and sat in the driver's seat trying to catch my breath. The dogs, finally, had stopped barking. Which was something. And I looked at the dashboard clock.

Twelve thirty. My heart sank. It's over, I thought. And I drove slowly home.

I DID not see Babette for two weeks, but then at the beginning of August, I was on the sidewalk on Main Street walking down to the beach and there she was coming the other way. She saw me and looked away. And she spoke not a word as she went by me. And I never spoke to her again.

THE Churches were in the process of selling that group of beach houses that year. It took a while. They were in poor condition. But finally, a decade later, there was this young artist, Andy Warhol, and his friends, who bought the property.

Jackie Kennedy and her children came there. Her sister, Princess Lee Radziwill, and her children came there. Some years later, my mother told me that the Rolling Stones were in town, staying at the Churches, as many people still called it, and they were often in the store.

"I really like Keith Richards," she said.

"What did he buy?"

"Toothpaste. Shampoo. But he's very funny. And then I played golf with him once. I was up at the club with a girl-friend and there he was, alone, looking for a game. He joined us. Said his name was Keith and left it at that. But I knew who he was."

As for the Tweeds' house, in 1966 it got sold to TV person-ality Dick Cavett. He lives there today, although where he lives is different in a strange way from what had been there before.

One day in 1977, when he and his wife, Carrie Nye, were in the city, fire broke out in the house and it burned to the ground. When the fire department finally put out the blaze, all that remained were the foundations and one of the two stone chimneys. It was over.

But it was not over. The Cavetts decided that, whatever the cost, they would rebuild the house to exactly the way it was. They made inquiries. But there were no plans for it. So they took out the hundreds of photographs they had snapped when they were at the house, and from these photographs and from the measurements of the ruins taken by the builders and archi-tects, the house was rebuilt stone by stone and panel by panel, a process that took two years and millions of dollars.

People say, visiting the house today, that it never burned. That somehow, through a miracle, the house burned down but did not burn down. They cannot tell it from what had been there before, it was done so well.

A coincidence in all of this involved my discovery of who the architect was for this project. His name was Jim Hadley. I had gone to undergraduate school with Jim Hadley and we had worked on the humor magazine together. But I belonged to Sigma Alpha Mu, and he belonged to Delta U. One was the Jewish fraternity of mostly very earnest and serious pre-med students, the other was the big party house. Hadley drank. In fact he drank so much as an undergraduate that though I had hoped I could turn over the editorship of the publication to him when I graduated, it was in the end impossible. The party house was his priority.

Now, years later, there he was, sober as a judge, meticulously designing the old Tweed house for the Cavetts.

"You ought to see it," he said, while it was under construction. "Everything is being filmed. There's a documentary being made of the rebuilding of this house. And it will be shown on PBS."

And it was.

Jackson Pollock

JACKSON Pollock died in a massive car crash on August 11, 1956. It took place on a curve heading north on Springs-Fireplace Road in East Hampton. And it happened because Pollock was drunk. He was also angry. Angry at the two young lovelies half his age in the convertible car with him because they wanted to go to a party and he did not. His wife was in Paris at the time.

"You want to go to this party?" he screamed. "How about *this*?" And he stepped on the gas, his blue Oldsmobile issuing a big puff of blue smoke, then surging forward to sixty miles an hour, then to seventy, then to eighty. The girls screamed as Pollock failed to make the turn. The car skidded, slid off the road into the woods, bounced off a tree, and rolled over several times.

When the police found the wreckage, they found Pollock still in the driver's seat, decapitated. One of the young women was also dead. The second had been thrown from the car and was injured, but recovered. She wrote a book about Pollock. The world-famous painter, the founder of drip painting, was in love with her, she said. She loved him too, she said, and would for the rest of her life. He would be divorcing his wife, he had told her. He hated his wife. And she was away in Paris, anyway.

On the occasion of the fifth anniversary of Pollock's death in 1961, articles appeared in other newspapers. He had been a nasty drunk, a conflicted, paranoid, confused man. There had been rumors that he had picked bar fights with the locals and had from time to time wrecked bars. Could it have been true?

The following summer, after thinking about it for almost a year, I decided to find out and then write what I found in my newspaper in Montauk. I would drive the sixteen miles from Montauk to East Hampton, then go to one of the bars he went to, and ask people about him.

On my way there, I began to question whether I could really do this. Would people want to talk about him? Perhaps they would pick a fight with *me*. I was, after all, just a college boy, and someone clearly who did not grow up in this place. I was also a momma's boy, still living at home. What did I know about bars?

Well, it was one o'clock in the afternoon. It wasn't likely that anybody was drunk. Yet. And maybe there wouldn't be *anybody* there.

In my convertible with the top down, I turned onto Springs-Fireplace Road, came to a curve in the road, then another curve in the road. Which was Pollock's curve in the road? As I approached another one, I saw there was indeed a woods adjacent to it. I actually looked for flattened foliage and broken tree trunks. None there. And none there at the next turn.

What house did Pollock live in anyway? I knew it was along here somewhere but I didn't know where. Perhaps I could go knock on the door and speak to his wife, Lee Krasner, now back from Paris. I could ask her how she felt about Pollock dying like that.

What a joke. I'd really go to some stranger's door and ask them how they felt about some great personal tragedy in their life? Other reporters did that. Disgusting. I would never do that. Not for my paper.

I made a left on Fort Pond Boulevard and began to look for a tavern named Jungle Pete's, which I had read somewhere was one of Pollock's hangouts. The road here was straight but very narrow, with small fishermen's homes on either side, set in the heavy foliage that marked that area. About a half mile down, I came to it. It was the only commercial establishment on the street. Set in, well, the Jungle.

There were about ten vehicles parked in front of the place. All of them were trucks of one sort or another. Pickup trucks, vans, trucks with camping rigs on them, trucks with fishing poles in them. I pulled in with my tail-finned convertible, all chrome and buffed steel. I turned off the engine. Through the open windows, I could hear conversation inside, lots of people talking, sometimes at the same time, sometimes with voices raised. There was the sound of a pinball machine. A jukebox playing music. I set the brake and got out. I was very aware of how out of place this looked—a shiny new car with tail fins and the top down (so I could experience what Pollock and the girls must have experienced). And so I got back in the car and pressed the button that put the top up. It groaned, came up, and then I got out again and locked the car.

I climbed the two steps to the entry door of Jungle Pete's,

JACKSON POLLOCK IN HIS STUDIO.
(Copyright © Joe Fig)

hesitated, took a deep breath, and went into a smoky barroom. Immediately conversation stopped, then slowly started up again. I took a few steps forward and went to the bar and I looked around. Rough, weathered men in workshirts were drinking beer. There were a few women. I ordered a tap beer, the bartender poured it, brought it over. And people pretended not to notice me.

After a fashion, I tried to strike up a conversation with the man sitting immediately to my left.

"Hi."

Nothing.

I tried the man on my right. "Jackson Pollock used to drink here?" I asked.

"Sure did, bub," he said, not looking at me.

"I'm writing this new newspaper in Montauk," I said, "and I was wondering what he was like."

"He was like? He was like anybody else." There was an edge in his voice.

Over at the other side of the bar, two men began talking loudly. One was getting red in the face. The bartender walked over.

"All right, all right," he said.

"Some people say he drank too much," I said.

"He drank too much. We all drink too much." He turned his stool to face me. He was about fifty, his face lined from being in the sun. "Don't care to talk about him. Or anybody else for that matter."

Down at the other end of the bar, it was clear to me that everybody was talking about everybody else for that matter.

At this point, for the first time, I noticed a certain common accent to the speech in this bar. It was kind of hard and flat, sort of like a Boston accent, but faster and sometimes almost unintelligible. And there were odd words and phrases thrown in here and there. "Bub." And "Yes, yes," repeated twice like that.

The man next to me spoke again. "He was a good man," he said. "We all liked him. Smart. I wouldn't want to say anything bad about him. ANYBODY WANT TO SAY ANYTHING ABOUT JACKSON POLLOCK? GOOD OR BAD?" he shouted over the din. Nobody replied.

On the other side of me, the man took his beer, got up from his stool, and walked across the room. Perhaps it was deliberate, perhaps not.

I'd been there long enough.

I took a few more sips of my beer, noticed that I really did not like it, paid, and walked out, closing the screen door quietly behind me.

Standing at my car was another man, looking in the window. He stood up as he saw me coming.

"Finest kine," he said. "A real beauty. You buy this?"

"My dad bought it for me. I did something good. He liked it. So he bought it for me."

"Probably get a lot of girls with this rig," he continued.

I wondered what he wanted. "Sometimes," I said. "I live in Montauk. You from here?"

Obviously.

"Yeah."

"My dad owns the drugstore in Montauk now."

"What brings you up here?"

"I run the new newspaper in the town in the summertime. People have been writing about the fifth anniversary of Pollock's death. I'm trying to find out more about him so I can write a story."

"Well, people don't like to talk about him."

"So it would seem."

"He got famous and all. And most of the time, he was really a very nice man. But then he'd get drunk. Pretty bad when he got drunk. Nasty. He'd break things. Then he'd pass out. So we'd take him home. Next day he'd be fine. We got used to him. I wouldn't want you to say anything bad about him." He paused. "Well, I will tell you one thing," he said. He looked around to see that we were alone. "Once I went over his house looking for him. He wasn't in the house. So I went to the studio knockin' on the door. Jackson? Jackson? The knockin' jus' opened the door, all by itself. So I walked in and right away realized I'd just walked across a big painting on the floor. Filled the whole room, almost. Paint was stickin' to my shoes. Uh-oh. The next day I told him what happened. And he said, 'I saw it. Looked good. Worked it into the painting.' "

"Can I write about that?"

He hesitated. "No," he said.

"Okay. I won't. I promise, I won't." I unlocked the car, got in, and started it up. Then I thought of one last thing. "You know the spot where Pollock crashed?"

"Yeah. But you don't really want to write about that either. People be here, strangers, tourists, all lookin' around. Ghoulish. Nobody want that. We kinda keep to ourselves."

"Yeah."

"Drive careful," he said. And he went inside.

I didn't write a word about Jackson Pollock for years and years.

Howie Carroll Jr.

SOMETIME during the first year I published the Montauk newspaper, I stumbled upon what I believed then, and still believe today, is the most extraordinary photograph ever taken in Montauk. It was taken by a *New York Daily News* photographer at four o'clock in the morning, outdoors at the Montauk Railroad Station. A flashbulb lit the darkness. In the background, dimly, is a side view of some of the passenger cars of a Long Island Rail Road train, a few uniformed conductors standing and smiling in the entryways. But these railroad cars are just the backdrop of the true subjects of this picture: forty-five drunken sportfishermen, fully dressed, carrying fishing tackle and other gear while running happily across empty railroad tracks toward the camera. You would have thought they had died and gone to heaven.

The caption of this picture, which was destined for the *New York Daily News*, read: "4 A.M. September 1, 1951. New York City fishermen disembarking from the Fisherman's Special to run for a place on one of the Montauk fishing boats at Fishangri-la."

The first time I saw this particular picture was in the reading room at the East Hampton Free Library. I had done much of my research about the history of the area in this library, assisted by the librarian, Mrs. Dorothy King. She would bring me things to read. I would read them at a table, take notes, and hand them back. This photograph, however, was a complete puzzle.

For one thing, though the Montauk Railroad Station was just a few hundred yards from the bay, there were no fishing boats there. And there was no Fisherman's Special. At this time, in 1960, just nine years since the picture was taken, there were between the tracks and the bay only the abandoned remains of a Navy Torpedo Testing Range from World War II. So what

THE DOCKS AT FISHANGRI-LA.
(Courtesy of the Montauk Library)

was Fishangri-la? I asked Mrs. King about it, and she said she had no idea.

"I remember the speech during the war when President Roosevelt used the name Shangri-la," she said. "American bombers had dropped bombs on Tokyo. It was a complete surprise to the Japanese. Everyone wondered where these planes could have taken off from. Roosevelt said they had come from the magical island of Shangri-la. He had made up the name."

About the same time I stumbled upon that picture, I was encountering stiff resistance from fishing boat captains to the idea of buying ads in my newspaper.

I'd be down at the docks on Lake Montauk, meeting the captains as they came through the breakwater to tie up at their slips. The fishermen, sometimes twenty to thirty of them, would come off carrying bags of fish. Then I'd go on board and talk to the captains.

"A newspaper in Montauk?" Captain George Glas said. "Not interested."

"All the people at the motels will be reading this newspaper," I said.

"All the people at the motels are not who is boarding my fishing boat. My people live in Astoria or Far Rockaway. Working class. And they drive out here to fish for the day. That's my customer."

"Maybe you'll pick up some new customers from the motels."

"I doubt it."

I tried Captain Paul Forsberg of the *Viking*, and I tried Captain Dick Rade of the *Marlin II*. I tried a charter boat fisherman, Captain Bert Tuma. Not interested. I wound up just listing all the fishing boats in the paper, and if the fishermen wanted their phone numbers and a few words of description about their boat, I'd sell it to them for $15 for the whole summer. A few bit at that.

That first year, one who did was a young captain's mate named Howie Carroll. Like me, he was also twenty years old. A bit odd. But he saw what I was about and he talked his captain into spending the few bucks.

I liked Howie Carroll, at least at first. He was local born and raised into a fishing family—both his father and uncle were boat captains—and I liked that. On the other hand, he was rough around the edges. He was small and thin. Puffy around the eyes. He was also bucktoothed and wild eyed and often unshaven. He was a town character, or a character in training anyway. I had a beer with him at Salivar's.

"People are kinda interested that you're starting a newspaper," he said. "But they don't trust you."

"Why?"

"Not from here," he said as if that explained everything.

We talked about girls. Most of them could be found working as waitresses at the Montauk Manor Hotel. There were maybe twenty in all. Where they went after work—after it ended at 11:00 P.M.—the boys followed. The Surf and Sand. The Blue Marlin. The Memory. That was it for girls.

"I'll see you there," I said.

"Aaaah," he said, "maybe. I gotta get up at four most mornings. The boats leave at five."

About a week later, when I saw Howie down at the docks

having just gotten off the boat on which he worked, he barely recognized me. Puzzled, I looked at him closely. He was drunk.

What I didn't know then, and didn't come to find out until just recently, was that there was a very personal connection between Howie Carroll and that amazing picture I had seen in the East Hampton Free Library. It was among the things that I believe eventually killed him.

Well, I wasn't a newspaper reporter for nothing. And if that photograph had created a mystery, I would solve it. And I soon did, though it was a long time before I realized the connection with Howie Carroll.

Talking with people down at the docks later that summer of 1960, I learned the following: The fishing village had not always been where it was now. The first fishing village in Montauk had been down on the arc of the bay by the railroad station. The property, at the time, which was about 1900, had been owned by the Long Island Rail Road, which had built the tracks just a few years before in the hopes of making a seaport on the bay. Though the railroad built a warehouse there and a few docks, and later a two-story railroad station where the tracks ended, nothing much came of it. Eventually, by 1900, there was just one train out from the city and one train back. And few people taking the ride.

Then, some fishermen from Nova Scotia built a bunch of fishing shacks on this railroad land between the tracks and the bay. They also built some fishing docks. And by 1925, there was a thriving village with a restaurant, a post office, and a school. The population was estimated at about four hundred Canadians there for the spring, summer, and fall. It was a true shantytown, and the Crash of 1929 and the Depression that followed only added to it.

In September 1938, the deadliest hurricane ever to hit eastern Long Island swept through. The sea broke open the dunes at Napeague, cutting off Montauk and turning it into an island for nearly two weeks until the waters subsided. But much worse, the flooding inundated the low-lying Montauk Fishing Village, destroying an estimated three-quarters of the buildings and killing six people.

After it was over, the villagers tried to rebuild, but it was apparent to everyone that this low-lying area was not a good place for a village. During the next year, most of the Montauk fishing fleet transferred its operations to the more sheltered waters of what is known as Lake Montauk, a former lake where a developer, Carl Fisher, had dynamited an inlet to link the lake with the open waters of Long Island Sound. Two years after that, when war broke out, back at the arc of the bay, the navy took over the railroad and condemned the land on which the remains of the village stood. There a naval base would be built.

Bulldozers came in and leveled the place. And soon there rose a military facility where navy torpedoes could be tested. There were about a dozen enormous concrete buildings of various sizes, and they were used as warehouse space for torpedoes, a manufacturing floor, an officers' club, a lab, and a marine hangar where seaplanes and boats could be sheltered. A long military dock stuck out into the bay.

For four years, between 1941 and 1945, the U.S. Navy would bring newly manufactured torpedoes to Montauk by railroad, put dummy charges into them, load them aboard PT boats, launch a seaplane, and then fire off the torpedoes, with the plane overhead following the bubbles and noting the trajectory. If the torpedo could pass inspection, it would be repacked into a crate and shipped back to the Brooklyn Navy Yard for deployment to the Pacific. The others were worked on in Montauk until they could be retested and finally pass inspection.

After the war, an enterprising businessman bought the abandoned torpedo testing station and turned the former officers' club into a fisherman's bar called Fishangri-la. On one side was the railroad. On the other, the arc of the bay and the navy dock. Fishangri-la became the destination for avid New York City fishermen who came out on the Fisherman's Special leaving Manhattan at 1:00 A.M. On board, they could order drinks from the bar car if they wanted—and after three hours, they would arrive at Montauk and leap off the train to run out to the old navy dock and onto one of the dozen or so fishing boats now berthed there.

One of these boats was called the *Pelican*. In 1960, when I learned about Fishangri-la, I was told that there had been this one fishing boat, the *Pelican,* that had come to grief in a storm, costing the lives of about fifty fishermen and putting an end to fishing from the bay once and for all. Don't ask about the *Pelican*. It was the town's dirty little secret. We now have tourists staying in the motels. They didn't need to know. They might like to know that as a result of the *Pelican* disaster, whatever that was, laws were passed about how many people you could put on a fishing boat before it was considered illegally overloaded. So everything is fine now and this will never happen again.

As far as my friendship with Howie Carroll, it all seemed

completely disconnected from the *Pelican*. Also, largely because of his drinking, we became distant. He got his Captain's License and, like his father and uncle before him, as he told me, he became captain of his own boat. But now he was drinking more.

"You should put an ad in the paper," I said to Howie one day over a game of pool at Salivar's.

"Can't afford it," he said.

One day, I went down to the docks and saw Howie Carroll fast asleep on a bench. It was eleven o'clock in the morning. His boat was not in its slip. It had gone out without him.

"He's sleeping it off," someone told me. But what this meant, as far as I was concerned, was that my friend would probably lose his Captain's License. Certainly he was unfit to captain a fishing boat that day. The whole thing made me feel very sad.

A number of years after that, I learned that Howie Carroll had taken a turn for the worse. I didn't see him at all then, and then one day I learned that he had died. From drink. He was just fifty-three years old.

As for the *Pelican* disaster, through the 1970s and 1980s I barely even thought about it. Nobody ever talked about it. And I had been warned off it and I respected that. What was the point when there were so many other stories to tell in the newspaper?

But then, around the year 2000, I had a change of heart. Soon it would be half a century since the disaster, and surely there would be very few people who were there at the time still around. It was time to tell the story. And as I learned about it,

mostly by researching in the library, I discovered that the story
was as gruesome as you could imagine.

In the early morning hours of September 1, 1951, there were
eleven fishing boats lined up along the navy dock. The fishermen were all friends, more or less, but they were also competitors. The Fisherman's Special would pull in at 4:00 A.M.,
and the fishermen, with their pockets full of money, would run
across the tracks to find a spot along the railing of a fishing
boat. The rule was that if you ran out of railing, you set up for
a row of fishermen behind those on the railing. And you filled
that up until the captain said that was it. There were no other
rules. How could one possibly disappoint a fisherman who had
partied in the bar car or slept across the seats of a passenger car
for three hours just so he could go out on a boat fishing? Somewhere, somehow, they would find room for everybody. This
was the third summer of Fishangri-la. Nothing bad could happen at such a happy place.

There is another photograph, taken by a *New York Daily
Mirror* photographer, of several Montauk fishing boats, loaded
with fishermen, heading out from the navy dock just after
dawn on that morning. The boats are heading away from the
cameraman, and the last one out has its name clearly visible on
its stern. *Pelican.* It is forty-two feet in length. The other boats
appear to be about the same size. All are loaded down with
happy, eager fishermen, two and three deep. There was a lot of
money to be made that Saturday morning.

I T may have just been chance that the *Pelican* was the last boat
leaving the dock. But it also might have been because the

Pelican was considerably slower than the other boats that day. One of its two engines was out of service. And they were waiting for a part to arrive to fix it. With one engine, they could do ten knots instead of eighteen. They'd just have to be careful. They'd go out only a short distance off Montauk Point. They'd never be out of sight of the mainland.

It was a sunny day. Predicting the weather back then was not what it is today, but nevertheless it was expected to stay sunny. The captain explained to the passengers as they fell behind the other boats that they were on just one engine. There was a collective groan. But, he said, we'll have a good time anyway and there are plenty of fluke off the lighthouse.

The storm clouds came up very quickly. Over ship radios, the word spread. It looked pretty nasty. Better head for cover. The *Pelican* had not even reached the lighthouse at that point. Fishing had not even begun. But the captain made the bold decision. They would turn the ship around and head back home. Short trip. These things happen.

The *Pelican* had just struggled to begin turning around when the storm hit. There were gale-force winds, a bristling rain. Many of the fishermen went inside, but there was not room for all of them. Most just stayed on deck to tough it out. The word was that the storm would pass quickly.

But now waves had begun to form, and the *Pelican,* taking them broadside, began to roll with them. With the wind pushing the vessel away from shore, the single engine was not enough to allow the ship to make headway. It might be better to just drop anchor for a bit.

No one was fully sure of what happened next, but survivors

later said that a huge wave hit the *Pelican* on the port side coming as if from nowhere. A rogue wave. The *Pelican* listed thirty degrees but then righted itself. And with the next wave, the sea washed briefly over the deck.

Now somebody saw a third big rogue wave coming. He pointed and shouted, and as fast as everyone could, they raced for the starboard side of the ship. Just from the shifting weight alone the *Pelican* listed badly. And then the wave hit. Already halfway up, the wave turned the *Pelican* entirely over and upside down. People on deck were thrown into the water. People were smashed against the railing. People were trapped in the small cabin upside down. There was a lot of screaming and yelling. Almost nobody had thought to put on a life jacket.

The storm blew for only another hour. In the blinding rain, the other ships were busy heading into the shelter of Lake Montauk. So it wouldn't be until two hours later that the Coast Guard first heard of the disaster and began to look for survivors. An hour after that, they came upon the upside-down hull of the *Pelican*, drifting slowly southeast just off the Montauk Lighthouse.

Nineteen people survived. Forty-five were lost, and some of their bodies were not found until the next day, floating in toward shore.

The captain of the *Pelican,* Eddie Carroll, Howie Carroll's uncle, was never found.

Balcomb Greene

At around six p.m. one Saturday night in 1961, I got on Montauk Highway and drove toward the Montauk Point Lighthouse six miles from the center of town. It was a beautiful summer's evening, the sun low on the horizon in the west, the start of what ought to have been a great night for a party.

I had invited a young woman named Lenore Grisar to accompany me, and as we drove she chattered away, but I wasn't paying much attention. The party was being held at the extraordinary oceanfront home that Balcomb Greene had built with his own hands, and I was very excited to finally see it.

We turned off Montauk Highway onto a dirt road just past Second House, about halfway to the lighthouse. This was the original Montauk Highway, the one that had been cut through the woods in the eighteenth century when George Washington had ordered the Montauk Lighthouse constructed. It was overgrown now with deep ruts, rarely used by the public because Camp Hero, a U.S. Army base built there during World War II, had cut it in two. It ended in barbed wire on its way to

BALCOMB
GREENE.
(Courtesy of Mrs.
Balcomb Greene)

the point, and then picked up again briefly on the other side of the wire just before the lighthouse.

Before the road ended the first time, however, there were three turnoffs, even smaller than the dirt road we were bouncing along. These were the long dirt driveways leading to the oceanfront homes. And we were to turn at the one that had a white wooden post with the letter *G* on it. Greene.

Balcomb Greene was surely one of the most extraordinary individuals ever to make their home in Montauk. He stood six foot five, never wore shoes or socks, used clothesline as a belt to hold up his rolled-up jeans, and always seemed to be splattered with oil paint. He had a lined, clean-shaven face, big eyes, and a full head of hair, and he was not only tall but gaunt. And he hardly spoke. Which is why I had been invited to come to a party at his house by his wife, Terry.

I first saw Balcomb Greene in my father's store. It had been

1956, five years earlier, when my dad had me working there stocking the shelves and manning the cash registers. This was before I started the newspaper. Conversation in the store had stopped. There he was.

As I recall, he was looking for aspirin. He had picked up a bottle and brought it to the counter and set it down. I rang it up. He withdrew some coins from his pocket and paid for it. He left.

After that, I would see him in the store or on the street occasionally. He would nod at me and grunt. That was it. An amazing-looking man, lost in thought.

I really thought that Balcomb Greene, this abstract expressionist painter, was one of the greatest painters of our time. I didn't know much about painting. But I'd seen pictures of his work in magazines. There were great triangles of sailboats leaning into storms, abstract pieces that were barely recognizable but evocative of the scene nevertheless. I knew what I liked.

I had been told that three years after World War II ended, in 1948, Balcomb Greene came out to Montauk with his then wife, Gertrude Glass Greene—she later died—and bought a piece of land in the woods on the ocean, hacked through a road, put in an electric generator and a well, and then built, with his own hands and with the help of a few friends, a glass and cinder-block home where he could paint and live undisturbed.

For a number of years after his wife passed away in 1956, Greene lived there entirely alone. Then Terry appeared on the scene, a beautiful young woman he had met in Paris. She came out on the Long Island Rail Road to visit him. And she had stayed.

We turned into the driveway. The car bounced along, vines

and branches brushing against the windshield, and we made our way down a slight grade until, coming around a bend, quite suddenly the house appeared in front of us.

It was far less imposing than I had expected. Where we parked there was a long cinder-block wall, one story high, with a strange-looking butterfly roof on top. There was a single door. We knocked and were led inside. People were already there, drinking wine and eating hors d'oeuvres. The entire front of the house facing the ocean was an enormous living room extending nearly sixty feet from end to end. If the outside from the rear was modest, this was an utterly spectacular view of the sea.

For some reason, the whole thing depressed me.

Terry welcomed us, and Balcomb grunted and nodded. Paintings covered the walls, some of them five feet high and six feet long. Beyond the house, visible from a window facing east, was a studio where the paintings were created. The whole thing was a statement, a statement of a man's life, in full. And there it was.

I do not remember much about this party, other than that there were about a dozen people there and Balcomb, much to my surprise, occasionally spoke. Mostly, I sat on a sofa with a drink in my hand and said nothing. Lenore, a beautiful young woman, mixed.

When I had first seen Balcomb in the store five years earlier, I had already been told about his appearance, so I was ready for him. There was, however, one thing that nobody told me about, but which I believed must have been true.

When my parents, my sister, and I moved to Montauk in 1956, Camp Hero, the big army base out by the point, was still active. One evening after dark, during that first year, we were having dinner at our home on South Fairview Avenue about seven miles away, when there was a flash of light and a tremendous roar coming from the direction of the lighthouse, followed by the rattling of the dishes on the shelves in the kitchen. A few minutes went by and there was another roar and rattling. We looked out our dining room windows then. After a while, a third one came, accompanied by a flash far away. And that was that.

The next day, my dad found out that what we had heard and seen was the firing of the largest guns ever made in World War II by the United States military. These sixteen-inch guns were fitted onto the decks of giant battleships. Four of them also had been fitted into two concrete pillboxes at Camp Hero, and were being tested out. The big shells, the size of torpedoes, were fired at surplus warships anchored far out to sea.

For the first three years that we lived in Montauk, we heard the occasional sounds of this bombardment. We got used to them. Then, in 1960, they stopped. The army base was being abandoned, though the Montauk Air Force Station, built adjacent to it in 1952, was getting beefed up. A huge radar tower was being constructed. If the Soviets were to fire an atomic warhead at New York, it would be picked up at Montauk first. But next door, the big World War II guns were being mothballed.

During those years prior to the party at that house, I often imagined, when I heard the big guns being fired, Balcomb Greene, in his studio, playing a Wagnerian opera very loud in the evening, and occasionally wincing as the guns, just a few hundred yards down the beach, would thunder away, lighting the sky, shaking everything, and sending billows of choking black smoke his way. In the woods on the cliff, I imagined him painting furiously.

Now I knew that his painting to the Sturm und Drang of guns firing was over. He was now doing his painting in silence. Maybe that was the cause of my sadness.

Nothing, however, would have prepared Balcomb and Terry Greene, or even me, for what happened the morning after the party.

According to what they later told the press, they had slept late, until around eleven. It was a foggy April morning. As they were in the kitchen preparing a breakfast they planned to eat out on the deck, they heard the unmistakable sound of metal squealing and scraping against the boulders below them. Looking out into the mist, they began to see the bow of a World War II navy destroyer, its forward guns pointed upward at them, slowly emerge through the fog. With every wave and with loud crunching noises, this destroyer slid up further and further toward them until, finally, it stopped. Shipwrecked.

For the next two months, the Greene home resembled nothing so much as the centerpiece of a circus. Their isolation was at an end. The shipwreck of a U.S. Navy destroyer at Montauk was a national event. Reporters and photographers from all the New York daily newspapers—the *Times*, the *Mirror*, the *News*, the *Post*, the *Journal-American*, the *Telegraph and Sun*, and the *Herald Tribune*—camped outside their house. TV crews from CBS, NBC, and ABC, the three news stations that broadcast from Manhattan, were also there. Reporters from *Time* and *Newsweek* were banging at their front door.

After a few days of this, the Greenes protested, and from that point on, the spectators and reporters stayed away from the house, hacking a new path down through the woods to the beach to what became a campsite for them.

The battle to save the USS *Baldwin* went on and on. From time to time, I went down there, to take pictures or to have a look, but certainly not to knock at the Greenes' door. I didn't contact them at all during this time.

An admiral gave an interview at the site. The ship had been in mothballs in Boston and was being towed by a tug to the new mothball shipyard in Philadelphia when, in a storm, the line connecting the two had parted. The *Baldwin* drifted northward and resisted all efforts to board it or bring it back under control. Then came the shipwreck. Now the constant rubbing of the hull of the *Baldwin* on the rocks at Montauk was tearing the bottom to shreds, they feared. They were still going to try to pull it off. Perhaps the pumps placed on board could keep it afloat until they could tow it away.

At the end of two weeks, a first attempt was made to drag the *Baldwin* off the rocks. A steel winch cable attached to the *Baldwin* from a tow vessel tightened, then snapped and, like a whip, struck and killed a seaman. The refloating plan would be reexamined.

Historians gave interviews. This was not the first time a military ship had come ashore at Montauk. The first one had been the British man-of-war *Culloden,* a 42-gun frigate that had been out in Long Island Sound during the American Revolution looking for French ships to engage when a great storm came up. The *Culloden* lost its mast and foundered on the northern shore of Montauk near where the Montauk Jetty is now. It's still buried in the sand there.

As the days went by, investigators began to write that the *Baldwin* shipwreck was a scandal. It had been an unnecessary move. The towing cable had been too long. There had not been a second one as a safety. There had been a report that the storm was coming but they proceeded anyway.

In June of that year, 1961, on a cold, windy day, the navy, after succeeding in sealing off all hatches, smokestacks, doors, and windows above decks, forced air into the hold with pumps in the hopes of floating the vessel. The *Baldwin* gently rose on the bubble, drifted off the rocks, and was towed carefully out seven miles, where frogmen boarded it, removed some of the caps, and dove overboard to swim to waiting rescue boats as the great ship went down to its final resting place.

Finally, once again, the Greenes were alone. Balcomb Greene would continue to paint, accompanied only by silence, for nearly another thirty years.

Esther and Sarah
(and the Rolling Stones)

JUST as you come into the town of Montauk, one of the first things you see on your right is the Memory Motel. Today it remains almost exactly as it was when we first moved into town fifty years ago: a plain, one-story, L-shaped motel of about twenty rooms, with a low sheltering porch covering the long part of the L.

The way it was placed on the property gave a kind of welcoming quality to the town. The main part of the L sat parallel to and about forty feet back from Main Street, while the short part jutted toward the street at the far end. And so, as you drove into town, what you saw first was whatever it was that was in the embrace of the L, which for years and years, maybe thirty years, were two live, very tanned, heavily oiled women in nearly identical jaguar bikinis, lying facedown (or faceup) on aluminum lawn chairs. They were always the same two women. One blond, the other a redhead. The owners of the motel, my mother said. For a boy of sixteen, which is what I was when we first came to town, this was quite a sight.

"Look the other way," my mother sometimes said as my
father drove past. And I would.

I had a pretty good idea of what went on inside the Memory Motel, or at least I thought I did. Actually, for many years,
I never had the nerve to go inside. In fact, I was forbidden to
go inside.

"Don't go in there," my mother said. "I can't tell you the
reason. But just don't go in there."

This is a house of prostitution, I thought. Or worse. Worse,
it seemed to me, was that it was a lesbian house of prostitution.
I knew what lesbians were. I looked for motorcycles out front
but didn't see any. I looked for women in leather walking
around but didn't see any. I saw cars parked, but they seemed
just ordinary summer-people-on-vacation sort of cars. Once I
saw an inflated beach ball in the backseat of a Plymouth sedan.
But the truth be told, I never saw any of the people who were
staying there. There were always cars lined up, facing the rooms.
And sometimes they vied for space with the bikini ladies. But
whoever owned these cars was either always inside, or somewhere else, perhaps at the beach. The motel, and indeed all of
Main Street, was just two hundred yards from the beach.

As I thought about it during those early years in Montauk
when I worked for my father in the drugstore, I came to realize
that the first thing you really noticed when you came into this
resort motel town was not really the Memory Motel—what a
name that was—but the two bikinied ladies. I wondered what
the rest of the motel and restaurant owners thought about this.
Montauk was a fishing and family resort. Or it was supposed
to be.

One morning, in 1962, I got up the courage to enter the Memory Motel for the first time. It was eleven on a Tuesday. The two ladies were not lying on the beach chairs. So it seemed safe. There were only a few cars out front. I pulled up and I took a deep breath.

I had been running my little summer newspaper for two years at this point. And this was surely the only retail establishment in Montauk I had never set foot in. I did not deliver the newspaper to the Memory Motel. I did not go in and try to sell them advertising. Largely as a result of the longtime instruction from my mother, I treated the Memory Motel as if it didn't exist. It had a big wooden sign on the fascia of the roof that read MEMORY MOTEL. Below that as far as I was concerned was nothing. Until now.

I would enter the motel, I knew, with the sales pack of the newspaper under my arm. I would try to sell an ad. But not very hard. Hopefully, they wouldn't take one. Then I'd leave. But I'd find out what was going on in there finally.

There were two doors where the two sides of the L came together. One had a little sign above it that read OFFICE and was closed. The other had a little sign above it that read BAR. Through a screen door, I could hear music emanating from the bar and I could hear pool balls clacking against one another. I wouldn't even look in there. I knocked twice on the office door. Nobody answered.

Well, I thought, looking at the screen door, I've gotten this far. And so I took another deep breath and walked in.

Even in the middle of a sunny morning, the place was dark. It smelled of beer and Clorox. Curtains billowed inward from

ESTHER AND SARAH AT THE MEMORY MOTEL.
(Courtesy of the Memory Motel)

an open window, brushing the linoleum floor. My eyes ad-
justed and I saw two fishermen playing pool. And I saw, behind this big shellacked wooden bar with its empty bar stools,
a man of about sixty wiping shot glasses with a rag. It was the
most ordinary scene imaginable.

"Hi," he said, looking at me curiously. "Can I help you?"

"Yes, is the owner in?"

"Where are you from?" he asked.

"The newspaper. I wondered if she, or he, ahem, would
like to buy an ad."

"Wait here," he said. "I'll get her."

And he left. I turned around. And there, occupying the entire opposite wall of this bar was one of the most remarkable

things I had ever seen. It was a work of art. Made entirely of carved plywood pieces attached to the wall, it was a map of the world. The wall was eight feet high and twenty feet long. I walked over. In the middle, there was North America, with Greenland and Canada at the top, attached to South America at the bottom. The two continents together were four feet wide and seven of the eight feet high. Then there were oceans painted a deep blue. And then there were islands and other continents, all a half-inch thick, all painted, and all in their proper places, from Japan over by the screen door to the Hawaiian Islands over by the one window. Inside the wooden continents, narrow white lines served to indicate the borders of the countries, and the names of them, also in white, identified each of them on a deep maroon background.

And there was more. Dotted lines in white, crossing the oceans, indicated at least five different voyages going around the world. Ports of call were indicated. And each of these voyages had dates written along the dotted lines, such as April 7–November 3, 1953.

The bartender walked back in with the blond woman. She looked about forty-five, wasn't nearly as pretty as she looked while lying on the beach chair, and she had on no makeup. She wore a robe and there were circles under her eyes. I had woken her up. But she would attend to business whatever it was. I wondered if she was wearing the jaguar bikini under her robe. Impossible. And where was the other?

"Can I help you?" she asked.

I took a copy of the newspaper out of my pack and handed it to her.

"I publish this newspaper," I said. "I was wondering if you might like to take out an ad in it."

She turned it over and over as if it were some foreign object. Normally, I would have at this point launched into a long and upbeat explanation about the newspaper and how important it was and how it could surely improve her business. But I really didn't want her to buy an ad. It would contaminate the other ads. And everybody would know it. She obliged.

"No," she said, handing it back.

"Well, thank you anyway," I said.

She looked at the bartender as if to say, "You woke me up for this?" And then she turned and went out through the door and back into the office.

I turned to the bartender. "That's quite a map," I said.

"Oh yes, these are all their travels. They're world travelers. Been all over."

"And they had this map made?"

"Somebody made it for them. I guess it reminds them of their travels. Pretty neat, huh?"

It was.

I left. And driving away, I thought how ordinary all of this was. How nicely this map had been made. They must really like looking at it every day, looming there as a huge presence to remind them of some pretty extraordinary times. I wondered if they had been accompanied by male companions. I thought not. I was pretty sure they must be a couple. I'd met women couples. This was a far cry from a motorcycle lesbian house of prostitution. But then, I really wasn't positive. And on the other hand, this really wasn't my cup of tea. I wouldn't be going back, is what I thought as I drove on.

And how did they get the money for those trips anyway? And what did they do in the wintertime when all the motels in town were closed up tight?

I N May of 1975, a seminal event took place at the Memory Motel that explains why nothing about it has ever changed from that day to this.

Earlier that spring, unbeknownst to anyone in town, the Rolling Stones took up residence at the Church Estate, directly on the ocean and alongside a deep woods out near the Montauk Lighthouse. Although referred to as the Church Estate, it wasn't owned by the Churches any longer. It had been bought, in 1972, by Andy Warhol and his friend, the film director Paul Morrissey, as an oceanfront retreat from the Warhol factory in Manhattan. Three years later, in early May, Warhol rented his estate to the Rolling Stones for a month. He would not be coming out to Montauk during that period. And the Rolling Stones needed a quiet place where they could rehearse and practice for their upcoming world tour.

I wasn't there when all this happened—I was away on vacation when the Stones arrived—but on the warm day that the Stones drove through Montauk for the first time, Mick Jagger noticed the MEMORY MOTEL sign, and the two well-oiled women getting some sun.

Two days later, after several all-night binges out at the estate, Jagger got it into his head that he and the others should hit on the MEMORY MOTEL. It wasn't all that busy at that time of year. They'd take it over for the night.

Some of the people in the entourage who were familiar with Montauk suggested that they not go down there. They predicted it wouldn't work out. There were better bars in town. But Mick insisted.

Twenty minutes later, they were on their way down there in three cars. They parked out front and went inside. It was about 10:00 P.M., and the place was filled with some of the regulars at that time, which, contrary to my imaginative fantasies, consisted of fishermen and their friends and families out to catch porgies and stripers either from the beach or out on one of the fishing boats. They would be going to their rooms soon. The boats left at five in the morning and the men, and perhaps a son or two, would be on them. The women and younger children would go to the beach.

Esther and Sarah appeared, not in bikinis but in normal clothes. And they observed what appeared to them to be about ten dirty, unwelcome hippies with beards, headbands, bell-bottoms, and ponytails accompanied by an equal number of scruffy long-haired women who seemed to fawn constantly over them. An argument ensued. The owners were told these were the Rolling Stones. They didn't care. Things were thrown. And Esther and Sarah threw the Rolling Stones out and told them never to come back again.

I sometimes saw Esther and Sarah around town after that, sometimes separately, sometimes together. Once I saw Esther at a Chamber of Commerce meeting, and she spoke intelligently, expressing her views about extending the tourist season or something. But I never really spoke to her again, at length anyway, and I was pretty sure she would not remember me.

The two women got fat as they grew older, but they still lay out there in the parking lot in front of their motel in their bikinis, which were still as outrageous as ever. Nobody stopped them. But surely, as a symbol of what you might expect as you entered Montauk for the first time, it wasn't the same.

Also, my mother moderated her views. It was clear to her now that this was a lifelong love affair between these two and, with the changing times and people coming out of the closet everywhere, she was now giving them the benefit of the doubt. They did shop in the store after all.

One day, she said this: "When you think about it, they came out here for the beach, but they need to be near the office. So they sunbathe in the parking lot." It made sense.

Then one day in about 1985, Esther came out alone, set out two beach chairs, lay out on one, and then nobody came out to lie on the other. Sarah had died.

For years afterward, this is what Esther did. It had been Sarah's beach chair. It would always be Sarah's beach chair. And the townspeople felt so sad for her. And then Esther died.

Not long ago, the new people who own the Memory Motel began to promote the place as a sort of shrine to the Rolling Stones. There were young people there now. They'd come in and look at the guitars up on the walls, the gold records in their frames, the pictures of the Stones everywhere, and the big map showing all the trips around the world. Once, the new owners called me and asked me to write about their place for the paper, and I did.

In researching it, however, I found that Esther and Sarah had bought the place in 1954 from an older WASP couple who had an oceangoing sailing ship and it was *they* who had the big map made because it was *they* who had gone on these five round-the-world trips—in their own yacht.

I also learned that Esther and Sarah had the same last name. They were sisters.

Sometimes I imagine young girl groupies in the Memory Motel today, drinking beer and tracing the Stones' five world-wide tours that are commemorated on the giant map.

Then they go over to the jukebox and, putting a quarter in, select the song that the Stones wrote for their album *Black and Blue*.

We spent a lonely night at the Memory Motel.
It's on the ocean, I guess you know it well.

Russ Corser

O N December 22, 1963, exactly thirty days almost to the minute after President John Kennedy had his head blown apart in Dallas, I got out of a taxicab at a small airport just outside of New London, Connecticut, grabbed my two bags, put my head down, and marched through a biting wind and snowstorm to the little terminal building. There was a separate entrance to the café, and through the frost on one window I could see one light was on. Russ Corser would be there.

I came in the door, which the wind slammed shut behind me, set my bags down off to one side, clomped the snow off my boots, and clapped my mittens together. Even the short walk from the taxi to the café had chilled me.

Corser turned on his stool at the counter. A waitress, the only other person in the café, was refilling his coffee mug.

"You sure you want to do this?" he asked.

"Yeah."

"Well, it's your dough. And I can get you through if we stay low. But it could get bumpy."

"I'm here," I said.

He thumped down the coffee mug, fished out a quarter, and set it on the counter. Then he stood up. He was a tall man with a full head of white hair parted in the middle, a style popular years earlier. He was about sixty, but he moved with the grace of a much younger man.

"Let's do it," Corser said. And he sighed deeply.

Only one thing about this conversation bothered me. The business of flying low. On previous occasions—and there had been many—when I flew with Russ Corser across Long Island Sound from New London to Montauk, he had always proudly told me that no matter what, if there was any trouble with his plane, we were always high enough to glide down and be able to set down on land. He flew this great arc—up seven thousand feet and then slowly back down. Now we would be sticking low and close.

Russ Corser liked to talk a lot. I think being high up in the sky opened him up. He had been a fighter pilot during World War II, and still wore the leather-and-fur flying jacket he'd worn in his air force days, with the tiger patches on it. He'd been in the Flying Tigers squadron with General Chennault in China.

Now he walked over to where my luggage was and put on that leather jacket, which was on a hook on the wall there. Then he stopped.

"Not a problem," he said.

I'd flown with Russ maybe a dozen times in the two years I'd been in grad school at Harvard. I'd take the train down from Boston, take a cab out to the airport, and for $19.95, Russ Corser and his New London Flying Service company would fly me home. Fast and direct. We'd fly for thirty minutes, over fishing boats, ferries, and submarines from the Groton Naval Base, and there would be Montauk—with the town and the people six miles to the west of the lighthouse, and between them, facing out on Montauk Harbor, the little airstrip that had been bulldozed through the dunes just four years before. There was a little two-room shack at one end. That was it. Not a house or a car or anything else for miles. A good place for an airstrip.

On prior trips, Corser had told me more about himself. He had become a stunt pilot after the war, then gave that up to run his little one-plane airline. He'd been married twice. Had one son who had died in a car crash. Now he lived alone.

When it came my turn, I told him about all the women I was dating at Harvard. Every girl in Cambridge wanted to date a Harvard man. And I told him I really hated the course I was taking, which would lead to a graduate degree in architecture. The buildings now being designed were cereal boxes, all cold and bare. I didn't want to design them. I wasn't even very good at designing them.

We walked out single file through the storm, Corser in the front, me in the back, toward the single-engine Cessna, which stood there trembling in the wind. Corser brushed the snow off the wing where the step was and slapped it with a mitten. Then he opened the metal door and motioned for me to get inside. I hopped up into the copilot seat. In a moment, I heard my bags being loaded into the cargo bay in the back. Then that door closed. Then Corser scrambled in next to me and arranged himself in the pilot's seat.

"Thought you might be late," he said. "Heard on the radio the trains were delayed."

"Got through fine," I said.

"Why fly today? You were originally going to fly across tomorrow. The storm should be done by tomorrow."

"Classes were over. To tell you the truth, I just wanted to get home and be with my parents after all that happened." I was referring to the assassination. "And I thought I'd just surprise my parents by coming home a day early."

I watched him switch on some dials, then listened to the rising hum of electricity as it coursed through the various parts of the aircraft.

The engine coughed, died, coughed blue smoke and died, then coughed a third time and caught. The propeller started to turn until it became a blur. Corser smiled.

"Where were you when it happened?" he asked.

"I was on a construction site," I said. "In Milton, Massachusetts. The architect's wife called around four in the afternoon. I think it had happened two hours before. We had worked for two, maybe three hours pouring a foundation. The president was dead the whole time, and we didn't know. It was such a shock. Everybody was crying."

"Here, too. I was out here working on the carburetor," he said. "Gladys told me. She was crying. I couldn't work anymore. So I went home. Here we go."

Corser pulled a lever and the aircraft lurched forward and bumped through the snow and down the runway toward the far end. You couldn't see more than fifty feet because of the snow.

"Not gonna talk anymore," he said. "Gonna fly this thing."

At the end of the runway, he turned the plane around, revved the engine to its maximum power, put on a headset, and spoke into it. Through the din of the engine, I could not hear any of what was said, though it was clear he was having a heated exchange with the traffic controller. Then, he slammed the plane into forward gear, throwing me against the seat, and we were headed back down the runway, bumping along, faster and faster until we were off the ground and flying. The snow whizzed by. White. Sideways. I closed my eyes.

My thoughts drifted off toward that hillside in Milton, Massachusetts. Briefly, I thought of the architect, shouting into the telephone up at the construction shack, "No, no, no!" Surely a member of his family had died.

It was late November, and I was there to take a semester off from the Graduate School of Design at Harvard to "get the feel" of construction, as my professors said. Then this horrendous thing had happened. We worked for another fifteen minutes on the construction site and then we were all sent home.

There was a lurch. And I opened my eyes. We were

skimming low over the ocean. Under the curtain of snowflakes, I could see the whitecaps. God.

"Nothing to worry about, nothing to worry about," Corser was saying. "We're almost there. Any minute."

And then, there it was, the runway, in front and slightly below, rising up toward us as we approached, slower and slower, the wings waggling, until we set down and wobbled and rolled down the ice to the far end until the plane came to a complete halt. Then Corser revved the engine again, turned the plane completely around, and brought it over to the small wooden shack that served as the Montauk Airport.

Corser reached across me and opened my door from the inside. Then he and I got out and together walked with our heads down into the wind toward the cargo bay. Corser got my luggage and set it down on the runway. Then he looked at me.

"I'd better be off," he said.

I fished two tens out of my wallet and handed them to him, he shivered, and he climbed back into the plane, revved the engine once again, and then the Cessna bumped down the runway, leaped into the air, and then got smaller and smaller, disappearing into the storm. A shudder of fear went through me.

For a moment I felt nothing. And then suddenly it occurred to me he was leaving me alone. Ten degrees out. Nobody for miles. And nobody knowing I was coming. I would freeze here. I was terrified.

Leaving my bags where they were, I ran down the runway in the direction the plane had taken off. But it was no use. He was gone. Now I was breathless, puffs of white smoke appearing in front of my face. I would have to think of something else.

The shack. I ran to it. It was padlocked shut. Next to it was a pay phone on a wooden pole. I ran to that. Fished some coins out of my pocket. But the slot for the coins was frozen solid. I was running out of time.

What could I do? I could run around the harbor, a distance of four miles, to get to town. I'd leave the two suitcases here on the runway. Who would bother them? Perhaps a car would be coming the other way for some reason. Not likely. I'd never make it.

Then I looked out across the harbor, and saw, one mile away, a light in the window of the United States Coast Guard Station. Ordinarily, I would never have thought to even look in that direction, because the station was on the other side of the harbor, across the water. One could not swim across the harbor in ten-degree weather. Out of the question. But one could walk across the harbor. It was solid ice.

Fifteen minutes later, frightened, bruised, and freezing, knees banged up from slipping and falling, I was shivering in a club chair in the living room of the Coast Guard Station, in front of a roaring fire. They had put a blanket over me. And they had given me a cup of hot chocolate.

Behind me, a coastguardsman was talking on the phone.

"Yes, Mrs. Rattiner. At the Coast Guard Station. Why is he here? He walked across the ice. It's a long story. Sure, I'll put him on."

They brought me the phone.

"Surprise," I croaked.

John Steinbeck

N the spring of 1963, I attended a meeting of the board of trustees of the Village of Sag Harbor to discuss a plan to bring tourists to that town in August by holding a "Sag Harbor Old Whalers Festival." I sat in the back of the meeting room on the second floor of Town Hall on a folding chair with the other reporters and took notes of the goings-on for my paper. Out the window, and across the street, I could see the Black Buoy Bar & Grill and several other bars. Below and two doors down, I knew, was the Sandbar, another notorious place. But it was 7:00 P.M., which was a good time, because it would be hours before some of the drunks would be tossed out onto the sidewalk from these many run-down establishments.

Sag Harbor was in terrible shape in 1963. Many of the downtown stores had gone out of business. On the little lanes surrounding the center of town, about half the beautiful old homes were unoccupied and abandoned. It struck me at the time, when I first went over there to have a look at the place, that there was something simply awful about what had happened to that town. It had been founded in 1707 and within ninety years had become one of the great whaling port cities in America. The downtown was built at that time—rows of stores all attached to one another curving from Long Wharf on the water, up Main Street to the Presbyterian church, and some of the great whaling captains' mansions on the hill at the back of town. During the next half century, hundreds of whaling ships were built at Sag Harbor for the whaling business. The ships would go out for a year at a time and return with barrels of whale oil and dozens of new workers from Fiji, Japan, the Canary Islands, and China. The town had a Customs House, the first electric generator for Main Street electricity on Long Island, a spur of the railroad coming to Long Wharf from Bridgehampton seven miles away, and about three thousand residents living in small houses on charming little winding streets. But whaling ended in 1849 and the community went into a steep decline. The steeple of the Sag Harbor Presbyterian Church, which had risen to the greatest height of any building on Long Island, blew off in the hurricane of 1938. The Customs House closed. The railroad spur to town was torn up for its steel during the scrap effort of World War II. And the population mostly left. By the time of this meeting, the village had been trying to hold on to the few factories that provided employment for some of the remaining nine hundred blue-collar residents. A noon whistle sounded every day in the center of town to announce the lunch break. And men were to be seen walking wearily to or from work wearing hard hats and carrying lunch pails. At the few small factories, they worked on assembly lines making wristwatch casings and helicopter gas tank caps. No wonder they drank.

JOHN STEINBECK
(FOREGROUND) AT THE
SAG HARBOR OLD
WHALERS FESTIVAL.
(Courtesy of the John Jermain
Library, Sag Harbor)

Just how bad things were, back then, could be best understood by the sign put up by the Chamber of Commerce leading
into the town from the Sag Harbor Turnpike. It read, simply,
SAG HARBOR. During the summer season, from hooks under it,
they put up a second sign reading WHALING MUSEUM OPEN.
But for the winter season, from October to May, they'd remove
the WHALING MUSEUM OPEN sign and just hook up a sign reading CLOSED. You'd be driving along and there would be this
sign reading SAG HARBOR CLOSED. And nobody even cared.

"So what I was thinking," the mayor was saying, "was that
we ask John Steinbeck to be the festival's honorary chairman."
There was silence. John Steinbeck lived on Garden Street in
town with his wife Elaine. He stayed there most days pecking
away at his typewriter. He had moved there ten years before.

"Why would he want to do that?" Councilman Harris said.

"Well, I thought he wouldn't have to do anything. We'd just have a big parade to start the thing. And we could have him in a convertible car at the front, waving to people and welcoming them to the festivities." The idea was greeted with silence. "Then he could go home. Or he could judge the beard-growing contest, if he wanted to."

Most people left John Steinbeck alone. He'd get his mail at the post office, eat lunch at the Paradise Restaurant with Elaine or one of his friends, get the morning paper at the Ideal Stationery Store three doors down, and then walk home. Everybody knew he liked the town—maybe it reminded him of one of those broken-down port towns in California during the Great Depression when he was in his heyday—but he wanted his privacy now. So nobody would even think of walking up to him and asking him for his autograph. It was that way in all our towns at that time. And people were proud of it. Famous people were tucked away and protected.

"Well, we could just ask him. He could just say no."

"I'm still not in favor of any of this," one of the other councilmen said. "Who the hell wants to come to Sag Harbor? And why the hell would we want anybody here? We're fine."

They were not fine. The Bulova Watchcase Factory, the biggest of the three factories in town, had said it might have to close. If this festival worked, there would be tourist money. If it worked.

"I'm worried *too* many people will come," said the village secretary. "Everybody will get drunk. There will be a riot."

"I've only got three officers," the chief of police said.

In the end, after what seemed to me an interminably long debate, a vote was taken and by a margin of 4 to 3 it was decided to have a Whalers Festival for a four-day weekend at the very end of August. And by the same margin of 4 to 3 it was voted to ask John Steinbeck if he would be the honorary chair of it. Nobody was happy with any of it. Nobody was talking to anybody, it seemed.

It was eight thirty in the evening when we headed silently down the stairs and out into the street. On the sidewalk in front of Village Hall, the trustees simply grunted at one another and then walked off in different directions to find their way home. None of them went to the Black Buoy or the Sandbar, I noted. It was a cool, mid-April night and the lights on Main Street, dim as they were, were lit. I found it a little disconcerting. I had personally seen drunks come crashing out the doors of some of the bars on the street with people shouting obscenities after them. So this colored my thinking about walking down the street alone. What if one of them just crashed out as I was walking by? It was a chance I'd have to take.

As for John Steinbeck, I had never met him. But in college, I had read some of his novels. I had never been to Monterey, but doing my undergraduate work in English, I had read *Cannery Row,* the book he wrote about the rough-and-ready wharf there that sounded a bit like Sag Harbor. Also, I knew by this time that Herman Melville had set a chapter of his book *Moby-Dick* in Sag Harbor. And that James Fenimore Cooper had written one of his *Leatherstocking Tales* while staying at the American Hotel in town. That hotel was still there, four doors down from Village Hall toward the Sandbar. It was a real dump in 1963, with all the upper floors boarded up and just a sleazy bar and restaurant on the ground floor.

In the weeks that followed, I really wondered if John Steinbeck would accept the offer to be in the lead car at the Whalers Festival. Frankly, I thought he would. He was sixty-one at that time, and the work he had been famous for was far behind him. He had written *Of Mice and Men* and *Tortilla Flat,* two great best sellers, in the mid-1930s. And then he had followed those up with his masterpiece, *The Grapes of Wrath,* the defining novel about the Great Depression, in 1939, which won both the Pulitzer Prize and the National Book Award. After that it was mostly downhill. He was compared, often, with the novelist Ernest Hemingway. But Hemingway had written masterpiece after masterpiece, and though he became depressed when he got older and killed himself by putting a shotgun to his head in 1961, he died laden with honors.

But then, the year after Hemingway died, the Nobel Prize for Literature was awarded to Steinbeck. What a delightful surprise for one of our local residents. Steinbeck was still writing, and his newer works in the early 1960s were pretty good, *Travels with Charley* and *The Winter of Our Discontent,* but when a reporter asked him if he thought he deserved the Nobel Prize, he had a one-word answer. "No," he said.

He'd accept the offer of honorary chairman of the Sag Harbor Old Whalers Festival all right. And he did.

And so, there I was, four months later, along the sidewalk next to the reviewing stand at the opening day of the four-day

Sag Harbor Old Whalers Festival. The whole town was turned out, as best it could, with American flags hung from the windows and little flags and pennants like those you might see hanging from the trees for a new gas station opening. There was a display of paintings of whales and whaleboats in the windows of one of the abandoned stores. And there was a huge, motley crowd of people on hand—parents with small children, tourists in Bermuda shorts with cameras hanging around their necks, teenagers in T-shirts that said OLD WHALERS FESTIVAL on them holding hands with each other with one hand and eating ice cream cones with the other, and motorcycle gang members with leather jackets and key chains. The police, beefed up with some of the officers lent by nearby towns, stood around uncertainly. Soon, there would be concerts, dancing, the results of a beard-growing contest, a reading of *Moby-Dick,* and a re-creation of Meigs Raid, the famous nighttime raid by patriots from Connecticut, who rowed across Long Island Sound to surprise the British encampment at Sag Harbor during the American Revolution. There would also be a costume party and contest, with contestants dressing as pirates, whaling men, Indians, and harpooners. There would be a chili-making contest. And there would be whaleboat races, whatever that was, at 5:00 P.M. that day.

But for now, there was the parade. It was just before noon. Off in the distance—Main Street curved around in an arc from Long Wharf to the Presbyterian church, so you couldn't see from one end to the other—we could hear the sound of a marching band coming up the street. It was the Pierson High School Marching Band, with baton twirlers and flag bearers just behind the Sag Harbor officers driving the two Sag Harbor Police cars with their lights flashing.

And then, behind the marching band, came John Steinbeck. He was sitting atop the backseat of a brand-new convertible waving to the crowd, and what struck me about him was how different he looked from the pictures I had seen of him. He was not an unpleasant-looking man. But he looked something like one of my uncles. He was overweight and ponderous looking, with a bulbous nose and a scraggly gray beard. With his position high up on the convertible top way in the back, you could see he was potbellied and thick around the middle. This definitely was not the slender, athletic-looking writer who had written this screed against poverty and big business during the Depression. But then, that was thirty years earlier. Of course he would look like this now.

His car passed by—it was being driven by the president of the Chamber of Commerce—and then it was gone round the bend. And at that moment, there sounded the loud, townwide noon whistle, its long, low moan drowning out the marching band and everything else for a while. It was lunchtime in Sag Harbor.

The highlight of the festival came later that day. The crowds of people wandered down to the shoreline just to the west of Long Wharf, and there witnessed eighteen men standing next to six wooden whaleboats lined up onshore, getting ready to launch their vessels into the harbor. There were real harpoons in these boats. They had gotten them from the Sag Harbor Whaling Museum. And the eighteen men, waiting eagerly for the start of their race, looked out into the harbor at something I had never in my life seen before. It was a full-size, floating, fake white whale, twenty-five feet long. I learned later it had been built of an old rowboat, bicycle pedals, two-by-fours, and some white Styrofoam. And there was a man inside. You needed someone in there to paddle it out with the bicycle pedals and anchor it in the proper place.

The starter called to everyone to get ready. And then, with a great pull of the chain, BLAM, the 12-gauge shotgun shell inside the small salute cannon, on loan from the Sag Harbor Yacht Club, exploded. Fire came out the end, and then a puff of smoke wafted into the air. With great splashes and yells, the eighteen men carried the six boats into the water, climbed in, and began rowing frantically toward the white whale. The people cheered. About eight minutes later, one of the boats arrived alongside and the harpoonist threw one of the harpoons into the Styrofoam. It stuck. Then the men rowed madly back to shore, trailed by the five other whaling boats, which followed after they had placed their harpoons. The winner had been the Sandbar. The Black Buoy was last. John Steinbeck was nowhere in sight.

I don't think, for safety reasons, that today they would ever allow a man to sit inside a great white whale like that as actual harpoons were thrown at it. But nobody seemed to think anything of it at the time.

When it was over, the Whalers Festival was declared a big success, and Steinbeck was invited to be the honorary chair for the second year. But he declined. Many of us wondered if it was some sort of slight to the festival, but then it was reported by the town pharmacist that he was quite sick. He died in December 1968. He was sixty-six years old.

The nation mourned their Nobel Prize winner. But there was little mention of Sag Harbor anywhere. The body was transported west, to California, to the small town of Salinas, where he is buried. You can visit him there today.

As for the Village of Sag Harbor, its festival was really very poorly attended in subsequent years, and considering that a fight broke out on Main Street during the 1965 festival, the village decided not to hold it again. Over the next few years, the town declined even further. The Bulova factory closed; the Grumman Factory, where they manufactured airplane parts, closed; Sag Harbor Industries, where they manufactured helicopter gas caps, closed. All moved to North Carolina, where labor was more plentiful and far cheaper.

I really wondered if Sag Harbor could ever rise up from the desperate straits it was in, but it did. A few brave New Yorkers bought some of the old abandoned whaling homes, gutted them, and fixed them up. The American Hotel was purchased and reopened by Ted Conklin as an elegant, formal restaurant, and a few abandoned stores reopened as antique shops or country furniture stores. Today, a small whaling home that could have been purchased for $7,000 back then wouldn't sell for less than $700,000. The town is packed with upscale summer visitors, and there are huge 150-foot yachts at Long Wharf. The late Betty Friedan lived here, as did the late Spalding Gray, and there are many other well-known figures on the national scene living here, including Jon Stewart, E. L. Doctorow, and Jimmy Buffett, some of them in homes that might sell for $20 million. And they are even about to begin construction on an exact replica of the great steeple atop of the First Presbyterian Old Whaler's Church.

In the spring of 2006, down in Washington, the government released the latest batch of historic documents from their files. These had been classified up until that spring. Now they were declassified.

One of the documents declassified consisted of a memo from adviser Jack Valenti to Robert McNamara, the secretary of defense in the administration of President Lyndon Johnson in 1966. President Johnson was in the middle of the Vietnam War in 1966 and was looking to read any advice he could get. So McNamara forwarded the memo to him. In the memo there is a reference to John Steinbeck, who had sent Jack Valenti a letter. I think this memo sheds considerable light on what Steinbeck was doing in the years after the Whalers Festival in the backyard of his own home. Among other things, he was firing guns. Here it is.

January 14, 1966

From: Jack Valenti
To: Robert McNamara

Dear Robert:

From time to time, John Steinbeck, the Nobel Prize–winning novelist, writes me. He's a fascinating man, with a kind of imaginative flair for war and its weaponry. I excerpt from his letter, for it bears on your business. It presents three different suggestions.

> *I am glad the bombing has been stopped and the peace feelers are out, and for reasons beyond the basic*

humanitarian ones. I hope the bombing will not be necessary again, but will you offer my suggestion that if bombs are indicated, we should throw everything we can into one colossal strike and then stop again? You see, I was in the Blitz in London. People can get used to anything except what they don't expect. Daily or nightly attacks can be taken in stride; it's when the pattern is broken that they get uneasy. A big strike, a pause for talk, and then if necessary another, but at irregular intervals, has devastating effect. And after each one, the question—will you talk now?

The two other suggestions may well already be used, but if not, should be. In bush country the rifle is an inferior weapon for big game. If you see something moving, your chance of hitting it with a rifle is slight. An open-bore 12-gauge or, if you're man enough, a 10-gauge automatic shotgun loaded with 00 buckshot makes a much more effective weapon. At forty yards one spread of 00 will bring down several running men and with only casual aim. Of course, you can spray the area with automatic rifle fire, but the weight in ammunition is much greater. For a man with a good wrist, a 12-gauge single-shot pistol chambered for buckshot would be effective; I never knew anyone to hit anything with a .45 unless he shoved it in his opponent's mouth. But, oh boy, let me tell you that out at Sag Harbor I have a 10-gauge starting cannon that fires black powder blanks. One day, just to test it, I wadded in a handful of buckshot and got behind a tree to pull the string just in case it should explode. At fifty yards it made a pattern that would bring down a squad. It is just an idea, but I believe that the scattergun has a very definite psychological effect. A twig will deflect a rifle bullet but not a charge of buck.

My third idea has been bugging me for some time. I think the most terrifying modern weapon is the napalm bomb. People who will charge rifle fire won't go through flame. The hand grenade is pretty good, but the necessary weight of metal for fragmenting makes it hard to throw and limits its range. Did you ever throw one with a bent arm? It will put your shoulder out for a week.

What I suggest is a napalm grenade, packed in a heavy plastic sphere almost the exact size and weight of a baseball. The detonator should be of very low power—just enough to break the plastic shell and ignite the inflammable. If the napalm is packed under pressure, it will spread itself when the case breaks. The detonator (a contact cap) should be carried separately and inserted or screwed in just before throwing. This would allow a man to carry a sack full of balls without danger to himself. Now, we probably have developed some fine riflemen, sharpshooters, etc., but there isn't an American boy over thirteen who can't peg a baseball from infield to home plate with accuracy. And a grown man with sandlot experience can do much better. It is the natural weapon for Americans. Six good men could ring an area with either napalm or white phosphorus faster than you could throw a magazine into an automatic or a machine gun. And an enemy with a bit of flame on his clothes or

*even in front of him is out of combat. This weapon
would also be valuable for cleaning out tunnels and
foxholes. Mounted as a rifle grenade, the Steinbeck
super ball would also be valuable for burning off
cover of extra ambush country or of tree-borne sniper
fire.*

SOMETIMES I think of John Steinbeck, and in my mind I
see him floating silently and slowly up Main Street, waving
and smiling, a friendly older man with not a care in the world.

The Flesh Eaters

LATE in the afternoon, on the nineteenth day of shooting *The Flesh Eaters,* all the actors and crew went out to the two-car garage, behind the Surf and Sand, opened the doors, and stared at the monster.

"Five people on each side," said the director, Jack Curtis. "We can do it."

I had never seen the monster before, though I'd been told it was in there. Now there was no missing it. It was eight feet high and nine feet wide, had two bulging eyes on stalks, and ten hairy arms attached to a great dome of a body. It was horrible. A pickup truck had been backed up to the front of the garage. The task was clear. Ten people would lift this thing up and we would place it carefully across the back of the bed of the pickup—it would never fit inside—and then we would secure it.

"Let's go, everybody. We haven't got all day."

Ten people, including me, had no trouble at all picking this up. It was papier-mâché.

"Dan! In the truck!" Curtis shouted.

I hopped up. And the rest of the people, hand over hand,

dodging wayward wobbling arms, slid it up toward me. How did I get into this? I'm supposed to be a newspaperman. I am a newspaperman. But truth be told, at any time, if a movie crew came to town and set up to shoot some scenes, I was there. I would take pictures. I would write about it. And, if possible, I would offer up myself to be part of the crew. Perhaps I could hold the director's coat or, from the outside where I would not be seen, rattle a tent flap to signify a storm while a scene was shot of a mad scientist working with test tubes and electricity in his makeshift beachside laboratory. (Which is already what I had done for this film.) Perhaps I could have a small part in the movie. Perhaps I could be the star. I came cheap.

The star in this movie was a well-known journeyman actor at the time named Martin Kosleck. He had played in a series of B movies in the 1950s, almost always as an evil Nazi officer, and then he had retired. Now Jack Curtis had brought him back from retirement for one last film, *The Flesh Eaters*. Once again as a Nazi scientist, he would build a machine on a deserted island that would conquer the world. It was a role he could not refuse.

By the time we were loading the monster, we were well past halfway through this four-week shoot. At the end of a typical day, I would come home and tell my mother and father about where in Montauk we had shot that day—they were only concerned that my movie career would not interfere with my getting the paper out, which I assured them it would not—and then I would have dinner, hang out with my family for a while, and then head back to the Surf and Sand Inn for the evening. The Surf and Sand Inn was a big nightspot and bar

MARTIN KOSLEK IN
THE FLESH EATERS.

with half a dozen small rooms upstairs for rent. It faced out on the Old Montauk Highway and, across the street and down a cliff, the Atlantic Ocean.

It had a regular bar crowd, a jukebox, and, along the windows, half a dozen tables where people could have steak, fried fish, or burgers. There was a large dining room toward the back.

Curtis had booked the rooms upstairs at the Surf and Sand for that month for the making of this film. He didn't reserve the whole inn, so it continued up front to function as usual, but the booking did include the dining room. Private.

In the evening, director Jack Curtis, the cameraman, the

rest of the leads, and Martin Kosleck would sit at a table drinking beer and, together, with thick scripts set out in front of them, turn to identical pages and make the plans for the next day's shooting. I would join them, the scribe, just barely tolerated, who had to be there to get the information for his newspaper story.

One night earlier in the week, on the tenth day of the shoot, I had made a move on the leading lady. I was emboldened by alcohol, no doubt, but there was no doubt about it. *The Flesh Eaters* opens with an aging, over-the-hill female movie star who drinks too much going out on a dock in New York City to charter a seaplane for what should be a routine flight to Provincetown, Massachusetts. She's supposed to star in summer stock there. Attending this movie star is her secretary, a beautiful young woman in her early twenties, who handles all the details for her employer. The plane takes off with the handsome pilot and the two women inside. It develops engine trouble in a storm and, crippled, successfully sets down in the water halfway to Provincetown next to an uncharted and uninhabited island. They wade ashore. And there they encounter Martin Kosleck and, ultimately, the flesh-eating monster.

The move I made was on the secretary. She was about my age and I was sitting next to her.

"I think I'll turn in," she said.

"Perhaps I should come up?" I said. "I've never seen the rooms upstairs."

"Sure," she said.

We went upstairs, into her room, and I sat awkwardly on a chair while she proceeded to get ready for bed. This consisted of her sitting in another chair in front of a mirror and taking off or peeling off different parts of her face. We talked about this and that. She knew, I think, exactly what I was about. But she was having no part of it.

"So this is your room," I said.

"Yes," she said. "Bedtime."

She peeled off her long eyelashes. She took the earrings out of her ears. She unpinned her hair and put it up in rollers. But the worst part was when she used a tissue to remove the makeup on her face and then replace it with cold cream, the goo of choice at that time.

In the end, she looked like the monster in the garage. And it was also completely apparent that she was far older than she looked when all made up. She was at least fifteen years my senior. Disillusioned, I backed out the door, said my good-byes, and fled.

The afternoon of the monster shoot, after it had been secured with clothesline on the back of the pickup, the cameraman, the young grip, and the lighting man leaped up to join me in the truck and keep the monster steady. We rumbled along the Old Montauk Highway, going up and down the hills, the many arms waving, and, following two cars filled with the actors that led the way, headed for town. I wondered if we would parade through town like this, or go out Second House Road and around town. I did know we were headed to the beach.

We passed the Second House Road turnoff and my heart leaped. We were out in the open, up high, the sun shining down on us, the wind in our hair, with this big monster, and we were going straight through downtown. Maybe I would see some people I knew so I could wave at them when we went by. We turned at Edgemere Street, went up Surfside Drive, and, halfway up, stopped and unloaded the monster and carried it through the dunes.

The shoot involved lots of white smoke—created with dry ice and fans—as the monster slowly wiggled its way out of the sea toward Martin Kosleck. I watched from afar, having been politely told that there was nothing for me to do in this penultimate scene. And there she was, the heroine, as pretty as always, running into the strong arms of the pilot as the monster advanced.

The Flesh Eaters was distributed nationally in 1964 as one of the follow-up movies to the hit *The Blob*. It did achieve considerable commercial success. As they left the theater, people were given small pieces of sponge impregnated with a powder that turned to fake blood when dropped in water. You did that when you got home.

As for me, I went on to cover, and if possible work in the making of, many movies filmed in the Hamptons during the next forty years. These included Sidney Lumet's *Deathtrap*, starring Christopher Reeve and Michael Caine; Alan Alda's *Sweet Liberty* (in which I played an extra strolling the sidewalk of Sag Harbor one evening); *Masquerade*, starring Rob Lowe; Woody Allen's *Interiors*; *Eternal Sunshine of the Spotless Mind*, starring Kate Winslet and Jim Carrey; *Rocket Gibraltar*, starring Burt Lancaster; and *Something's Gotta Give*, starring Diane Keaton and Jack Nicholson. It's been a wonderful film career for me and I have many memories. But no awards.

IN 2002, at the *Dan's Papers* "They Made the Movie Here Film Festival," which at that time was in its tenth year, we had a showing of *The Flesh Eaters*. When the movie ended and the lights came up in the Duke Auditorium of Chancellors Hall at Southampton College, the first thing the host of the event, Guy de Fraumeni, the noted film critic who has been a judge at the Sundance Film Festival, did was ask if there were any questions. An older man stood up.

"That was the *worst* movie I've ever seen!" he said.

Frank Mundus

THE East Hampton Cinema on Main Street is where the world-class filmmakers who live here hold movie premieres. I can think of at least a dozen films that have been introduced here, where they have rolled out the red carpet, put up the felt ropes, and positioned the paparazzi alongside to shoot the stars as they come in. But whenever I pass this theater, what I remember most is the very first premiere ever held here.

As it happens, it was not only the first one but also the biggest and most successful one. The film is still among the ten highest-grossing movies of all time and the top fifty best films ever made, and if you haven't seen it by now, you should. The film is *Jaws,* and it made the film reputations of three men connected with it: Steven Spielberg, the director; Richard Dreyfuss, the hero; and Roy Scheider, the police chief of the town of "Amity." As for the killer shark, in the end, it lost, but it scared the wits out of just about everybody who went to see this film when it came out in 1975.

The idea for this film, of course, had been in the making long before 1975. Around 1968, a writer named Peter Benchley had come out to Montauk and had become fascinated by a wild and unpredictable character he met there named Frank Mundus. Mundus would head out to sea in his forty-foot fishing boat searching for giant killer sharks that in many cases were bigger than his boat. He would harpoon them, run with them until they tired, then bring them alongside and shoot them until they were dead. Then he would lash them to the side of his boat and bring them in. Peter Benchley modeled the fearless and irascible character of "Quint" in his book after Frank Mundus. Universal Studios bought the movie rights. And so it was Quint, or Mundus, who was the maniac in the movie who went out with Scheider and Dreyfuss in his fishing boat on this final desperate quest to kill the man-eating shark.

At seven o'clock on a Friday evening in July 1963, I drove down to the docks with a single stack of my *Montauk Pioneer* newspaper to deliver to the fishing boats. I had come from the center of town, four miles away, where Main Street was alive with tourists walking around, buying souvenirs, window-shopping, playing miniature golf, or eating in the Shagwong or Trail's End restaurant.

Unlike the center of town, the docks are quiet at seven at night. The hundred fishing boats there, rocking gently in their slips, are tied up. The fishermen have gone home. The captains have gone home. They will not meet up with one another again until four o'clock the following morning.

I parked at the most southerly end of the docks, nearest to

Uihlein's Boat Rental, and taking a bunch of newspapers out of the backseat, I got out of the car and climbed over the railing to the deck of the *Viking II*. Going to the entrance of the locked wheelhouse door, I slipped a few newspapers under it. Then I steadied myself and, tucking the remaining newspapers back under my arm, made the short leap to the boat just adjacent, where I did the same thing.

It occurred to me at this moment—because this was the first time I had done this—that what I was doing was illegal. I was trespassing. Well, so what? Everybody loves the paper. Or should.

A few days earlier, I had been encouraged to leave newspapers on the boats by a Montauk Open Boat captain named George Glas of the *Helen II*. I had been down at the docks trying to sell my advertising, and he had been just one of the three fishing boat captains who had bought anything. The others turned me down.

"You ought to just put a few on the decks of each boat," Glas had said. "People do read 'em. It might help you out."

Captain Glas, like many of the others, fished for porgies, fluke, and blackfish out at some place called Cox's Lodge. As many as fifty people could show up at his boat at four in the morning, pay $15, and come aboard for the trip out there. They'd be out all day and get back to the docks at three in the afternoon, exhausted, sunburned, and lugging bags of fish. Glas would tie up, spray the decks with fresh water from a hose, and count the money. Then I could talk to him, as I could talk to anyone else. Except for Mundus. He wouldn't talk to me.

"What's wrong with Mundus?" I had asked.

"He's pretty rough," Glas said. "Goes his own way. Started doing this 'Monster Fishing' for sharks a few years ago. It's not a sport. He goes out and shoots them. Nobody likes him."

So there I was. Not too many papers would fit under the door of the wheelhouses, which was a good thing. Leave too many, they'd use them as fish wrappers. Probably use them as fish wrappers anyway. Can't help that.

As I went from boat to boat like this, each time doing the same thing, my mind tended to wander. But then I'd slip or lose my balance for a moment and I'd get refocused. What a hell of a job it was, running a newspaper. I imagined a headline: EDITOR FALLS OFF BOAT, BANGS HEAD, HOSPITALIZED.

And there was Frank Mundus.

What was he doing down at the docks at seven o'clock at night? I stopped. He was a big, sweaty, burly man with a cowboy hat and boots. He stood there with a huge carving knife, and at his feet there was a cut-up shark, maybe six feet long. Above him was one of the biggest signs in the harbor. MONSTER FISHING. CRICKET II. CALL FRANK MUNDUS. And the phone number.

"Don't put none of that here," he said, waving at the fishing boat behind him.

"Okay."

I just stood there, staring at him.

"You ought to write about me shark fishing," he said. "You'll sell more of your papers."

"The paper is free."

Mundus didn't say anything.

FRANK MUNDUS
ON THE DOCK
AT MONTAUK
HARBOR IN
1968.
(Courtesy of Frank
Mundus)

"You ought to advertise in the paper," I said. "Explain what you do. People say what you do isn't fishing."

"Well, they ought to come out and try it before they say that. You want to go shark fishing?"

"I get seasick," I said. "I can't even go out in a boat."

"Well. We just come in today. Late. Caught six fish like this. This is the last one."

"I put thousands of copies of the paper in the motels. All those people come out here. They read all the ads."

Mundus seemed a little weary.

"How much?"

"A small ad? You could get one about two by three inches for ten bucks. Want to try it?"

Mundus took a wad of money out of his pocket and peeled off two fives.

"Write something nice," he said. He pointed to his sign. "Now beat it."

My heart leaped. But this was the first and last time Frank Mundus would ever take an ad in my newspaper. Two weeks later, when I came back to talk to him there on the dock, he was brandishing a gun. Cleaning it, it seemed to me. He looked up.

"Not interested," he said.

And I walked off.

About a week after that, my dad came home to dinner from the drugstore to tell the family there was quite a bit of news in town. At the time, my uncle and aunt were visiting with their kids. The closest in age to me was Johnny, who was sixteen, seven years my junior.

"Mundus has a monster shark he is bringing in," Dad said. "It's bigger than his boat. So he's going slow. They expect him in around midnight. Everybody is going to be there."

We all went down to the docks at midnight and the whole town was there. But Mundus was nowhere to be seen. The word was going around that a wind had sprung up and things were going even slower than he thought and he'd be in around 3:00 A.M. Some people were going to wait. But my dad said we should go home. We could see this big fish, which reportedly was about the size of our car, in the morning.

But I could not sleep. I stayed up in bed staring at the ceiling until about 5:00 A.M., then tiptoed over to the guest room and woke up Johnny. It was still dark.

"Psst. Get up. Let's go see that fish."

He blinked and grinned. In the darkness we got dressed quietly and tiptoed out the front door. Ten minutes later, we parked the car out at the docks, where, under the strings of used-car-lot lights, the fishermen from the city had already arrived for the new day. They stood around drinking coffee or talking animatedly as they boarded one boat or another, getting ready to go off on another day of sportfishing.

I asked somebody about the shark.

"On the beach in back of Gosman's," a man with a baseball cap said. "But all the excitement's over. Everybody's gone home."

Gosman's was a small clam bar up near the jetties, about a hundred and fifty yards away. It wasn't open and was dark, inside and out. But I knew the way around it. Did I want to go around? A shark the size of a car? I looked at Johnny. Hey, no problem.

Struggling hand over hand, we walked slowly and awkwardly down a dark alleyway around to the back of the restaurant looking for a fish. There was no fish.

"Somebody must have moved it," I said.

But then Johnny, who was behind me, screamed. He had taken a step off to one side and, in the dark, had tripped and fallen over something. It was the carcass of the shark. I went down as well. And now I was screaming. The shark was lying on its side, motionless, every bit as big as advertised. It was dark gray, its skin cold and tough as sandpaper, and at one end, a single eye stared out above what appeared to be a tongue lolling out. And there were all those razor-sharp teeth. We got to our feet, retreated backward, then ran back to the car and drove home. No one even knew we had been gone.

Later in the morning, we returned to find the newspapermen there, the TV people holding interviews, Mundus yelling at everybody, telling them to keep back and running back and forth with his gun. The shark, which now was beginning to smell, had been winched ashore at 3:00 A.M. by a big truck owned by another fisherman who had agreed to lend it for the effort. The pull had stripped its gears. The shark weighed, people guessed, more than four thousand pounds, though no one would ever know because there was not a scale in Montauk big enough to lift it. Nothing like it had ever been seen before in these parts.

Before the day was out, it would have to be cut up and disposed of. Mundus was going to have the head stuffed and mounted. Maybe get it hung up over a bar down there, maybe Salivar's.

SOME thirty years later, in 1992, the Coast Guard issued an order that every fishing boat captain, including the oldtimers, would have to take a new written test.

Mundus, who was surely the most prominent fishing boat captain in Montauk by that time, demurred. He would take the test, but maybe at the end of the fishing season. The Coast Guard insisted. And then Frank Mundus announced that he would retire rather than take it. Suddenly, a rumor swept through town. Frank Mundus, it was said, had never properly learned to read. (And now I knew why he did not particularly appreciate my newspaper!)

The following year, Frank Mundus, now sixty-eight, took up with a young Englishwoman he had met in a mail correspondence. He had been widowed twelve years earlier. Now he married her and moved to the Big Island of Hawaii. There they live on a twenty-acre farm near Naalehu, where they raise sheep, hogs, and occasionally wild boar that weigh more than five hundred pounds.

WHILE writing this book, I came across a photograph of Mundus, taken in the 1960s, standing on the dock and peering at the camera through the skeletal jaws of one of the great white sharks he had caught. It was a terrific shot of him and I thought it ought to accompany this chapter. When I tried to contact him in Hawaii to get his permission to do so, however, I learned that he was back in Montauk. At the age of eighty-three, he had just arrived here to spend a month, seeing old friends and going out fishing every morning in the *Cricket II*, which, amazingly, had been brought back out of drydock and restored by some filmmakers interested in making a documentary about him.

"He's staying at the Star Island Yacht Club," his wife told me over the phone. "But I'm staying here. Somebody's got to feed the animals. We've got a whole farm of them, including a nine-hundred-pound hog named Fritzi that Frank just bought. I'm sure he'd see you, though. It's best in the afternoon, when he gets back in."

I found Frank, weathered and suntanned, sitting at one of the outdoor picnic tables they have set up there between the yacht club and the docks. There were his filmmakers and a small crowd of well-wishers talking to him. Spread out in front of him on the picnic table was some of the paraphernalia he had for sale and also some of the books written about him. Behind him, in its slip, bobbed the *Cricket II*.

I listened to Frank reminisce for a while, asked him if he remembered the young man who once sold him an ad in the *Pioneer,* which he said he did. And I bought one of his books, which was called *Monster Man.*

Then I asked him if he would be willing to let me use the photo of him looking through the shark jaws for this book. I had a copy with me. He took out a ballpoint pen, asked me to hand him the photo, and, when I did, swiftly wrote the following on the back of it:

> *Dan Rattiner is welcome to use any pictures of me in any way he wants. Frank Mundus. June 13, 2007.*

Well, I thought, so much for the rumor that he wouldn't take his fishing boat captain's test because he couldn't read or write. And so much for the theory that that's why he didn't appreciate my newspaper.

Uncle Ed

THE richest man I knew growing up was my Uncle Ed. Architect, engineer, builder of Manhattan office buildings. His greatest claim to fame, however, was as an inventor.

"He invented the S clip," my mother said proudly. "Every time a construction company in America builds a skyscraper that has concrete floors, they have to use S clips. And for every S clip they use, they pay Uncle Ed fifteen cents."

Uncle Ed at one time owned most of downtown Garden City, Long Island. I remember at the age of fourteen accompanying him from his apartment in Manhattan to an attorney's office in Garden City to sell some of his holdings, going out via the Grand Central Parkway in a limousine driven by his chauffeur, and being told by him the secret of business.

"If you're in the living room and they're playing poker in the kitchen, don't place any bets."

Once a year when I was growing up, the whole family would assemble for a dinner in the home of one of the uncles and aunts somewhere in or around New York City. There'd be maybe fifty people at the dinner. But all conversation stopped when Uncle Ed and Aunt Bertha's limousine pulled up. Uncle Ed was a little man, five foot three, with a thick neck. Aunt Bertha towered over him. They'd come in. Ed would sit down in a club chair and the children would gather around. He'd tell stories.

"I was in the war, you know," he'd say. He was referring to World War I. "There was this long line where you waited to get your uniform. At the front, they'd measure your neck. 'Fifteen inches,' the sergeant would call out. A man at a table would give you a small uniform. 'Eighteen inches,' would come the call and you'd get the big uniform. The sleeves of my jacket came out to *here*." He held his left palm about a foot beyond his right hand. "The pants came all the way over my shoes. The ends wriggled on the ground when I walked.

"My job was to guard the Parsippany Reservoir in New Jersey. One dark night, some German soldiers came creeping quietly along the shore. There were ten of them, then fifty of them. They were one behind the other, all along the curve of the reservoir. What was I going to do? I only had one bullet. I had an idea. I picked up my gun, grabbed the barrel in one hand, and slowly bent it into a small curve, like this." He showed us by motioning with his hand. "Then I put in my one bullet. Aimed. And when I pulled the trigger, BAM! This bullet went out, went around the curve of the reservoir, through each German, then came around the whole reservoir and plink! Right back into the breech of the gun. What do you think of that?"

We told him he was making it up, but he swore it was true. That's just how it happened. He even had a medal. We howled.

And there were many other stories. He had won a bid in

UNCLE ED TELLING ONE OF HIS STORIES.
(Courtesy of Dan Rattiner)

Manhattan to build a five-story parking garage. How had he done it? The plans called for the facade of the building to be made of six-sided masonry pieces that could be stacked up into a lacy fencing. You'd drive right up to the masonry and stop. You could see out. But it would be hard to see in.

The masonry pieces called for were expensive. So what he'd done was call a sewer pipe company. They made six-sided sewer pipe. You'd buy it in ten-foot lengths. "How much to buy it in ten-*inch* lengths?" he asked.

"Why would you want to do that?" they asked.

"Just give me a price," he said.

And so they did. It was far cheaper that way. And it was just as strong.

Another time he won a bid to restore a dilapidated dock along the West Side Highway in Manhattan. He had given such a remarkably low bid that not only had he won, but his competitors came to the awarding-of-the-contract ceremony to see how he did it. He had arranged for helicopters to hover over the end of the dock and hold it up with cables while new pilings were put in below.

Then there was the time he was sitting on the subway one morning, heading to the downtown opera house he had under construction. Across from him sat a man reading the *Daily News.* On the front page was the headline OPERA HOUSE UNDER CONSTRUCTION COLLAPSES.

"I felt sick," Uncle Ed said. "Right then and there on the subway, I took a slide rule out of my bag, and by the time I got to my stop, I had figured out the mistake I had made with one of the stress calculations. But it wasn't my opera house. It was another opera house."

Thus were the legends of Uncle Ed.

Over the Christmas break after my second year at graduate school studying architecture in 1963, my father spoke to me after dinner at our home in Montauk.

"It's time for me to build a new store," he said. "The lease on the old building will end in two years. I have this property on the plaza right in the center of town. Do you want to design the building?"

"Sure," I said. But deep down I was not so sure. I did some pencil drawings, made some plans, even called Uncle Ed for his advice, but then I didn't like what I had done and started over. And thus it went for a week. Two weeks after that I gave up.

"I don't think I know enough," I said.

"We'd really like you to do it," Dad said.

"I know."

"You think anybody else could do it?"

"Uncle Ed," I said.

Uncle Ed came out to Montauk five times in the next six weeks, and often I'd come home from delivering the newspaper to find his limousine in front of our house. Inside, he and Dad huddled over drawings.

At one point, he asked how I was doing at architectural school.

"Terrible," I told him. "I'm not interested in buildings. I'm interested in the stories about buildings. I have a wonderful professor named Mitchell who teaches the main engineering course. He tells hilarious stories, like you do. So I got an A. But it is not about architecture."

"Tell me one of his stories."

"One of his lectures was about the premise 'God Is on the Side of the Erring Engineer.' He told us a story. It was very much like the one about the opera house. He had designed a small bridge that went over the Mystic River near Boston. He designed it with a full load of trucks in a traffic jam on the road going across. Then he figured the pilings to be able to bear a weight twenty times that."

"The standard multiple," Ed said.

"One day, he told us, he saw a picture of his bridge in the local Mystic newspaper that terrified him. So he got in his car and raced down there to watch his bridge collapse. The picture showed a dredge in the river, one metal arm wrapped around the support for the bridge, and the other arm scooping up muck off the bottom. He'd never figured any sideways stress like that. But the bridge held."

Soon the drawings for the store were finished, and the firm of Ed Pospisil Builders appeared on the lot with a bulldozer to dig a hole. The construction was under way. It would take just under a year. But during that time Uncle Ed suffered a stroke. Now he was in a hospital in Manhattan.

"He was just walking down the sidewalk in front of the apartment house when it happened," my mother said. "But he's getting better."

"What about the building?" I asked.

"It could be a problem."

But it wasn't. From his hospital bed, every day, Uncle Ed monitored the progress of the construction. My mother and father were his eyes and ears. Did the indoor light fixtures arrive? Was the plate glass for the front in?

One time, my mother told me the most amazing story. Uncle Ed called her to look and see if any of the six big wooden trusses that had arrived the day before had been lifted onto the walls yet. They would span the space and, eventually, support the roof.

She went and looked, then called him back.

"None are up yet," she said. "The workmen are just standing around."

Uncle Ed had my mother go out and get Ed Pospisil and bring him to the telephone. He gave Ed quite a tongue-lashing. "Yes sir," Ed Pospisil said. "No sir." By the end of the day, two of the trusses were up.

Six months later, the whole town turned out for the grand opening of the new store. It was a beautiful day. And on the counters inside were platter after platter of delicious things to eat—chicken in gravy, spaghetti, roast ham, cupcakes, chocolate chip cookies—all brought there by the residents of the town. They loved my parents. And they loved the new store. It was the biggest store in town. And everybody who came in, including the customers, ate up.

The ribbon cutting was scheduled for three that afternoon. In attendance would be my mom and dad, Mr. Pospisil, and the leading dignitary of the town, Perry B. Duryea Jr., who at that time was the majority leader of the State Assembly. He would do the honors cutting the ribbon. As for the architect of this beautiful store, my mother explained that he was still at home in the city, recovering from his recent stroke. He could not travel.

But then, at five minutes to three, just as everybody began to assemble on the sidewalk in front of the new building, the familiar black limousine pulled up and out he came. He got out slowly. The chauffeur came around to help him. Bertha took a wheelchair out of the trunk, but he waved it off with his cane. He would walk. And he did, arriving in his good time to his proper place with the other dignitaries at the ribbon cutting. Flashbulbs popped as the ribbon was cut. A few short speeches were made. The ceremony ended with Father Nichols saying a prayer.

For the rest of the afternoon, Uncle Ed held court, in his wheelchair, just in front of the entrance to the pharmacy in the back. Customers and friends would come over and shake

UNCLE ED HOLDING COURT AT THE GRAND OPENING
OF THE NEW WHITE'S DRUG AND DEPARTMENT STORE.
NOTE PIES AND CAKES.
(Courtesy of Dan Rattiner)

his hand and he would thank them and smile. It was a wonderful day.

Five years later, Uncle Ed walked slowly from his office in
what was then the Architectural Design Building on 40th
Street and Park Avenue to his apartment, one block away, at
39th Street and Lexington. It was normally a ten-minute walk.
With his cane, Uncle Ed could negotiate it in about twenty.

The apartment house where he lived—and I visited it many
times—was a nineteen-floor brick affair known as the Concord. It had been built in the 1920s and Ed and Bertha were
among the first tenants. But now, a major Manhattan commercial developer had bought the building and was in the

process of trying to force everybody out. That spring day, the Concord was a very forlorn place. Ed and Bertha were the last tenants still in the building. And they were not moving.

Ed came through the lobby to the elevator. He set down his bag. And with the tip of his cane pressed UP. The elevator came, and he got in, and it slowly rose.

As he passed the fifth floor, Uncle Ed heard what he thought was jackhammering. It *was* jackhammering. And as the elevator rose up higher and higher, the racket got louder and louder, until, finally, at the fourteenth floor, where the doors opened and Uncle Ed got out, he saw three men with a jackhammer, blasting away at some concrete in the ceiling to expose the steel skeleton that was the bones of the building. They were beginning the conversion to office suites with or without Ed and Bertha moving out. Maybe the noise would drive them away.

Uncle Ed set down his bag in the hall and took out a tape measure. He asked the men to stop what they were doing for a minute, which they did, and he asked them to reach up with the tape measure and give him the depth dimension of the exposed beam. When they had done that, he thanked them. Then he put the tape measure back in the bag and walked down to apartment 18 at the end of the hall, put his key in the door, and went inside.

There was Bertha. "We're staying," he said.

"Hello?" He was on the phone. "Can I speak to Mr. Wickham? Mr. Wickham? This is Ed Klausner, your tenant at the Concord. No, I am not calling about moving. I want you to know your workmen are up here, cutting the concrete away from the steel beams, enabling me to measure them. They are thick enough for residential construction. They are not thick enough for commercial construction. The city will not let you convert this building to a commercial use. You'll be right over? I'll be right here."

One month later, Ed and Bertha were ensconced in one of the most magnificent apartments in the entire city of New York, a triplex apartment designed as a country house at 88 Park Avenue, the same distance from Ed's office as the Concord, but southwest, not southeast. I visited there often. It was an absolutely fabulous place, with dining rooms, libraries, many bedrooms and bathrooms and servants. And it was all being paid for by Mr. Wickham, who happened to find this place just coming on the market, and who would be willing to move them there, pay the rent and, as a matter of fact, all their utility bills, maintenance, and staff for the rest of their natural lives.

Now, whether this story is true or not, I cannot say, because it was told to me by my Uncle Ed when I visited them in the new apartment. But there you are. And there they were.

Ed passed away four years later, in 1972. He was seventy-two. As for Bertha, she was just getting started. She made herself a career as a literary agent, hosting lunches and dinners for the literary lights of the city in this magnificent setting for the next twenty years. Ask any writer in New York if they heard of the International Literary Agency. That was her. My Aunt Bertha.

She finally passed on in 1996 at the age of ninety-six. By that time, the rent was being paid for by the estate of Mr. Wickham, who was able to successfully complete the conversion of the Concord to commercial use, but had been unable to outlive his tenant.

The Ladies Village
Improvement Society

LIKE anything you love, sometimes it's just nice to get away from it. And so, every once in a while, I'd get in my car and head out from Montauk, in the only direction possible, west, off the peninsula, to East Hampton sixteen miles away.

If Montauk was the land of vacationers—working-class people from western Long Island with two weeks' vacation coming out to the motels for sun, fun, swimming, and fishing—East Hampton was its polar opposite. It had a quiet, leafy Main Street, with giant elm trees lining both sides and overarching the boulevard, with rows of stores beneath, anchored in the east by a big colonial wooden windmill on a broad lawn, and on the west by the town green, which included a pond, a cemetery with tombstones dating back to colonial times, a tall flagpole that had been fashioned from the mast of the *John Milton,* a long-ago sailing vessel that had shipwrecked on the ocean beach nearby, and the Mulford Farm.

Word travels fast in a small town such as East Hampton, and in 1964, people in the town were already familiar with this upstart newspaper I had founded in Montauk. Like just about everything else in Montauk, they didn't like it.

On a Saturday afternoon in the third week of July, I drove to East Hampton to enjoy the first day of the Ladies Village Improvement Society Fair. It was an annual event, during the third week of July every year, and the Ladies Village Improvement Society had run it every year since 1896, a year after the group had been founded in East Hampton, as a force for temperance and high moral standards and especially to lend their support to the issue sweeping the land at that particular time: the prohibition of liquor. By the 1960s, the LVIS consisted of elderly blue-haired society ladies—wealthy summer people from Manhattan—who pruned the flowers in the flower boxes along Main Street, saw to the mowing of the lawns in public spaces, went to visit merchants who put large signs in their windows to tell them they would have to remove them (which they would), and kept an eye out for any signs of the hoi polloi (people eating ice cream on the street, or in Bermuda shorts, or women with skirts too short). These people, along with Italians, Jews, Negroes, or other minority groups, would be duly noted, and then frostily stared at. As a member of one of these minority groups, I was stared at.

I parked my car along the narrow road, James Lane, that separated the Mulford Farm from the town green. Parking was prohibited along this stretch, but for the LVIS Fair, or for the churchgoers on early Sunday morning, the rules were not enforced.

I'd been to the fair before and I had always liked it. It was fun. Corn and crabcakes for sale. Cupcakes and cookies.

Lemonade. Games. Small pens with sheep and goats in them you could pet. A pony ride. Square dances.

The year before, I had gone to the fair on the morning of the first day with a stack of my newspapers, hoping to put the stack on one of the two folding bridge tables at the entrance so people could pick a copy up as they went in, but I had been told no, they would not do that. So this year I didn't even try. I was just going to have fun. And I had invited a girl, Corinne, who was a waitress at the Montauk Manor, to come with me. I loved the fair.

We walked down the row of cars parked on James Lane to the entrance and got to the back of the line where you paid to get in. There was an excitement to the place—the smell of spices and farm animals, a man with an accordion singing square dance tunes over a PA system. A breeze rustled the leaves in the trees.

The line moved quickly. The LVIS had, with the help of the Village Highway Department, no doubt, built a five-foot-high snow fence along the road. There was a big sign on the fence farther down, the sort the LVIS would usually frown upon, but which they made exception for since it said COME TO THE LVIS FAIR, JULY 24, 25, AND 26, MULFORD FARM. At the front of the line, there were the familiar folding tables set up. Cardboard posters about the fair had been taped to the front. Behind the tables, two ladies were selling tickets and making change, moving as fast as they could. Lots of people were coming and they wanted the line to move quickly.

As we moved forward, I noticed that about ten feet behind the two women, several small boys had created an opening in the snow fence. They would slip through without paying. And in a few minutes some more kids would come and slip through. Apparently the word had gotten out. The women never even turned around.

We got to the front of the line. I'm a good guy. I thought I'd tell them about it.

"I just thought you ought to know that just behind you there's kids sneaking in," I said. "There's a break in the fence."

Both of these elderly women, who had been looking only at the tickets, the money, and the change, now stopped what they were doing and stared at me. They knew exactly who I was.

"This is none of your business," one of them said. "Who do you think you are?"

"I just thought you'd like to know . . ."

"We know what we are doing," she concluded.

Now the other woman spoke. "Do you see how we keep our town?" she asked me. She would not wait for a reply. "East Hampton was voted the most beautiful town in America last year by no less than the *Saturday Evening Post*."

"How many tickets?" the first one asked.

"Two," I said.

"That's one dollar."

We paid and went in and had a wonderful time. But I could not get the idea of the *Saturday Evening Post* out of my mind. This magazine was, along with *Look* and *Life* magazines, the largest-circulating big-format magazine in the country. Perhaps five million people read it every week. You couldn't help but notice that East Hampton was beautiful. But this was quite an honor indeed, to be selected by the *Saturday Evening Post*.

THE LVIS FAIR AT MULFORD FARM, 1912.
(Courtesy of the Ladies Village Improvement Society, Inc.)

As the years rolled by, I occasionally—when writing about East Hampton—noted that it had been voted the Most Beautiful Village in America by the *Saturday Evening Post*. Soon the phrase began to appear on the front cover of the brochure put out every year by the East Hampton Chamber of Commerce. Then it was in advertisements and articles written about the town. People running for office in the town would use the phrase. For a while, it was even on a small sign that the mayor had authorized be put up at the entrance to the village.

I didn't think much about any of this until one day, perhaps twenty years later, I was at a party and was introduced to a very interesting, elderly man still active in the advertising business. We talked for a while about our careers. Before he had been an ad man, he said, he had worked at the *Saturday Evening Post.*

I mentioned the business about East Hampton.

"I don't remember any of that," he said. "And I would. I was there until it closed. And I worked there for almost twenty years before that."

I did the math. He would have been there at the time they had this contest.

"Are you sure?" I asked.

"I'm sure."

I told him how I had heard about it.

"I think you got it wrong," he said.

The following autumn, I went to the New York Public Library in Manhattan and was directed to their publication annex, which was directly across the street and down one block, at the corner of Fifth Avenue and 40th Street.

I spent five hours at this library. They did indeed have a complete set of the *Saturday Evening Post* and they also had a card catalog that might refer you to any article in any of them. I looked through the card catalog. There had been an article about single girls living together in a residence in East Hampton in 1975, which would have been eleven years after the LVIS Fair I went to. There was no reference to any contest or to East Hampton having won any contest.

I flipped through the pages of all the issues of the *Saturday Evening Post* for 1961, 1962, and 1963 and did not find anything.

Then I thought maybe the blue-haired lady had the wrong

magazine. I looked in the card catalog for every reference to East Hampton during the 1950s and 1960s. There were articles in *Holiday* magazine, an article in *National Geographic.* But no contest. And nothing even close. It didn't happen.

Today, East Hampton is still advertised as "the Most Beautiful Village in America." I have written numerous articles trying to set the record straight. None of them do any good.

Richard Nixon

ONE of the most controversial individuals of the twentieth century was Richard Nixon. In 1966, I had the opportunity to interview him person-to-person in Montauk. But I turned him down. Thus separates journalists who get nominated for Pulitzer Prizes from those who don't.

It came about like this. It was a day in August. Outside, in Montauk, people were swimming in the ocean, sitting around the pool at the motels, driving out to the tip of Long Island six miles away to admire the lighthouse. Or shopping in one of the many stores, including my father's new store in the center of town. It was a beautiful day. I was in my office.

This was my first office, the first office this newspaper ever had other than my bedroom at my parents' house. Those first three years, I had a big cardboard sign Scotch-taped to my bedroom door, with the words READ THE MONTAUK PIONEER on it. Inside was a desk and a chair, a bed and a dresser and a closet, all the same furniture that had been there since we had moved to Montauk in 1956. If I needed to use the telephone, I went downstairs to the kitchen. There was a phone in the kitchen.

This sixth year, the sixth summer I ran the newspaper, however, I saw a way I could have an office in downtown Montauk. My dad's new drugstore, which he had built on land he had bought, was put up around the corner from the old store, which he had rented. And it was three times as big. Early on in the construction of the new store, Dad decided to continue paying the rent on the old store for a year after it closed. Everyone was used to going to the old location. So he had a big sign on the door: WHITE'S DRUGSTORE NOW AROUND THE CORNER, with an arrow. He thought one year would be enough to get people used to the new address. After that, the landlord could rent the old space out to whomever.

GURNEY'S INN IN THE 1960S, WHERE
RICHARD NIXON STAYED.
(Courtesy of Gurney's Inn)

As for me, as I helped the workmen carry all the merchandise from the old store to the new during that first week in June—the business continued in both locations for two days—I had an idea for the old one. It was very forlorn looking. Dust and dirt everywhere. Some of the counters, empty, still there. What if I set up an office for the newspaper in the prescription room? I asked my dad and he was fine with it. My mom wasn't so sure. She didn't want her twenty-three-year-old son in such a dirty place. But in the end, she relented. I'd only be there for the summer, after all. That fall, I would be going back to grad school. That I would pay no rent went without saying.

And so, on that afternoon in August, I was sitting on a tall chair in the prescription room, my feet up on the old stained counter, when the phone rang. I picked it up.

"Montauk Pioneer," I said.

"Hi, Dan, it's Nick Monte."

Nick was the owner of Gurney's Inn, an oceanfront hotel in Montauk.

"We have a celebrity staying with us. Richard Nixon."

"I heard he was there," I said.

Actually, when I had been at Gurney's trying to sell Nick an ad two months earlier, I could see several plaques on the wall, with personal letters written to Nick on stationery from the vice president's office, extolling the virtues of the inn and telling Nick how much he, Richard Nixon, and his wife, Pat, had enjoyed their stay the month before. One was dated July 1960. And it was engraved right there on the brass plaque. Anyone coming in could read it. Dick Nixon had been at Gurney's to write his acceptance speech for the Republican nomination for president. He wanted peace and quiet. And he got it. But that had been six years earlier.

On this day, in the summer of 1966, Richard Nixon was at a political low point in his life. He had not yet become president of the United States. He had not yet become the first man to resign the presidency. But he was going through a different kind of disgrace.

Perhaps a brief history of Richard Nixon is in order at this point. Nixon graduated from law school in 1937 and became a lawyer in California. His first political campaign, for the U.S. Congress in 1946, pitted him against the liberal Democratic incumbent, Jerry Voorhis. And it set the tone for many campaigns to follow. In it Nixon, a vehement anti-Communist, accused his opponent of dangerous left-wing leanings. He won easily. The new congressman then gained public attention as a member of the House Un-American Activities Committee, playing a prominent role in the committee's investigation of Alger Hiss, a respected former State Department official accused of spying for the USSR in the 1930s. Then, in 1950, Nixon decided to run for the Senate. In another miserable, dirty campaign, he won—some say stole—the election from popular incumbent congresswoman Helen Gahagan Douglas, labeling her the "pink lady."

In the summer of 1952, General Dwight Eisenhower, a World War II hero, was persuaded by the Republican party to run for president of the United States. He selected Richard Nixon as his vice presidential running mate. And the ticket won in a landslide.

Nixon's connection with Montauk came about because of a

meeting Nixon had with Soviet premier Nikita Khrushchev in 1959. It was called "the kitchen debate," and the two men spent a half hour in Moscow at an international trade fair debating the merits of communism versus capitalism while sitting at a Formica counter of a kitchen unit designed by New York designer Raymond Loewy. These kitchens could be assembled in a day. In fact, they were actually being assembled in Montauk, by the hundreds, in a Levittown-like complex of residences near Montauk Harbor called Culloden Shores, named for the British man-of-war HMS *Culloden* that shipwrecked there during the American Revolution. At that time, you could go into Macy's Department Store in Manhattan and on one of the upper floors walk through a complete home designed by Mr. Loewy, the very home you could buy at Culloden, furnished under Mr. Loewy's direction down to the sheets and silverware, chairs and sofas. You paid $14,599, they gave you the key to the front door, and the place was yours. The Culloden, with about two hundred homes in it, remains in Montauk today, with the houses selling—when the owners deign to put them up for sale—for almost a million dollars each.

In any case, the first collapse of Nixon's career, not the one with Watergate much later, took place in 1960 when Dwight Eisenhower, having served two terms, retired from the field, leaving his vice president to run against John F. Kennedy. The upstart Kennedy defeated Nixon in the election by a narrow margin. And Nixon withdrew from the public eye. Two years later, he announced his candidacy for governor of California. He ran. He lost. And at a disastrous news conference afterward, he lost his temper and told the reporters, essentially, that they had been responsible for his defeat because of the way they lavished praise on his victorious opponent, Pat Brown.

"I am gone," he told them. "You won't have Nixon to kick around anymore."

And that was the last anyone, including me, had ever heard of Richard Nixon until I got that call from Nick Monte. Nixon and his wife were back in Montauk.

"So I was thinking perhaps you ought to write a story about Mr. Nixon for your paper," Nick continued. "He could make some time for you. You could come over."

What went through my mind, amazingly, was that Nick Monte was really after a little free publicity for Gurney's Inn. I had lots of other motels and inns in the paper paying good money for big ads. Gurney's had bought only a small ad that year. Nick should *buy* an ad and feature Richard Nixon. As a matter of fact, I was not so sure that doing a piece about Richard Nixon staying at Gurney's Inn would do Gurney's any good.

"Here, let me put him on," Nick said.

And so there he was, Richard Nixon. The nobody.

"Hello, Dan. May I call you Dan? Mr. Monte has told me all about you and your wonderful newspaper. Perhaps we could get together."

I moved one of my feet. A box containing a bottle of aspirin clattered off the stained counter and hit the floor.

"How long will you be in town?" I asked Richard Nixon.

"Three more days."

"Well, let me see if I can fit you in. Tell Nick I'll call him back. It's going to be a very busy week for me. I'll let him know."

And that's how I never interviewed Richard Nixon.

Saving the Montauk Lighthouse

IT started with an innocent phone call. I was sitting in my office, the prescription room of my father's old abandoned drugstore, with the deadline for the newspaper approaching and I still had no idea what to write for the lead story.

I hated that. Sometimes I'd read a columnist's piece in one of the dailies, his picture at the top the size of a postage stamp, and I'd know right away that he had written the column without knowing what to write about. They paid him to write it five times a week. He came to work. He sat down. He typed something, blah, blah, blah. A total waste of time.

Now it was happening to me. And I wasn't going to put up with it. I looked around, searching for something, anything. Behind me, down two steps, was the stockroom, a dark space filled with empty boxes on dusty shelves. The big wooden plank I knew so well was still set up there. On Sundays, when the store was still here, my dad and I would come down at six in the morning and start assembling the Sunday papers that had been dropped in front of the store at 4:00 A.M. The big one, of course, was the *New York Times,* consisting of ten sections, all

THE DERELICT SHINNECOCK LIGHTHOUSE, DEEMED A
SAFETY HAZARD, BEING BLOWN UP IN 1948.
(Courtesy of the Montauk Library)

of which we would have to insert, one section inside another.
The day before, Dad would have had to guess how many to
order. Three hundred? Four hundred? He'd guess by the weather
report: more if the weekend was predicted sunny, less if it was
predicted rainy. And so there we would work, he and I, assembling the newspapers there in the back to get them ready for
when the crowds would begin to come. After services, parishioners from the Protestant and Catholic churches up the street
would arrive at 7:30 A.M. and 8:00 A.M., respectively. My dad
and I would smile and greet them as they made their purchases,
usually of two or three of the newspapers right there out front.
Sylvestor's Day. Blah, blah, blah.

Thinking of this was getting me nowhere.

What about something with the Montauk Lighthouse?
One of the things that always touched me when we were selling

the Sunday papers was the Sunday finery of these Montauk families. The wives would be gorgeous, the daughters in dresses with ribbons, and the sons in Sunday suits. But the men, for the most part, were fishermen, and their Sunday best was usually ill fitting and well worn, complementing the lined, tanned, weather-beaten faces of men who worked on the sea. They'd give me money for the papers with rough hands.

For some reason, I thought of a postcard we had in the store that showed the classic view of the Montauk Lighthouse. It was a long, side view, and on the rocks down front, at the edge of the sea, were two small fishermen in rubber waders, their lines far out in the water, surf-casting. The thing about this photograph was just how much land there was from the edge of the cliff to the lighthouse. The picture had been taken in 1917. It was a considerable walk. Perhaps two hundred feet. As a matter of fact, not far from where I was sitting on my stool at the prescription counter, there was a circular metal stand at the front of the store, empty now, though at one time you could turn around and select from it this very postcard, as well as others of various scenes of Montauk.

Earlier in the week, that summer of 1966, there had been an item in the paper that said the chief coastguardsman at the lighthouse—with nothing better to do, I supposed—had made his annual measurement of the distance from the lighthouse building to the edge of the cliff. It was fifty-six feet, four inches. This was one foot six inches less than it had been the year before. Erosion was the problem, of course.

I did the math. At this rate, sometime around 1990, the

lighthouse would fall into the sea. And there was my lead story. I called the Coast Guard.

"Chief Petty Officer Coastguardsman Hutchinson," a brisk voice said at the other end.

I asked to speak to the man in charge, was told he was the man in charge, and so told him who I was and what I wanted. I wanted to write about the future of the lighthouse.

"The story I read said the cliff has lost almost two feet from last year."

"Yes, it has. We get big storms. The dirt on the cliff comes loose and slides down. We had one last week, you may remember."

In front of the lighthouse, there was, and still is, a sixty-foot-high white rectangular lookout tower with a slit window up near the top. It was built during World War II as a position from which to fire guns at an incoming Nazi naval invasion. We talked about that for a while, and how that was now even closer to the edge.

"That will probably be the first to go," I said.

"What do you mean?" he said.

"Well, it's closer to the cliff than the main lighthouse is."

"Well, we don't know about that. All we know is that this year was less than last year and last year was less than the year before."

"Were you doing this ten years ago?" I asked.

"We started making the measurements eight years ago. I have it right here. Eight years ago, the measurement was sixty-one feet, seven inches."

MONTAUK
LIGHTHOUSE.
(Courtesy of the
Montauk Library)

"But if you do the math," I said, "and this keeps up, the lighthouse will be standing for only another forty years."

"That really doesn't matter," the coastguardsman said.

I was puzzled. And then he told me something that sent an electric shock through me.

The Coast Guard was planning to turn off the light in the Montauk Lighthouse. The lighthouse was the symbol of Montauk. It would be nothing without it. And now he was telling me the Coast Guard had issued orders, earlier in the year, to send surveyors out to Montauk Point to look for an appropriate site inland on which to build a steel tower.

"They're talking about a thousand feet back," he told me. "The lighthouse was originally built three hundred and fifty-five feet back." I knew that. It was common knowledge. "They'll put up this tower, probably twice as high as the lighthouse, and they'll put the light up there. And they can operate it by remote control from Star Island. It's a whole new technology."

"What will happen to the old lighthouse?" I asked.

"You'll have to ask headquarters about that."

An hour later I learned that the Coast Guard was suffering through a budget crunch. It had been going on for several years, and up and down the Atlantic coast they had been evaluating which lighthouses they could shut down and which ones they could run remotely with the new technology. They wouldn't need a staff, maintenance, communications, or living quarters. These were enormous savings. Already they had shut down several lighthouses off Virginia and North Carolina. In fact, one of the earliest lighthouses they had shut down had been the one on the beach in front of the Coast Guard station in Hampton Bays. I never knew there had been a lighthouse on the beach in Hampton Bays. What had happened to it? I asked. They had put it up for sale as a government surplus property, but nobody wanted it. So they dynamited it to rubble in 1948. There were liability problems in keeping it in an abandoned condition on the beach like that.

I felt physically sick.

THERE were just two days until the paper had to go to the printer. What could I get done in two days? Well, the first thing I could do was go to the library to learn just what there was to know about the Montauk Lighthouse. Maybe it was something valuable, besides just something of sentimental value to Montauk.

At that time, there was no library in Montauk. There was a bookmobile that came to town once a month, sent there by the county to park in the public parking lot behind my father's store for half a day. I had borrowed books from the bookmobile and returned them a month later. But now there was no time for that, obviously.

Instead, I got in my car and went to the one place, sixteen miles away, where I had gone when I had started the newspaper six years earlier in order to learn the history of the area, the East Hampton Free Library. I loved that library. It was an old building, with book-lined rooms filled with comfortable over-stuffed leather chairs and sofas, much like you might find in an English drawing room. Air-conditioning was not in common use then, but to sit in these rooms on a blazing hot day was a pleasure. Breezes blew through the open windows. And in the shadows, things were dank and cool. You read in silence.

When I told Mrs. King, the librarian in the history room that held the Long Island Collection, that I wanted to see the Montauk Lighthouse document, she seemed surprised. I had read so much in there. Seen the deed that Chief Wyandanch of the Montaukett Indians had signed with an *X* to sell all of eastern Long Island to the white men. Seen the documents the library had relating to the Nazi spies who came ashore at Amagansett one night from a submarine intent on wreaking havoc during World War II.

Had I not seen the material about the Montauk Lighthouse?

I sat down. Mrs. King soon brought me the documents. The site for the lighthouse was chosen by a French architect named Ezra L'Hommedieu during the presidential administration of George Washington. He had ordered the walls to be built six feet thick at the bottom and three feet thick at the top, one hundred and ten feet up, of large stones brought down from a quarry in Maine.

What had raised my eyebrows was the business about George Washington. The U.S. Congress had authorized the funds to pay Mr. L'Hommedieu and the builder, John McComb Jr., in 1796. It was one of the first authorizations of funding ever taken by the United States of America. It was very possible that this was the first lighthouse ever built by the United States of America!

I was amazed that the Coast Guard would even think of tearing the lighthouse down. For the rest of the day, all I could talk about was the lighthouse.

Later in the afternoon, I was sitting back in the prescription room with a friend I knew, Ron Ziel, a photographer and a history buff. He had stopped by to talk to me about a tourist railroad he hoped to build on the old abandoned railroad bed between Bridgehampton and Sag Harbor. It would be seven miles long. He had presented the plan to the town and they had taken a dim view of it. Ron's specialty was photographing old steam engines. But then I got the conversation around to the lighthouse. I told him the story I had learned, and he remembered a photograph he had seen.

"There is a picture on the wall in a barber shop in Hampton Bays where I get my hair cut of the old Shinnecock lighthouse in Hampton Bays," he said. "It is being dynamited. There is a puff of smoke around its middle and the top half is bent one way and the bottom half is bent another. It is halfway down."

Four days later, I drove around town delivering the new edition of the *Montauk Pioneer*. There were 135 stops altogether. I had started at one end of town and, hoisting the bundles of newspapers on my shoulder, which my father had taught me how to do while working with the Sunday papers in the drugstore, I ran upstairs into motel lobbies, ran into restaurants to put bundles on top of cigarette machines, ran into and out of fishing tackle stores, souvenir shops, and real estate offices, leaving twenty-five copies on their counters and desktops. Soon there were people standing perfectly still, holding the newspaper and, with eyes wide, reading the lead story.

The headline on the front page read LIGHTHOUSE DYNA-MITED. Under it was a photograph, the full width of the paper, showing the Shinnecock lighthouse halfway down, the puff of smoke clearly visible. And under that there was the long story about the future of the Montauk Lighthouse. At the end there was a call to action. On Saturday night of Labor Day weekend, which was three weeks away, everyone should assemble in the public parking lot of the lighthouse at nine, and in the darkness turn on a light to protest what the Coast Guard intended to do to the Montauk Lighthouse. People could bring candles, sparklers, flashlights, lanterns, whatever. It would, I hoped, be a tremendous display.

That event was probably the largest protest ever held in the history of Montauk. Police estimated that more than two thousand people attended. The police department had sent officers there to direct incoming cars; the fire department was there with fire trucks in case anything untoward happened; there was a fife and drum corps from Babylon, Long Island; a performance of flaming-baton majorettes from somewhere else up the island; speeches made by the town supervisor and by the Speaker of the Assembly in Albany, Perry B. Duryea Jr., who just happened to be Montauk born and raised. Offshore, in tandem with our display on land, lights flashed from the decks of sportfishing boats that floated just off the lighthouse.

Three days after the demonstration, an editorial appeared in the *New York Times,* describing the event and urging the Coast Guard to reconsider its decision. And one month after that, the Montauk Lighthouse was named to the recently created Historic Register of the State of New York (it was added to the National Register of Historic Places in 1969). A year later, at a second display of lights held at the lighthouse, people excitedly pointed out that at the top of the lighthouse there were coastguardsmen shining lights back at us in support. It was one of the most moving experiences I have ever had. And six months later, the commander of the First District of the United States Coast Guard issued a press release announcing that the plans for the Montauk Lighthouse had been scrapped.

"From here on," he wrote, "we will set aside funds to see to the preservation of this historic treasure. Our first job will be to give the lighthouse a new coat of paint, something it has not had in almost twenty years."

But there was more to come. Six months after that, in the late spring of 1967, a woman named Giorgina Reid came to see me at what were then our brand-new newspaper offices in East Hampton. She was a small woman of about fifty with a lively manner and sparkling brown eyes and she lived with her husband, Donald, in Rocky Point, Long Island, on the north shore

about 40 miles to the west. Their house was right on the edge
of the cliff overlooking the Long Island Sound. One night, in a
storm, they lost a good part of that cliff. But Giorgina Reid
was not going to take this lying down. She read up on what to
do about this very alarming situation. And she had developed a
way of seeding a cliff face, using planks and topsoil and beach
grass to make a sort of terracing.

"It worked," she told me. "I've written a book about it.
And if it can work at Rocky Point, it can work at the Montauk
Lighthouse."

She handed me a copy of her hardcover book. It was called
How to Hold Up a Bank.

Every Sunday, for the next twenty years, Giorgina and her
husband and a group of volunteers would come out to the
Montauk Lighthouse and, with permission from the Coast
Guard (and a signed insurance waiver), climb out on the cliff
face and build terracing. There were gains and losses over the
years. But mostly there were gains. And after a few years, the
Coast Guard funded the method, and sent teams of workers
out there to work under Giorgina's direction. Today, the Montauk Lighthouse is still fifty-five feet from the edge of the cliff
face, which is entirely terraced in beach grass. It is an amazing
achievement.

ONE of the most vivid memories I have of this time is
reading the letter I received from the president of the
Franklin National Bank, a bank with branches all over Long
Island. This bank was owned by a man from Milan. The bank
would do anything in its power to see to it that the Montauk

Lighthouse remained where it stood, he wrote. If there was anything he could do, please let him know.

The letter was written on official bank stationery, and on the top, in addition to the name of the bank, was its logo, which appeared not only on all its correspondence but also on its checks, its deposit slips, all its official documents, and in all its advertising, both on television and in print—a stylized but unmistakable drawing of the Montauk Lighthouse, with the beam of its light shining triumphantly over all.

I N 1976, I received a letter from the Commander of the First District of the United States Coast Guard. In it, the commander said the Guard would like to hold a ceremony at their headquarters on Governors Island to honor Giorgina Reid and me for the work we had done for the Montauk Lighthouse.

At first I thought it was some kind of joke. So I called Giorgina and Donald, who still lived in their house in Rocky Point overlooking Long Island Sound.

"I got one too," Giorgina said, referring to the letter. "I think this is really classy of them."

"It sure is," I said.

We agreed to meet up at what was then the Howard Johnson Restaurant at Exit 64 on the Long Island Expressway, leave one of our two cars there, and travel into New York City together.

We followed the directions given us by the Coast Guard, and we parked in an official U.S. Coast Guard lot at South Ferry on the tip of Manhattan next to a government dock. A small white cutter, with a gun on the bow, was waiting for us, and the coastguardsmen on board, also all in white, took us the short distance across to this off-limits island, just off the tip of Manhattan. What a spectacular view we had from there. We could see the Statue of Liberty, the Verrazano-Narrows Bridge, Brooklyn, New Jersey, and all the skyscrapers of lower Manhattan, including the newly completed World Trade Center, and also the Staten Island ferries, which plowed by.

The island, which has since been abandoned, was a genuine military base at that time, with coastguardsmen in uniform walking around, foursquare brick buildings with white Georgian-style columns out front, parade grounds and walkways, barracks and comfortable-sized residences for the officers.

We were given a luncheon—no speeches were made—and then we were each presented with a framed award by the commander of the Coast Guard. Photographs were taken of us shaking hands with him as we were handed these awards. Each described some of what we had done. Mine bore the headline CERTIFICATE OF APPRECIATION. Hers bore the headline CERTIFICATE OF ACCOMPLISHMENT.

Bob Kennelly

LATE in 2006, a very large home in East Hampton was picked up, turned sideways, and moved about half a mile to a vacant lot owned by the Druker family. This took place in the estate section of the town and, as you might expect, everything about it was writ large.

The house had been built by Bruce Ratner, the billionaire real estate developer who is in the process of moving the New Jersey Nets basketball team to Brooklyn, something he can do because he bought that team a few years ago.

The house was meant to be for the private use of his family, and he had hired an architect named Francis Fleetwood to design it in the "cottage" style of the late nineteenth century. Construction of the house—six baths, seven thousand square feet—went on for two years between 2002 and 2004 at a cost of $3.2 million. But then the Ratners spent only a short time in it. Very soon thereafter, Bruce Ratner sold the house, and the fourteen acres of oceanview land upon which it sat, to the retired vice chairman of Goldman Sachs, Roy Zuckerberg, who decided he loved the fourteen acres but didn't like the house.

Instead of tearing it down, however—there are homes out here that are built and torn down before anybody lives in them—he sold it to the Drukers, who did like the house and then paid the Davis House Moving Company $1 million to move it half a mile to their property, a project that was completed in December 2006. The house was about the largest structure ever moved from one site to another out here, and one of the interesting things about it was that the movers used a remote control device to activate the electric motors attached to each of the axles and wheels that were under it. It was moved high-tech. And representatives of numerous moving companies in these parts came as spectators to see how Davis would do it.

What I was thinking about, however, when I went down to Further Lane in East Hampton to watch this move, was a man named Robert Kennelly, an Irish American who moved houses by yelling at people, by backbreaking strength, and by huge steel I beams and railroad ties bolted to old pickup truck axles. I also thought of the ripping sound that something makes when it comes through a wall, which it did at Bob Kennelly's office one time when I was in it.

"THEY'RE moving one of the old fishermen's houses down at Fort Pond Bay," someone told me on a sunny July day in 1966.

I went down to the bay, where Montauk's first fishing village, now long abandoned, once stood. And there was Kennelly in Bermuda shorts, a workshirt, and sneakers, crawling in and around and under a two-bedroom house tied at one end with a heavy chain to the back of a pickup truck.

There was a man who was going to get hurt, I thought. Something is going to fall on him.

The house had been lifted about six feet off its foundations, suspended up there and held high with crisscrossed railroad ties that formed a pier under each corner. Several telephone poles with truck wheels on the ends of them were underneath the house, waiting for it to be dropped down so it could be towed away.

Kennelly was yelling. There were five workmen that I could see, maybe six. And they were running around, looking at him occasionally, getting their orders, and then running again. This went on for about a half hour. And not much else happened. I took pictures. And I tried to interrupt him at one point, hoping to interview him for the newspaper, but he would have none of it.

"Can't talk now," he said. "Call my office."

I did. From the phone in my dad's abandoned prescription room, I learned that his office was in Southampton on County Route 39. It was about a forty-five-minute drive. But he would be back later.

"Could I come by?" I asked.

"Sure. Just stop over. He loves reporters. He said he'd be here at three. Come at five."

Kennelly's office, which was located just to the east of the auto upholstery place, consisted of several buildings, all quite small, mostly sitting on wooden skids, with all sorts of employees running around. Apparently when they would move something—moving houses is a big deal in the Hamptons for some reason—if there was something left over, a shed or an

BOB KENNELLY, ON THE TAILGATE OF A TRUCK IN 1971.
(Courtesy of Lyle Smith)

outbuilding or a garage, Kennelly would ask if he could have it. People would say sure. He'd find something to do with it later on.

Kennelly worked in one of these buildings, a small, one-room corrugated-steel structure, not much bigger than one of the sheds he was storing. It was furnished with borrowed furniture—an old metal businessman's desk, a chair with a rip in it, and a couple of lamps that did not match. He was on the phone when I came in.

"The power lines still have to come down, lady. I'm trying. It's the lighting company. I said I'd call you when we have it arranged. Nothing happens until we do. Don't worry, I said I'd call you."

Outside, there was the sound of heavy machinery moving things, people talking in loud voices. What a place.

He smoked a cigar. He kept his feet up on the desk for the most part. Dog poop was stuck between a couple of treads. He recognized me.

"You can't just interrupt somebody when they're moving a house," he said.

"Sorry," I said.

I asked him how he got into house moving. It was such a weird question. His family went back to the time when the wealthy WASP summer people first came out to Southampton. They brought the Irish with them as servants. One of them was his grandfather.

"There are usually lots of kids in these families," he said. "My grandpa and my ma lived in the Murray Compound. It had a wall around it. That's where the Irish lived. I was one of ten kids. So we all got into different things. I got into construction. Then, at one point, we had to move something. So that's how it started."

Kennelly was the main moving guy on eastern Long Island, he said. There had been competitors, but they had come and gone. He could do it better, and cheaper. And no, he had never been injured, although once he had a close call when a house crashed down off its moorings before it was supposed to. It had been during the night.

"Most of what we move is houses that are too close to the beach. They get built too close. The dunes go. They have to be moved back."

I asked him if he'd like to buy an ad in the paper.

"Somebody would see the ad and say, I think I ought to move my house?" he guffawed. "No. We're in the Yellow Pages."

The following week, I did write a story for the paper about Bob Kennelly and the house he had moved at Montauk. And that, I thought, was the end of it. What an interesting man.

But it was not the end of it. About two weeks later, I got a call from Kennelly telling me I might be interested in watching him move an old historic cottage down Main Street in East Hampton. It was called "the Purple House" and it was being moved to an oceanfront compound owned by a very wealthy lady named Adelaide de Menil.

"She's collecting these old houses," he said. "Maybe making a little village out of them."

When the time came, I stood in front of the East Hampton Post Office with John Strong, an insurance man, and we watched Kennelly and this little colonial cottage come rumbling by. He waved. Adelaide de Menil was also part of the move. She had set up a camera on a tripod not far from where we were standing and had programmed it to automatically take a picture every twenty seconds as the house came slowly by. After the film was developed, she could watch the house move in fast time.

About ten years later, in 1975, I had another encounter with Bob Kennelly. Now it was my turn to call him up on the phone.

"You know about the Shoreham Nuclear Plant?" I asked.

"I know all about the Shoreham Nuclear Plant," he said.

Beginning around 1968, the power company on Long Island

had embarked on a plan to build a nuclear power plant on the north shore of the island in a town called Shoreham. It was now still under construction. Billions had already been spent even though protesters demonstrated against it almost daily. It was felt that the plant was too near a populated area. There was no way, if there was trouble, that the populace could be evacuated.

"I just read that the supervisor of Nassau County is in favor of the plant," I told Kennelly.

Nassau County, a bedroom community to New York City to the west of our county, wanted the jobs the power plant would bring. The county seat, Mineola, was about sixty miles from Shoreham.

"No."

"I got this idea," I told him, "that if this supervisor likes the nuclear plant so much, we pick it up and move it to Mineola. I'd like you to move it."

"Impossible," he said.

"I'm going to write about it," I said. "I know it's preposterous. SHOREHAM NUCLEAR PLANT TO BE MOVED TO MINEOLA."

There was silence on the other end of the line. Then he spoke.

"Call me tomorrow," he said. "I'll work up an estimate for you."

Two weeks later, I ran the article, front-page. Kennelly had won the bid. He was going to lift the plant up and have it moved to a barge tied up at the beach, towed to Great Neck Harbor, then brought inland and towed down a straight paved road that he would build to take it directly to a site right next door to the Nassau County Courthouse. The cost of the move would be $423 million.

About a week after the story came out, Kennelly called me again, inviting me down to his office.

"Five P.M.," he said.

Again we sat in his office, he behind the metal desk, I in the same overstuffed club chair with the rip in it.

"You won't believe how many of my relatives called me to congratulate me on winning this bid," he said. "Some I hadn't heard from in ten years. They were in California, Texas, North Carolina. They were all just calling me to say hello because they hadn't talked to me in years and oh yes, what about all that money." He started laughing.

At that moment, there was a commotion outside, and then a loud bang and a tearing sound, shaking the building we were in. Kennelly kept right on laughing. Outside, someone was cursing.

"No, no. Get back. Stop!" came a voice from outside.

The tear was in the corrugated metal on the side of the building about six feet up. It caved in toward us, then ripped open with a bang, and now there was a rusty ten-inch-high steel I beam slowly sliding in from the outside across the little office. It moved slowly, toward the desk. If it continued it would be two feet over the desk, right between us. "Hold on! Hold on!" came from outside.

Kennelly looked at the ceiling. He had stopped laughing, but he was still contemplating the $423 million. And the beam, which clearly he had seen, kept moving. Now it was right between us.

And then it stopped. And moments after it stopped, it began to retreat. Soon it had gone back out the way it had come in.

"I told them all to go to hell," he whooped, referring to his relatives.

Around 1990, Kennelly finally did get seriously injured. A house fell on him, crushing his thighs, and after that, he continued to work, but from a wheelchair. Davis House Moving came into the business. So did Dawn House Moving from Patchogue.

For years and years, after that, if you drove past Kennelly's property on County Route 39, you would see this big gash in the shape of the letter I, still visible on the side of the corrugated office where Kennelly sat. Just one of those everyday things that happen in the moving business.

Lieutenant James Kealy

VERY time I drive down the Montauk Highway between
Bridgehampton and East Hampton, I peer up a driveway
to look at a tiny cottage and studio. It is on the south side of
the highway, the expensive side, and it is officially in the section called Georgica, or at least on the fringe of that section,
which makes it worth even more. Most recently it sold for
about a million dollars.

As I look at it, I play the history of this house backward.
The current landscaping on the property is *House & Garden*
stuff: meandering walkways of stone, gardens of sculpted low
bushes and brightly colored flowers. Before that, there was no
landscaping, and the house had been up by the front of the property, by the road. And before that, the studio, which is today
beautifully finished with decks and skylights, had been merely
a single-car garage. And there had been no wooden stockade
fence then. Nothing to separate the house from the busy road.

That fence, which many years ago I had built, is still there.
And so are the cedar trees, which I got in the mail from the
government when they were giving them out free to whoever

wrote in for them. These cedar trees were nine inches tall when I planted them in front of the fence. Now they stand almost twenty feet tall.

Mostly, however, what I see when I look at this house is a friendship I made with a man who went by the name of Lieutenant James Kealy. I never met the man, but I have come to know him very well. It's a long story.

The shops in downtown East Hampton today are mostly shops you find in any resort frequented by the wealthy. Polo. Tiffany's. Cartier. Coach. There are two exceptions among the hundred or so downtown. One is White's Drug Store, the East Hampton "White's," owned by the Marmon family for more than fifty years through several generations. And the other is Reed's Photo Shop on Newtown Lane, run by John Reed Jr.

One day in the early spring of 1966, I went into Reed's Photo to get some film. Earlier on, I had bought a camera from John Reed Sr. It was a used camera, because I could not afford a new one, but it was a Nikon with a zoom lens that went up to 135 mm. You could get pretty close from far away with that. Good for newspaper work.

"What can I do for you today?" John asked.

"Nothing about photography," I said. "I'm looking for a place to live for the summer. I have almost no money. Someone said you might know of something."

At that time, many of the local people would rent their homes out for the summer season. You could make quite a bit of money doing that. It would pay the mortgage the whole year, if you could give it up for just the three months. And I knew John did that.

"It's the place I rented for the summer last year," he said. "Cheap. Not bad. But now, this year, things have happened there and it's just a little too chancy for me. What with my wife and kids and all."

"Like what?"

"The people who own it now tell me they are going through a divorce. It just started, and neither of them is letting the other live in the house. And neither of them is letting the other rent it out. I offered to renew. The husband, a guy named Mabley, who is in the trash hauling business, said his wife wants to make sure he is stuck with the mortgage. He said if he rents it to us again, she'll evict us. Too chancy. But maybe not for you, since you're single."

"Where is it?"

"On Montauk Highway, a quarter mile past the bowling alley on the south side. Between Cove Hollow and Jericho. I could give you the guy's phone number."

"Where are you living?"

"I'll show you."

At John's invitation, I went behind the counter and down a flight of stairs. The whole basement of his building, although not finished, was gaily painted and furnished for the summer.

"We can do three months down here if we have to. The whole thing about the divorce came up just last week."

The next day, I called up Mabley and we met at his house. He was a small man, thin, about forty, and there was alcohol on his breath. It was ten o'clock in the morning.

He took me through the house, and indeed, it was not

much. There was no central heating, but there was a gas space heater in the center of the house in the dining room. Certainly I would need no heat in the summertime. The whole house was just one story high, and measured on the outside, which I did later, just twenty by forty feet. It sat on cedar posts. And somehow, they had crammed seven rooms into this tiny space. Three bedrooms, a bath, breakfast room, kitchen, dining room, and living room. Two of the bedrooms were just six by seven feet, large enough to get a double bed in and stand up alongside. Though there were windows.

"I talked to my lawyer. If you want to make a check out to my bank paying the mortgage and taxes, you can live in it all summer or as long as you want. Unless she evicts you."

"How much is the mortgage?"

"Forty-three dollars and fifty-two cents."

He stared off into space. Out the window there was a garage. There was a big padlock on the door.

"My wife has her stuff in there."

"I think I'll do this," I said. "Let me call you back later in the day."

I didn't have a lawyer, but my dad did. He was Saul Wolf, of Scheinberg, Wolf, Lapham & DePetris in Riverhead, where Saul worked, and Mill Hill Lane in East Hampton, where he lived. Saul and his wife, Ann, were close friends with my parents. I called Saul.

"Live in it all you want," he said. "Change the locks. Possession is nine-tenths of the law. If you live there she has to go through an eviction process to get rid of you. This could take months. When she shows up, and she will, tell her to call me. I'll hold her off until autumn. And if you want to give her my business card, stop by the house. Ann will give you one."

Autumn was all I wanted. And so I changed the locks and moved in. One week later, Mrs. Mabley did indeed show up at the door. She was overweight, about forty, and very angry. She was also very small, and she had a Cockney accent. She didn't scare me. And I didn't let her in. Instead, I gave her Saul's business card. She left, cursing.

One week later, however, she was back. Calmer.

"I have some things in the garage," she said. "Mind if I get them?"

"Go right ahead."

She hauled out two suitcases and set them in front of the garage. She looked very forlorn. And so I invited her in.

"For tea," I said.

"Well, thank you very much."

As it turned out, I really got to like Mrs. Mabley. From Liverpool, she had worked as a barmaid, then come to America and married this drunken sot Mabley, with whom things would never work out. He beat her. He drank too much. She was now living in North Sea, a section of Southampton.

She asked me about this bright red Triumph TR-3 sports car I had in the driveway, and I told her I had just bought it as a used car from a man named Charlie Brown who owned a bar by that name in Hampton Bays. When I had bought it, he showed me his driver's license as identification. He really was named Charlie Brown.

"I had thought Charlie Brown's had been named after the

cartoon character from *Peanuts*," I told her. "He really was him."

A few months later, I went to visit Mrs. Mabley in North Sea, where she was living with another Englishman, a man named Sidney Law, who had a shop on North Sea Road where he repaired foreign cars. I spent many an afternoon talking to the two of them there as Law worked on my little sports car over some minor problem. Law could fix anything. Mrs. Mabley served tea.

That fall, I bought the house, the garage, and the quarter acre of land it sat on, for $9,250. This was the first house I ever owned.

O N a Saturday that October, at 11:00 A.M., I was ready. I had gallons of red and white wine, a barbecue grill in the backyard with the coals hot, and the refrigerator stocked with potato salad, ice cream and cake, Cokes, and hot dogs and hamburgers. Bowls of chips and popcorn were placed on tables, and the Beatles blared from the record player. All the windows were open. It was a glorious, sunny day. I was expecting about two dozen people.

Thus began one of the grandest house-painting parties in East Hampton history, an event still talked about by some people today, during which the entire exterior and interior of this house of mine got painted an earth-toned beige on the outside and a cheerful yellow on the inside. People came and went. I had gallons and gallons of paint, several wooden ladders, lots of brushes. The painters, for the most part, had not painted anything but a canvas before.

About five hours into this party, as it was beginning to finish up, the one neighbor who was close enough to have minded
all the noise—a Mrs. Collins—wandered over to the hedge
separating our two properties. She was an elderly woman.

"Come on in," I told her.

"Nah."

"Oh, come on. We still have plenty of food."

"Well, all right."

With people coming over to say hello, and a little potato
salad, Mrs. Collins soon cheered up, though she remained sitting on one of the folding chairs I had put out by the barbecue.

At one point, I sat down next to her.

"Nice party," she said. "The house never looked so good."

Mrs. Collins, I learned, was one of three sisters who owned
the North Main Street IGA supermarket in town. She was a
widow. Her husband had worked there too.

"Do you still work there?"

"Sure do. We've got to keep track of everything. I take a
shift."

I asked her what she knew about my house.

"People tend to keep to themselves," she said, "but I do remember how it got here. There was this handsome young man
in town named Lieutenant Kealy. He had been in the war, the
First World War, and now the war was over, and one day I saw,
glory be, a house moving slowly down Montauk Highway coming into town from the west. Half the town was out there, I
think, watching and helping walk it through.

"Lieutenant Kealy sat on a buckboard in front of the house,
which was on a big platform-type thing with wheels under it,

and he was driving a whole team of mules, straining under the weight of the pull. But they were moving along."

"My house was brought here by mules?"

"Well, the road had been paved ten years before. So it wasn't too hard. Lieutenant Kealy was sure pleased with himself. He backed it in here. They put cedar posts under it as they slid the platform out. Kealy had bought it for a dollar, he told me. This was one of the barracks they had built at the soldier training camp, Camp Upton in Brookhaven. After the war, they were selling these barracks for one dollar. Anybody who was a veteran and had been at Camp Upton was welcome to one for a dollar. All you had to do was haul it off."

"What did Lieutenant Kealy do here in town? Did he get married? Have children?"

"To tell the truth, I really don't know. Like I said, people tend to keep to themselves. Seems to me after about five years I no longer saw that handsome young man. Then some other people had it who I do not know, then some other people. Then those Mabley people had it for a few years. There was a lot of yelling going on then, I remember. And now you. Are you going to get married?"

The party ended around 5:00 P.M. with the house painted. People said their good-byes. My girlfriend, Arda, was in the kitchen, cleaning up. I was cleaning up the bathroom. And then I remembered something. And I looked up. In the ceiling in the bathroom, there was a hatchway. It had to go to the attic. I had never thought to go up there before. What, if anything, could there be of Lieutenant Kealy's up there? There was surely nothing of his in the main part of the house.

I looked to see if I could climb up by standing on the tub or the sink, but that wasn't going to work. So I used one of the ladders. And that made it easy.

In the waning afternoon light, with a flashlight, I poked around up in the rafters. There was no way to stand up there, but I could crawl around.

Inside of a half hour, I had found a whole treasure trove of things that belonged to the handsome lieutenant from World War I. And one by one, I transferred them down to Arda, who set them up on the dining room table.

Here is the best of what I found.

There was a white silk handkerchief with two crossed flag-poles on it, one bearing a French flag, the other an American flag. A caption read VIVE LES AMÉRICAINS!

There was the gun casing of an artillery shell, a heavy cyl-inder of brass that probably weighed ten pounds and was about a foot long and four inches in diameter. Somebody had crudely hammered a bas-relief that twined its way all around the outside of the casing. This was a flower, a chrysanthemum I thought, with stem and leaves. The equivalent of somebody hammering a sword into a plowshare.

There were several New York City daily newspapers, all dated exactly the same, May 22, 1927, and all bearing huge headlines on the front page, variations of LINDBERGH IN PARIS!

There were three silver-plated trophies, all tarnished, each one a silver cup with a handle, about a foot high, and inscribed. One read ROSELAND, 1ST PRIZE, FLAPPER CONTEST, 1926, JAMES C. KEALY. Another read ROSELAND, 1ST PRIZE, WALTZ CONTEST, 1926, JAMES C. KEALY. The third trophy, a little

smaller, read ROSELAND, 2ND PRIZE, CHARLESTON CONTEST, 1926, JAMES C. KEALY. Kealy, apparently, had been beaten.

So, Kealy was not only handsome, he was also a fine dancer. It was not hard to visualize him leaping around the dance floor, he and his partner, at the Roseland Ballroom, the popular dance parlor in business in Manhattan at 51st Street for almost the entire first half of the twentieth century.

There were also a dozen old 78 records that I brought down from that attic. All of them were from the late 1920s, and three of them were songs praising Charles Lindbergh, who captured the imagination of America by becoming the first man to fly solo across the Atlantic, from Roosevelt Airfield on Long Island, about forty miles to the west of Camp Upton, to Paris. One was LUCKY LINDY. Another was THE EAGLE OF THE U.S.A. And the third was LINDY DOES IT!

"What do you think?" I asked Arda. Arda was from Holland. And she had a master's degree in history.

"I think the lieutenant was in Paris in 1918 on the day the armistice was signed that ended World War I. This was said to be the biggest celebration, and the greatest outpouring of affection for American troops ever. I think the silk handkerchief was a souvenir of that celebration, as was the gift of that shell casing.

"I also think the lieutenant loved dancing and music and was a great fan of Charles Lindbergh. I think that is about all we can get from this."

Four years later, married (not to Arda) and with an infant daughter, we were home around three o'clock one Sunday afternoon when out on Montauk Highway in front of our house, there was the tremendous crash of metal on metal. It was an auto accident. Had to be.

I leaped up, ran out front, and saw one of the most horrible things I had ever seen in my life. A head-on collision. My wife, Pam, was right behind me. There were two cars and five people. And lots of blood.

"I'm going to get some towels," Pam said. "And some buckets of water." She ran back to the house. And I walked out into the street.

Both cars were all crumpled up. The white car was a big fifteen-year-old Buick. Alongside it, leaning against the driver's door, was a man of about sixty with a white beard who had been its only occupant. He had a bloody mouth, and the center part of his beard was red. But he was standing. He made no acknowledgment as I walked over to him.

Opposite the Buick, there was a small red car, a hatchback, and from the backseat, there was the muffled voice of a child.

"Why me? Why me?" it kept shouting. The child shouted this over and over.

I turned and ran over. There were two adults in the front of this car, a new Toyota, and one girl in the back. But she wasn't saying anything. The adults were apparently uninjured, but stunned, and they too did not seem to notice I was there. And then I found the source of the voice, a boy in the backseat who had been thrown forward in such a way that his head was now stuck under the back of the front seat. He couldn't get it out.

"Why me? Why me?"

I tried to pull the boy's head out, but it wouldn't budge. The seat would have to be moved up and forward. But there was a man in it. Not knowing what else to do, I returned to the front and helped the two adults, obviously the parents, out onto the street. The woman was covered with blood and had difficulty standing. I laid her down in the grass. But the man seemed okay.

Pam appeared. "I have towels, water, and a ladle," she said. "We can give people something to drink."

I walked over and thrust my bloody hands into the water. Then I dried them on a towel.

At this point, the police arrived, along with an ambulance.

They took over. The woman was being attended to. The man with the beard was now talking incoherently, trying unsuccessfully to explain to anybody listening what had happened. Now I noticed there were old hardcover books everywhere around the accident, on the street, in the grass. The white Buick had been filled with books. Some still lined the rear window shelf.

The boy was now pulled free. He was weeping, still shouting "Why me, why me?" His sister was fine, the father was fine. The mother was now sitting up.

So, nobody died.

The next day the people in the red car stopped by the house. They had spent the rest of the day in the hospital. Now they had a rental car. They wanted to thank us. All the injuries had been superficial and thank God for that.

That night, I told Pam we would have to sell the house. I could not see us raising children there on the side of a major highway, especially one with just two lanes. Within three months, we were gone, having moved to a much larger house on a residential street in Bridgehampton.

About five years after that, I noticed that my old Nikon had ceased working. I parked on Newtown Lane in East Hampton, and I walked with it into John Reed's photo shop. John was at the counter, and I set the camera down in front of him.

"You know that camera you sold me? Well, it broke," I said. "I think it's still under warranty. It's only been ten years."

He laughed. And he took it in and fixed it for free.

Willem de Kooning

"THERE he is!" whispered the young woman sitting next to me.

Throughout the three-hundred-seat John Drew Theater in East Hampton, the whispering began. And heads turned.

In the back, standing defiantly, seeming to tower over the entourage that had entered with him, stood Willem de Kooning, the Dutch painter who had vowed in 1961, just six years before, that he would never, ever again allow a painting of his to be displayed in Guild Hall, the East Hampton institution that housed the John Drew Theater. He had also said he would never set foot in there either.

But there he was, his eyes flashing fiercely, his face set. He was a tall man with a thick shock of blond hair, and he had made his career as a painter, working up in the woods of Springs in a studio of his own design. He was accompanied by his wife, Elaine, and what seemed to me several of his girlfriends. He had many girlfriends. And apparently, from what I had been told, a friend of one of his girlfriends had written the play we were about to see. And he had promised that, just this once, he would come.

The management of Guild Hall tried to make the best of it.

"I see that our friend Willem de Kooning has come to enjoy this evening's performance," a voice said over the loudspeaker.

There were a series of boxes at the back of the theater, where important people sat. De Kooning was standing in front of a seat in the front row of the very center box. He sat. And the rest of the people with him sat. And though I do not remember the performance I saw that night, I do remember turning around to look at that box from time to time to see if he was still there. He was. But during the applause at the end of the play, he quickly left.

De Kooning's decision to boycott Guild Hall in 1961 came about because of what might have seemed a very petty matter. It had to do with a beach, specifically Georgica Beach.

In the mid-1950s, when the most important people in the Hamptons were the writers and artists, there was a very famous picture taken of all of them on Georgica Beach. It was taken by a photographer from *Time* magazine, and in a subsequent issue, it was the centerpiece of a feature about all the famous artists and writers of the Hamptons. In this picture were Larry Rivers, Alfonso Ossorio, Balcomb Greene, Syd Solomon, Jackson Pollock, Lee Krasner . . . the list goes on and on. And among them, probably the most accomplished artist of the time, having ascended to that title after the death of Jackson Pollock, was Willem de Kooning. It was captioned "THE ARTISTS HAVE A PICNIC," and, from left to right, the people were named.

People later pointed out that the "picnic" was unknowingly arranged by the *Time* photographer, who called up several artists and said that he had been told the artists had a regular picnic on Saturday afternoons at Georgica Beach and asked if he could photograph it. This was the first anybody ever knew about a regular picnic—surely there had been irregular picnics—but if *Time* wanted a regular picnic, they would oblige. And so they did. After that, because everyone remembered the occasion fondly, Georgica Beach became the place to be if you were an artist or a writer in the Hamptons during the late 1950s and early 1960s.

But the area was growing. And times were changing. In the late 1950s, something called zoning laws were established. Until that time people could build anything wherever they wanted to, so long as they owned the property. There are, today, a few pockets in the country where zoning never properly took hold—Dallas, Texas, comes to mind—but here in New York it was taken up by every town and village in the state, one at a time and after great discussion and thought.

In 1960, the year I decided to begin publishing my newspaper, I went out during my spring vacation from school to every merchant and business owner in Montauk. I was determined to get a yes or no from each and every one of them about their buying an ad in the paper. And I did.

As I was presenting something new, there were several occasions when people I saw began to put two and two together and began to talk about another new thing—zoning.

"If you publish this paper," one of them told me, "you must come out against zoning. We have been fine without it until now. A man's home is his castle. Who are these people to

MIMI KILGORE AND WILLEM DE KOONING.
(Photograph by Kathryn Abbe; courtesy of Guild Hall, East Hampton Inc.)

tell us we can't build a house over here, or we can only build a business over there?"

My father explained the true nature of Montauk to me at that time when I talked to him about this at his store.

"People don't wind up in Montauk because they were just drifting through and stopped. People make a decision to come to Montauk. It's a peninsula. You are at the end of something. And people who make decisions like this are usually very determined, very opinionated, very iconoclastic people. They want things done their way. And so they wind up going to some place where they can get things done their way."

One day I went to what had originally been a private home on East Lake Drive that looked like a small French castle. It had a broad front lawn with a horseshoe-shaped driveway that led in from the street, past a sign that read CAPTAIN'S MARINA, and up to a heavily carved front door. I knocked, a man answered, and I asked to speak to the owner of the Marina.

Tony Erick told me that the house had originally been built by advertising man Marion Harper—the founder of Marshak Advertising—for him and his wife Virginia as a summer home. Soon thereafter they divorced, and for a long time the house lay unoccupied. Now Erick had bought it and had built a large dock out into the water of Lake Montauk where his customers would berth their boats.

"I've got about forty slips," he told me. "Then they passed zoning. They say I can't build any more. But I intend to anyway. And you see that spot over there?" He pointed to an open piece of lawn adjacent to the beginning of the dock. "I'm going to build a restaurant and tackle shop there. It's illegal, they tell me. We'll see about that."

Erick built his restaurant, and four years later the town ordered him to tear it down, and when he wouldn't, they sent in a wrecking crew and did it for him.

In 1958 the town passed a law banning the construction of new billboards. At the same time, a second law was passed that said the existing billboards could remain up for only the next five years. In 1963 they would have to come down.

This was a particularly bad blow to the merchants of Montauk. When you came through Amagansett, the last town before Montauk, twelve miles away, you went down a hill onto a paved road that went along a six-mile sandy stretch called the Napeague Strip. And there were a hundred billboards along both sides of the road that advertised Montauk restaurants, fishing boats, miniature golf courses, fishing tackle shops, tennis courts, beach pavilions, nightspots, and so forth and so on.

Each and every one of them wanted to be the first one you saw as you came down the hill, so the total length of this massive array of billboards was just a quarter of a mile, after which there was nothing but sand dunes and beach grass for the entire rest of the way.

In 1963 about ten of the billboards came down in accordance with the law, but the owners of the other ninety hired a lawyer who sued. Years went by. And while the matter was wending its way through the courts, the billboards remained up, in open defiance of the new town ordinance.

One night in 1966, someone—they never did find out who—got in what must have been a four-wheel-drive Jeep and, in the darkness, drove into the dunes along the side of the road and one after another knocked each and every one of the billboards down.

The next day, the town issued a warrant for the arrest of whoever did this. But at the same time the town government said that if anyone wanted to put a knocked-down billboard back up they would have to get a permit, and none were being issued. For years, the debris of these fallen billboards remained. And, slowly, they were taken away.

As for Willem de Kooning, his problem with Guild Hall and Georgica Beach was a new law restricting Georgica Beach to village residents only. That would be the new zoning. And that meant the artists and writers, who almost all lived up in Springs, outside the village, could not go there.

De Kooning deduced, probably correctly, that the only group as powerful as the artists and writers in Springs were the wealthy summer people who lived adjacent to Georgica Beach. His argument was with the village, not with Guild Hall. But Guild Hall was the cultural center of East Hampton Village, and among those on the board were the mayor and many of the New York summer people. De Kooning flung down the gauntlet. Six years later, he was, for that one time, back at Guild Hall. But Georgica Beach remains restricted today.

I N the summer of 1985, I was having dinner with a friend at a restaurant up in Springs called the Sea Wolf. Suddenly, just two tables away from us, there was a tremendous commotion. Willem de Kooning had fallen off his chair and crashed to the floor.

As there were only women at his table, I got up and walked quickly over. So did three or four other men nearby. And we got him up. He was a big man, and those at his table said we should come with them and help him outside to his car. He was extremely drunk.

I am sure he had no idea I was there. But he threw his arm around my shoulder, and I lifted him up. On the other side, someone else was lifting him up, and we half dragged and half carried him out the door, reeking of alcohol and sweat and slurring his words.

"I'm the greatest living painter in the world," he said. "I'm the greatest living painter in the world." He kept repeating this over and over again until we had gotten him into the backseat of his car and closed the door so we could no longer hear him.

Soon after that, de Kooning began to decline into a very unusual twilight of old age.

For the next twelve years, he would get up from his bed in his house on Woodbine Drive, get himself dressed, sit down at the table, and eat the hearty breakfast that would be placed before him. He would not speak. And he did not seem to know where he was.

Then he would get up, walk slowly into his studio, and paint. People whom he knew would come over, and they would talk to him and he wouldn't recognize them. He spoke a few words. But he had no idea who they were. He just painted.

Every day he followed this routine, and he painted many hundreds of paintings in what the art world came to call his "twilight period." The critics wrote in glossy art magazines about the work of this period. They still do. They say it was much like his earlier work, but gentler, simpler. There was something calming about it, as if the painter had come to terms with his paints and canvas, finally, and all the Sturm und Drang and tensions had come to an end.

On March 19, 1997, at the age of ninety-two, de Kooning's presence on this planet came to an end.

Frank Tuma Jr.

F Montauk had a straight man back then, it was Frank Tuma Jr. Tall, tanned, movie-star handsome, and amiable, he had black hair parted and slicked back, blue eyes, and a straight nose, and he wore, every day in this rough-and-ready town, a tie and a jacket. He was the only man in Montauk to do so. Had there been a multinational corporation with the need of a vice president/manager in Montauk—and as it happened there was one—he was the man for the job. He spent his working life in that job. And his handsome tan came from playing golf on the weekends.

At that time, the Tuma family was considered the equivalent of royalty in the town. Eddie Tuma and his brother Frank Sr. were fishermen. Eddie owned a charter boat, and Frank Sr. owned Tuma's Tackle Shop, a small two-room wooden building on Main Street. A few years earlier a photograph of Frank Sr. surf-casting off the rocks at Montauk Point had appeared on the cover of the *Saturday Evening Post*. "Mr. Montauk," the *Post* called him. And so "Mr. Montauk" he was called by everybody in town. Frank Sr. and Eddie had three children between

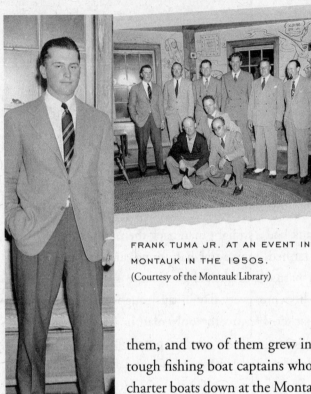

FRANK TUMA JR. AT AN EVENT IN
MONTAUK IN THE 1950S.
(Courtesy of the Montauk Library)

them, and two of them grew into rough, tough fishing boat captains who ran their charter boats down at the Montauk docks, along with about a dozen other charter boat captains.

And then there was Frank Jr. He grew up to look, act, and think like Bing Crosby. Or if he had been born later, Johnny Carson or Regis Philbin. Where did he come from?

Frank Jr. came home from college—an Ivy League college—at just about the time that a group of New York investors took over the Montauk Beach Company, a failed real estate development firm founded in the 1920s, which still owned a little over half of all the vacant land in Montauk. The new owners renamed the company the Montauk Improvement

Company, determined to "improve" Montauk by developing it. They launched the business slowly, year by year, cutting up chunks of land, subdividing it into lots, and offering them for sale to the general public. They were looking for a vice president to manage local, day-to-day affairs.

Never has a man been more appropriate for a job than was Frank Jr. for this one. They set him up in an office in an abandoned bungalow next to Tuma's Tackle Shop. So he was still in the family, so to speak. And soon thereafter, they fixed up the first floor of an abandoned seven-story office building in the center of town and moved him there so he could oversee all the salespeople selling the lots to the tourists. A big sign MONTAUK IMPROVEMENT COMPANY was erected across the front of the entire first floor of this building. As for floors two through seven, they remained abandoned, with paint peeling off the walls and thirty-year-old desks, chairs, and filing cabinets cluttering the rooms. Who knew that the bank of elevators at the back of the series of offices on the first floor did not work? Or that the grand staircase at the back of the main floor leading up to the mezzanine led to a debris-filled mess?

Frank Jr. worked for the next forty years as vice president of the Montauk Improvement Company and later, when Montauk Improvement ceased operations, as the successor to its holdings, which he named, finally, the Tuma Real Estate Agency.

When I came around that first year to see the merchants in town to sign them up for a full summer of ads in the newspaper, Frank Jr. bought a modest square for the Montauk Improvement Company, which he asked that I run next to the Tuma's Tackle Shop ad his father had bought. In the second and third years, he doubled the size of his ad. The Improvement Company was on the move.

In the spring of 1967, my father, as he said he would, had ceased paying the rent on his old abandoned drugstore space. So what had been the first office for my little weekly newspaper, his dusty old prescription room, would no longer be available to me. The new renters were already renovating the premises into a liquor store.

I looked around. Where else could I have my office in Montauk for the upcoming summer? My eyes lit on floors two through seven of the Montauk Improvement building. I walked over to talk to Frank Tuma Jr. I had no idea if this would be a hard sell to Frank Tuma Jr., so I just went and asked him.

"You want to rent an office up there?"

"No, I want you to let me have it for free. I just need a place to have a desk and a chair. There are plenty of them up there. I won't fix anything up. I'll just go there to hide out and write. And maybe people coming to see me would stop on the way to the stairs and buy a lot."

Frank's eyes twinkled and he smiled. He got it.

"Take your pick," he said, motioning toward the grand staircase.

I felt like hugging him. And up the grand concrete staircase I went, two steps at a time, bursting through the rusting steel fire door with the broken lock to the wreckage of floors two through seven. I was a kid in a candy store. I could take my choice of the whole world.

What a cold, spooky place it was. The old Montauk Beach Company had gone bankrupt in 1938, at the bottom of the

Depression. There were still calendars on the walls behind the desks, curling with age, from that year. There were old telephones that didn't work, with frayed wires attached to junction boxes at the base of those peeling walls. There were desks filled with stationery and papers, brochures for the Montauk Yacht Club, for the Montauk Manor Hotel, for the Surf Club, and for the Star Island Casino next to the Coast Guard Station on that island. And there were filing cabinets filled with correspondence and architectural plans, with deeds and legal papers. The Montauk Beach Company had been in the business of trying to develop all of Montauk. As I went up and up and up, using the fire stairs from the mezzanine floor to get to three, four, five, and six, I realized that the company must have gone bankrupt in one single day, and on that day the working people on every floor of this building had just left. Now, twenty-nine years later, it was still as they had left it.

Finally, I came to the seventh, and top floor, which was the old Carl Fisher penthouse apartment, the aerie from which this man, the founder of the Montauk Beach Company, the millionaire from Indianapolis via Miami Beach, had bought practically all of Montauk and tried to develop it all those years ago.

Unlike the dreary office-building floors below, this space had once been an imposing apartment, done in a classic English half-timber style, with huge rough-timber beams, above two magnificent fireplaces, one facing into the living room, the other facing into the bedroom—there was little doubt where the big king-size bed would have been. Each room, in all four directions, led to an open terrace surrounding the penthouse. The views of Montauk extended for miles in every direction—

to the lighthouse, the ocean, Amagansett, and the fishing village, respectively.

I imagined him, an overweight middle-aged man with a white floppy hat, his big paw around the waist of his fifteen-year-old bride, Jane, leading her into the bedroom. I imagined him out on the terrace with many of his millionaire friends—Firestone, Olds, Champion, and so forth—all from the automotive business in Indianapolis where Fisher himself had made his first fortune, with Fisher pointing out different lots that these millionaires could buy in the big City of Montauk, population 150,000, he planned to build. This seven-story skyscraper he built was just the first of what were to be many tall buildings marking the center of the future city of Montauk. Look out and you could see, already under construction, the golf course, the first of the three hotels, the polo field, the beach club, the boardwalk, the yacht club. It was 1926. And the sky was the limit.

I could make my office here, I thought.

IN the end, however, I chose the mezzanine. Coming up the stairs was nice and an adventure, indeed, but I fully expected, at any moment, some ancient man to creep silently out of a closet and come up behind me. I was spooked. The mezzanine it would be.

ONE hot August day, I was sitting at my desk—old wooden desk, old wooden chair on squeaky wheels—when a secretary from the Montauk Improvement Company rang me up on the extension phone that Frank had kindly installed for

THE MONTAUK IMPROVEMENT SKYSCRAPER, VACANT FROM
FLOORS TWO TO THE PENTHOUSE, IN THE CENTER OF
DOWNTOWN MONTAUK IN 1972. DAD'S NEW DRUGSTORE
IS IN THE FOREGROUND.
(Courtesy of Dan Rattiner)

me. (Wire out a window on the first floor, wire in a window on
the mezzanine floor.)

"There's a man here from IBM who would like to see you,"
the secretary said.

I had just come from the beach, and was in a T-shirt, bathing suit, and sandals.

"I don't know anybody from IBM," I said.

"He says he has an appointment. And he wants to show
you the new IBM typewriter."

"I never made any appointment," I said. "But, hmmm."

Wheels were turning. I'd heard IBM had come out with a revolutionary new typewriter called a Selectric. It had a little typeface ball you popped into it. I'd never seen it.

"Send him up," I said.

About two minutes later, a slender man in a dark suit and a narrow gray tie appeared at the top of the mezzanine stairs breathing heavily. Both arms were wrapped around a large, unusually streamlined, and apparently very heavy gray typewriter. In one hand, under the typewriter, he was grasping the handle of a shiny gray leather attaché case, which swayed as he walked. He was struggling.

"Are you Mr. Rattiner, the publisher of the Montauk newspaper?" he asked.

I stood up. I wanted to help him. But he waved me off.

"It's all right," he said.

"You sure you're okay?"

He came over to my desk—I quickly moved some papers off to one side to make some room—and he thumped the typewriter down, somehow managing to do it while swinging his attaché case out of the way. He had a crew cut. I would have judged him to be about forty-five. Then he sat down in the chair on the other side of my desk.

"I read about this typewriter in the magazines," I said.

"Wait until you see what this baby can do." He patted it. "But first let me tell you a little bit about it. And here's my card."

He reached into a breast pocket and pulled out one and handed it to me. GEORGE HARMAN, ASSOCIATE REGIONAL SALES MANAGER. INTERNATIONAL BUSINESS MACHINES. Then he shook my hand.

"Dan Rattiner," I said.

"George Harman," he said. He took out some color brochures. "Is that what you use now?" he asked.

He motioned dismissively to the old Remington upright manual typewriter on the desk. My dad had given it to me from the pharmacy.

"Haven't changed those things since the nineteenth century," he said. "But this is a revolution."

I let him explain the whole thing to me. Though there had been electric typewriters around for a few years already, none could do what this one did. It had silver balls, each about the size of a Ping-Pong ball, that slipped onto a post right in the center of the typewriter and had the alphabet on them in raised letters. You pressed the letter *A* and the ball twisted instantly so the *A* faced the paper, then struck the paper. A perfect *A*.

"You can actually choose different typefaces for your typewriter. How about that?" He opened a box—it contained half a dozen balls—and took out one and handed it to me. It said 10 PT. CENTURY on the top. I kept looking at where this went on the typewriter. But he was saving that for last. He wanted to talk about balls.

"You have BODONI, CENTURY, BOLD, ITALICS. Your choice. How about that?"

"Pretty amazing," I said. "You know, I really don't think I could afford one of these."

"They aren't cheap," he said proudly.

"And I've tried the electric typewriters, but I find that if you just look at them, they type the letter. The keys are so sensitive."

"We think we have solved that problem."

"And I hate the humming noise they make. I am just so used to the clack, clack, clack."

He stood up. "Well, I think it's time we plug this baby in, fire her up, and let you see what she can do." He grabbed the cord and looked around.

"There's no electricity up here," I said.

THE mezzanine floor above the Montauk Improvement Company offices remained the Montauk office for the newspaper through the remainder of the summer of 1967 and the summer of 1968. From time to time, bored, I would riffle through the tens of thousands of pages of business papers in the desks and files of the old Montauk Beach Company. They didn't belong to me. So I never thought to take any. Except once.

I came across a folder containing the correspondence between Carl Fisher and his manager in Montauk, Tom Ringwood, during the years 1936 and 1937. The Crash of '29 had devastated the company and brought all construction to a halt by 1932. Fisher had lost control of the company around 1933, had been put on a pension, and was drinking heavily while living out a restless retirement in his home in Miami Beach, which the company, now in receivership, had salvaged for him and his wife. But that did not stop Fisher from writing to Ringwood.

All the correspondence, both to Ringwood and back to Fisher, were carbons. I wondered about this for a while. But then I realized that Ringwood must have sent his originals to Fisher, keeping a carbon for himself, while Fisher must have had a secretary type the original, which he kept, while sending Ringwood the carbon. Fisher was, even in decline, the old boss.

Almost all the letters from Fisher involved requests. Could Ringwood have the living room rug in his abandoned Montauk mansion cleaned and sent to him in Florida? Could he have the housekeepers give the Montauk house a special cleaning toward the end of August? Jane was thinking of coming up there. (By sleeper train.)

What about the idea Fisher had had, linking membership in the golf course with that of the Surf Club, and then packaging them as free for a year if you bought a building lot? Had that worked? (It hadn't.)

Ringwood's letters were polite and respectful. Regarding Fisher's personal requests, he took care of them. Regarding the business suggestions, he said they were considering them.

About two years after this last letter was written, Carl Fisher died in Miami Beach of alcoholism. He was sixty-five.

There were roughly eighty sheets of paper in this folder. And I stole them one day, although I felt very guilty about doing it, hiding the folder in my Windbreaker as I walked through the salespeople's offices on the first floor.

In 2003, I had the opportunity, in an oceanfront home in Southampton belonging to Ambassador Carl Spielvogel and his wife, Barbaralee Diamonstein, to spend an hour with a very, very wealthy man named Mitchell Wolfson Jr. of Miami. Wolfson is a huge collector of Americana and has built a large museum to house his collection, the Wolfsonian, in that city. During our conversation, he told me he had an entire wing devoted to Carl Fisher, the founder of Miami Beach and Montauk. I asked him if he would like this collection of correspondence I had and he said he would love to have it. So I sent it to him. Though not before I made copies of these carbons, which I donated to the Montauk Library—built in the 1980s as the successor to the old bookmobile.

As for the rest of the material, it's gone. The Montauk Improvement Company sold the seven-story office building in the early 1980s to a developer from New York City. He emptied out the entire building, throwing the contents in the trash, then refurbished it and even hired Garden State Brick to put a new facade on the structure. The elevator was replaced. The rooms spruced up. And all sold off as condominiums to people who wanted vacation homes "conveniently right in the center of town, with ocean views."

Montauk Realtor John Keeshan sold them all, during a five-year span, but spent another five years trying to sell the penthouse, which finally, around 1992, got sold to a Manhattan family.

I've often wondered if they know the history of what they got.

Cecil Hoge Jr.

———————————————————

A T 6:00 A.M. on a summer's day in 1967, I got out of bed at my little barracks-building home in East Hampton to get ready to play a game of squash at the fabled Meadow Club in Southampton. I shaved, brushed my teeth, combed my hair. I looked nothing like anybody I knew who got to go to the Meadow Club. I was Jewish. There was no getting around it.

Who was not Jewish was Cecil Hoge Jr. Cecil was twenty years old, a prep school kid now at Yale with curly brown hair, a firm jaw, a winning smile, and a can-do manner. We had hit it off almost immediately, which was odd, not only because he was from one world and I was from another, but because I had hired him.

This was the seventh summer I had run the paper and it was expanding. The previous year, I had hired my first employee, Jim Lytton, who was down for the summer from his sophomore year at Wesleyan. I was, by this time, twenty-six. And I found him working at a gas station. Someone had told me he'd like to do newspaper work.

"I don't want to hire you," I told Jim. "I don't even want to be an employer. I'd rather do everything myself. But now there's too much to do."

"Make a list of what you want me to do," Jim said.

"Just *stuff*," I told him. "You'll see it when it happens. But for now, just try to keep busy."

Now I was going to have to worry about *him*.

Cecil Hoge Jr., the son of Cecil Hoge Sr. of Southampton, and the nephew of both Serge and Ivan Obolensky, all of whom had mansions in Southampton, was either the third or fourth employee. He wrote articles I assigned him. And he delivered the Amagansett route. It surprised me to see someone from his station in life work so hard, but he did. Discipline is what it was, I guessed.

That, however, was not why we had hit it off. Cecil had the same odd take on life that I did. Something I found funny, he found funny. It was enough.

What do you wear to play squash? I had never played squash in my life. I dressed in shorts, Keds sneakers, and a white T-shirt. I had no intention of standing out in any way at the exclusive Meadow Club. I ate breakfast. Cheerios and orange juice.

"I can't go to the Meadow Club," I had told him when he had asked me.

"Sure you can. I'm a member. You're my guest."

"But I've never played squash in my life."

"I could teach you. Have you seen it played?"

"No."

"Really?"

"You hit a hard rubber ball against a wall."

"See?"

The sun was just rising as I pulled out of my gravel driveway out onto the highway. I headed west. There wasn't a car on the road at that hour. The Meadow Club was fifteen miles away.

I had asked Cecil why it was that he wanted to play squash at seven in the morning, and he had said that's how early it had to be for him to reserve the court. But I didn't believe him. What I really thought was it had something to do with me. As in—he's a Jew. Cecil, determined to befriend me, was going to be smuggling me in. And then we'd be done before all the regular members arrived, is what I thought. But I had kept that to myself.

Montauk Highway bisects the Hamptons, going east/west, in a very real way. The area south of the Highway was where all the members of the Social Set lived. The lawns were mowed, the hedgerows that lined the narrow streets were tall, intimidating, and tightly trimmed. You couldn't see through them. You could hear the sounds, however. They included the thwack of tennis balls, the splash of swimming pool water, and the whirr of water sprinklers.

Behind the hedgerows, the Social Set drank Bloody Marys for breakfast, went to cocktail parties, coming-out parties, engagement parties. Everybody knew everybody else. They even had their own special phone book, called the Blue Book, so you would know whom to call. And they all belonged to clubs, to golf clubs such as the Maidstone or the National, beach clubs such as the Bathing Corporation in Southampton, or the Meadow Club, which was a croquet and tennis club.

That first summer I expanded my newspaper to include a separate East Hampton summer edition, I had put in a section about recreation. I had listed the boat rental places, the public tennis courts, the public golf clubs. I listed them, wrote a few sentences about them, and at the end included their telephone numbers.

What about the private clubs? I had thought. I included them too. Next to the clubs I gave the phone number and the words "for membership information." Two weeks later, I got a call from an employee at the Maidstone Golf Club. He wished us to remove reference to their club in my newspaper. No, they weren't looking for new members. The membership applications were from the children of the members, he said. They

TENNIS AT THE MEADOW CLUB IN SOUTHAMPTON.
(Courtesy of Dan Rattiner)

had a long waiting list. Please. I removed it. Too bad for them if they don't want new members, is what I thought.

Then there was north of the Highway. Kids on bicycles, jungle gyms, fishing boats on blocks in the front yards, dogs running around, horses, wetlands, cedars, and elm trees. Recreation was the Pancake Sunday breakfast at the firehouse, or pool at the tavern down on the corner. High school football games were a big deal.

Oddly, my little house sat south of the highway, but it was south by about a hundred feet. It was right *on* the highway. So it was north of the Highway. No hedgerows *on* the highway.

Cecil had really tried to bring me into High Society prior to his invitation to play squash at his club. He had invited me over for lunch at the Hoge summer mansion on First Neck Lane. And I had gone. I was introduced to his mother and his father, to his sister and brother, to various friends and guests who were out for the weekend. The house was airy and cool, with lots of wicker, rattan, and overstuffed sofas. An overhead fan whirred around. There was talk of somebody who had run off with somebody else. Ivan Obolensky and his wife stopped by.

The next day, I spoke to Cecil when he came to work and asked him how my visit had gone. "Not well." He grinned. "You did something. I don't know what."

What could it have been? I recalled sitting on the arm of a sofa for a while. Maybe that was it. Was I not wearing the right clothes? Had I coughed without covering my mouth?

So now it was three weeks later, and I was responding to my next invitation from Cecil, which was to play squash. And so I put on my turn signal, and drove slowly through the white pillars marking the entrance to the Meadow Club, up past the grass tennis courts and into a parking space. There was only one other car in the parking lot and it was Cecil's. He was already there, standing by the side entrance, a white gym bag over his shoulder.

"We've got just five minutes to get ready," he said, looking at his watch. "Then we've got an hour."

"Sorry."

Next to him was an older man in some sort of uniform. He had a metal ring with keys on it attached to his belt.

"You can let us in," Cecil said.

Then he introduced us. "This is Dan. This is Mr. McCann."

We shook hands.

"We better get to it," Mr. McCann said in a cheerful Irish brogue as he fiddled with the keys.

We went inside, into a locker room that smelled of sweat and hair tonic. Nobody was there and it was dark. Mr. McCann switched on a light.

"You didn't bring a racket?" Cecil asked, looking me over.

"No."

"Mr. McCann, see if you can find Dan a racket."

McCann, who was opening some wall cabinets, grumbled something about there not being rackets, but he went off to look anyway and came back with one. Also a ball.

"This is the only ball I could find, Master Cecil," Mr. McCann said.

"Thank you, Mr. McCann. Dan, do you want to change your shoes?"

Cecil sat down on a bench and zipped open the gym bag. "I have sneakers."

He looked at Mr. McCann, then looked at me. "You're not supposed to use rubber soles. Marks up the floor." He paused. "But I think it will be all right. This once."

He glanced at Mr. McCann worriedly but got a blank look back. He took off the shoes he was wearing and put on the special shoes from the bag, whatever they might be.

McCann now got two towels out of a cabinet and set them on the bench. Then he unlocked the door to the squash court and walked off. I never saw him again. Cecil finished lacing up his shoes and we walked to the door and went inside. We were, as near as I could tell, the only people in the building, other than Mr. McCann.

The court was a two-story-tall room with a hardwood floor and hardwood painted walls all around. High up on one side wall there was a small window that let in sunlight. A wire cage was mounted over it to protect it. You couldn't break the window.

"Here's how it works," Cecil said, coming to stand next to me. We both had rackets. He bounced the ball once in front of him—it made a loud rubber sound—and then he caught it.

He swished his racket. "Here's how you serve. You bounce it once, and then you hit it as hard as you can against the back wall. Then I have to hit it back. It's real simple. And we alternate shots. I hit it back against the back wall, then you hit it back against the back wall. The rules are you can let it bounce before you hit it, but only one bounce. If it's more than one bounce, you've lost the point."

"What about the side walls?" I asked. "I've seen a game where the ball's hit off the side walls."

"Bounce it off the side walls all you want. It doesn't count for anything. Use the ceiling if you want. But it must hit the back wall."

"I got it. So the side walls are to confuse people."

"Yes. Okay. You serve," Cecil said. And he handed me the ball. It was black, rubbery, and heavy. It would make quite a mark if it hit you in the head, is what I thought. I can do this.

"Ready?"

"Ready," Cecil said, and he crouched down just in front and off to the side of me and began to rock from side to side.

I'm gonna win this, I thought. I bounced it off the floor and I swung the racket as hard as I could. But I hit the ball on the wood of the racket, not the strings, and off it went up and sideways. I followed it with my eyes. It would hit the side wall way up.

But it didn't. It hit, and lodged, in the wire mesh in front of the window. And it just stayed there.

We stared at it for a while. It was about fifteen feet up, and there was no way whatsoever we were going to be able to retrieve it. "So that's *it*," Cecil finally said.

And it was. We stared at it a few minutes more, made feeble noises to each other about that being the only squash ball in the building and Mr. McCann had already told us that, and then we shuffled back out of the court to the bench and the lockers.

"Sorry," I said.

"It's all right," he said as he unlaced his shoes. But I could see it wasn't. He was angry. But he was trying not to let on. Finally, he stood up. He took a deep breath.

"Well," he finally said. "Thanks for coming." He clapped a hand on my shoulder. "Just go out the way you came in."

"You going to stay?" I asked. But I knew the answer already.

"I'll see you around noon. That's when you said I should come in."

"That's the time," I said.

Over the years since this incident, Cecil and I have maintained what I call a once-in-a-while friendship. We both got married, had children. At one point, I didn't hear from him for about ten years, but then he called me up and we picked it up as if it was yesterday. He had an article he wondered if I would run. Send it in, I told him. I did run it. His father died, and he took over the family business, which was a mail-order house with offices based in Port Jefferson. He had moved there, bought a house on the water, sent his kids off to boarding school.

He sent me another article. And our friendship marched on.

Cecil's mail-order business is largely based on fishing, hiking, and the outdoors. They sell tents, backpacks, shoes, jackets, nets, and cooking gear. They put ads in *Field and Stream, Outdoors* magazine, and *Backpacker* magazine. Not too long ago, they added a Web site and the business expanded dramatically. Cecil and his wife and kids are content.

The last time I talked to Cecil Hoge he had just come back from China.

"We visited the factories where they make inflatable canoes," he said. "You know our inflatable canoes are the mainstay of our business. We contract out the making of them. At the factory, I got the grand tour. Any idea how much it costs for the workmen there to make one canoe? I counted heads, I know what they pay them. I did the math."

"No idea," I said.

"Eight dollars and seven cents. Everything else, including me, is middlemen."

That's Cecil. I think about him every once in a while. And I also think of the wire mesh with the ball in it. Perhaps it is still there, still up there on the side wall at the Meadow Club, a memorial to one long-ago failed attempt at intercultural relations.

Jim Jensen

For three decades, beginning in the mid-1960s, Jim Jensen
was the news anchor for the *CBS Evening News* on WCBS-
TV in New York. The ratings were high, he won many awards,
and he was movie-star handsome. He reported the news in a
serious yet upbeat manner, informing the public about the assassination of President Kennedy and the inauguration of President Johnson, about the '67 Six-Day War between the Israelis
and the Arabs, about the Vietnam War and the refusal of Muhammad Ali to take a step forward and be inducted into the
armed forces.

I often saw him on television. I never met him. But once,
late one afternoon in the summer of 1967, his assistant called
me up out of the blue at my office in East Hampton, and when
she got me, she put him on.

"You son of a bitch," he said. "Have you any idea what a
disgrace you are to American journalism? Have you any idea?"

He went on and on. After a while, he got tired of berating
me, told me so, and then said he had no further interest in
talking to me. Then he hung up. That was the first and last

time I ever had any contact with Jim Jensen. Although I will
say that when I heard some years later after he retired that he
had died of a sudden heart attack, I said to myself, Serves you
right.

How I came to have this brief one-sided conversation with
a major American television anchor goes back to the year I
started my newspaper in Montauk. Going around selling advertising for it that first year I found easy to do in some cases.
But in others I got an argument.

"This is going to be a newspaper? But it's going to be *free*?"

"Yes."

"Who is going to read a free newspaper? There is no such
thing. People will not read a newspaper if they don't pay for it.
If they pay for it, they will read it. If they don't pay for it, they
may pick it up, but they'll throw it away."

"Not if it is really, really interesting," I said.

I went over the numbers back then, which was in the
springtime of 1960, with my potential advertisers. There were
30 motels in Montauk, with an average of 35 rooms. With two
beds a room, and with about 80 percent occupancy and a turn-
over of twice a week—I had called all 30 motel owners and had
asked them how often the tourists came and went—this meant
there were at least 3,000 new people in town per week. Add
that to the number of people who had summer homes, which
was about 500, and add that to the permanent population,
which was 900, and you got about 4,400 people in town at any
one time. Yet the local weekly newspaper sold only 220 copies
a week in Montauk, a fact I knew because I knew how many
were being sold in my father's store. And my dad's store and

the smaller store called Martell's were the only two places it was for sale. I could give away twenty times that!

"I'll pass," many people said.

The idea that nobody would read a free newspaper really stung. News should be free. Somehow I would show them.

The first hint of how this might happen took place later in that first year. I was home one afternoon when the phone rang. My mother took the call. It was for me.

"Hello?"

"Is this the editor of the *Montauk Pioneer*?"

"Yes."

"Well, this is Milt Harris. I'm the stationmaster at the Montauk Railroad Station. We've got a very angry group of people down here. You published the wrong train schedule in the paper."

"I did?"

"There's no afternoon train at four fifteen. There *used* to be a four fifteen. But they changed it to six fifteen. Have you any idea what you have done?"

"No."

"There's about sixty of them. You should come down here and talk to them."

I was twenty years old. "Why don't *you* talk to them?"

"I'm not going to talk to them. I'm upstairs, in the apartment above the waiting room. I'm not coming down. I've got the door locked."

I thought about it. What could I possibly say to these people? Nothing. They'd kill me. "I'm sorry but I'm not going to come down there."

"*Everybody* reads your paper," he said.

One of the great stories from the history of Montauk involved the failed attempt by developer Carl Fisher to make it into a resort city comparable to Miami Beach in the 1920s. He had built the seven-story skyscraper in the middle of town, but just a few years later, after the Crash of '29, it became vacant. It was still vacant in 1960.

The following year, 1961, I published a picture of our vacant seven-story skyscraper on the front page, and over it I superimposed a picture of Howard Hughes, with an arrow pointing to the penthouse apartment.

HOWARD HUGHES SECRETLY IN MONTAUK, I headlined.

At the same time this was going on, the richest man in the world, Howard Hughes, was holed up in his penthouse apartment in Las Vegas. Or maybe he wasn't there. Maybe he was somewhere else? Who knew? Thus I was launched on a career of publishing on occasion, just to wake everybody up, something entirely made up as if it were real. If it got people to talk about the newspaper, it was certainly okay with me.

There was another reason I liked the idea of making up some of the news every once in a while. Four years earlier, as a junior in high school, I had taken a journalism course with a charismatic teacher named Harry Friedlander. He talked to us about newspapers.

"Newspapers are sticklers about publishing the facts on the news pages," he told us. "You may believe everything they write in the front of the book. Then they have the editorial page. It is on the editorial page that they write opinions."

I raised my hand.

LONG POND
ON A QUIET
DAY.
(Photograph by
Joan Gray)

"But sometimes, doesn't a reporter have an interest in slanting a story one way or another?" I asked. "Wouldn't that put opinion on the news pages?"

"You don't do that."

"I don't believe it," I said. "*Everybody* has an ax to grind about something."

"Go tell it to city hall," he said.

Harry Friedlander also taught us how to write for newspapers. No matter what the story, he said, the most important thing goes in the first paragraph. Then the second most important thing goes in the second paragraph and the third most important thing in the third, and so forth and so on. That way, when the typesetters print out the story in galley form, as a single long sheet one column wide, the editor can, in order to make it fit, cut it anywhere and still know that the most important facts were still in there. They were at the top.

Again I raised my hand.

"That is why newspapers are boring," I said.

I would tell stories from the beginning in my paper, as a storyteller would. I would capture the interest of the reader, and then I would expand upon it. There would be no need for cutting. I'd tell each story from front to back, and it would be my job to make the pieces so interesting that the reader would simply be compelled to read them through.

And every once in a while I would break the bond between reader and reporter. You can't trust what you read. It may not be true. It may be just what the editor wants you to think. For example, in the 1890s, William Randolph Hearst, who owned the largest chain of daily papers in America, wanted to stir up war fever in order to sell newspapers. He sent reporters to Cuba who wrote back and said the Spanish rulers of the island really weren't that bad.

"You furnish the pictures," he said, "and I'll furnish the war." And he did.

No. Every once in a while I would tell a lie. And nobody would know when I would do that. Although I did expect that the lies would be so outrageous as to be obvious. People would at least suspect they were being lied to.

In 1966, visiting an island in the Caribbean, I befriended a young man, Bill, who was a skin diver. We had drinks in a bar one evening. And we talked about the Loch Ness monster, which had been in the news because there were people in Scotland who believed they had seen the monster in the loch. There were pictures. Fuzzy ones, to be sure. Bill had gone to Scotland and volunteered to join the team looking to find the monster, and he had taken many shifts as one of the watchers. He thought he saw something once.

Earlier that year, in Bridgehampton, I had driven with a friend down some dirt roads to the north of that town. Through the woods we passed close by two of the most beautiful and isolated lakes I had ever seen. They were called Long Pond and Little Long Pond.

Now, sitting in the Stone Balloon Café in St. Croix with Bill, I had a great idea. And so I wrote about the monster in Long Pond. I interviewed some students from St. John's University in New York City, who were camping there for two weeks and taking eight-hour shifts looking to photograph the monster. They had the pond under surveillance twenty-four hours a day. Spirits were high. They'd be there at least another week. They'd get a picture of him yet.

I gave the history of the sightings of the monster.

In colonial times, a woman had seen the monster and had come running into town to tell everybody. The people said she was a witch, and she got arrested and burned at the stake.

In World War II, a group of soldiers had set up a camp on the banks of the pond. But then, one night, the monster appeared, the alarm was sounded, and the subsequent fusillade of machine-gun chatter, cannon fire, and flamethrower bursts was heard as far away as Montauk. But the monster was gone in the morning.

I had a wonderful time making up this story of the monster in Long Pond. It may have been suspicious, but it was believable.

And then came the call from Jim Jensen.

When he slammed down the receiver, I found myself shaking like a leaf. What the hell was he talking about? I had absolutely no idea. It was something I had written, obviously. But what?

With very mixed emotions, I decided I would try to call him back. I got the phone number from Information at CBS and placed the call. I wanted to talk to him and I didn't want to talk to him. Finally, I got through to his assistant. I took a deep breath.

"Um, is Mr. Jensen there?"

She asked who was calling and I told her.

"Mr. Jensen already talked to you," she said.

"I know, but nowhere in the conversation did he say what it was about. It was a very one-sided conversation. Then he hung up. Have you any idea what this was about?"

"I certainly do," she said. "He read your story about Long Pond and the students from St. John's, and he sent out a crew to interview them. They choppered out at six this morning and have been looking all day. But it turns out there is no story. I guess you know that."

"Thank you very much."

"Please don't call again," she said.

Speed King

A T 8:00 A.M. on a beautiful but hot Friday morning in early
August of 1968, I drove to Speed's Luncheonette on Newtown Lane to treat myself to some scrambled eggs and coffee before going to work. There were two luncheonettes on Newtown
Lane at that time. One of them, on the east side of the street,
was called Eddie's, run by Eddie Cangalosi and his wife, Ruth.
On the west side, right next door to the little police station, was
Speed's. Oddly, Speed's had two gas pumps on the sidewalk out
front. They were right up by the curb, and I was told that in the
1930s, you could drive up and pump gas into your car there.
But people didn't do that anymore right there in the middle of
town. Though I believed the pumps did still work.

Speed was a slender older man in a white apron. He had
close-cropped gray hair and was slightly stooped and slow
moving—which was why everybody called him Speed—and
though of a pleasant disposition, he didn't talk much. Often,
when things were not busy, he could be seen standing in the
doorway under the SPEED'S sign, sometimes with a spatula in
his hand, just staring out, taking in the scene of downtown

SPEED KING IN THE SPRINGS
IN 1950.
(Courtesy of Dan King)

that spread out around him—roughly fifty stores occupying both sides of two streets, Main Street and Newtown Lane. His place was about ten stores up the lane from the traffic light where the two streets come together.

"Hey, kid," he said when I sat down at the counter. "How's the newspaper business?"

"I'll have a number three," I said.

"How you want it?"

"Scrambled. And with jelly for the toast. Also a cup of coffee."

"Comin' up," he said.

He wrote down my order and walked away. A few stools down, two people were talking about a storm that was coming up the coast. It was expected Wednesday, but it wasn't expected to be the worst thing that ever happened. Nothing like Hurricane Donna, which had hit eight years before. At a table, there was a couple, owners of the local Ford dealership, facing each other but each holding up and reading a section of the morning newspaper. Nobody, especially me, had any idea that before this day was out I would be in jail.

The food came and I ate, and after paying with a dollar bill I had with me, about ten after nine I drove off to my office, the front half of a former carriage house I had rented on Gay Lane behind the Amaden Gay Real Estate Agency. It was a big space. My office, with four employees at desks and layout tables, fit comfortably in the front. In the back was a furniture-making shop run by a guy named Harry VanTassel. When he used any sanding equipment he would close the door that separated the two spaces to protect us from the voluminous dust. A kindness. Another day he offered another kindness. We had a big bumblebee in our half of the carriage house. It poked slowly around, here and there, not bothering anybody, but we found its presence unnerving. We called to Harry, and he wheeled in his big commercial vacuum cleaner—the one that sucked up sawdust—and carrying his flexible tube and brush, he chased it up to a window and sucked it in with a FOOP! It was quiet at first, but then, after a moment, you could hear it rattling around in there. Then it settled back down again. Perhaps dead.

Anyway, on that Friday morning, I came in the front door and immediately, before I could even go to my desk, Marge Miller, the secretary, looked up at me. She had a very worried look on her face.

"A police officer was here," she said. "He's looking for you."

"Why?" I asked.

"I don't know. But he has a warrant for your arrest."

The other three employees glanced briefly up at me from whatever they were doing.

"Well, I'll go down to Town Hall and straighten it out," I said. I had no idea what this was about.

"You might want to go home and change," Marge said. I looked down. I was wearing sandals, a bathing suit, and a T-shirt with a pen in the breast pocket. "I think he wants to take you to jail."

"I'll straighten it out," I said firmly. And I left.

Driving the one mile from Gay Lane to the Town Hall on Pantigo Road, I tried to think what I might have done. I hadn't hurt anybody or stolen anything. Perhaps they just wanted to ask me some questions.

I pulled into the parking lot and walked in. The first place to start, I thought, would be with the town clerk. I never got there. As I was in the hallway about to go into the room where the town clerk's counter was, I felt a hand on my shoulder from behind me. A voice was connected to it.

"Gotcha," it said. I turned. And there was a police officer I had never seen before, in full battle regalia, blue cap with black visor, sunglasses, starched uniform, whistle and badge, billy club and gun on his hip. For the purpose of this story, the name on his badge was RICHARDS.

"You're under arrest," he said.

I looked at the door with TOWN CLERK stenciled on it. "I have to see the clerk," I said. "I have to pay the fine or something."

"No you don't," he said. "You're coming with me."

"I don't want to come with you," I said.

"You were supposed to be in court on Friday. Village Hall. You didn't show up."

I didn't say anything. But now I knew. There was a traffic light at the corner of Woods Lane and Main Street, but in the off season, it was just a blinking light. Last April, when there was nobody around, I hadn't come to a complete stop. And a cop, with nothing better to do, had pulled out from behind some bushes, turned on his flashing lights and siren, and pulled me over. I gave him a hard time, told him he should be out chasing criminals instead of hiding behind bushes waiting for the local citizenry. He gave me a ticket and I told him I would fight it. I had gotten a trial date in, uh, August. Uh-oh.

"What do I do now?" I asked.

"When you didn't show, the judge issued a bench warrant. So I pick you up, put you in the police car, and bring you in. You go to jail."

"I do?"

"Yes."

"But I have things to do."

"You should have thought of that before you decided not to show up."

"What about my car?" I asked. "I have my car here at Town Hall. What do I do with my car?"

"You could leave it here. Tell you what. I know where you live. You go in front of me and I'll follow you home. And no funny business. You leave your car there."

And so that's what we did. At my house, the barracks building formerly owned by Lieutenant Kealy, I drove in the gravel driveway. And he came in right behind me. I got out.

"I'll get my wallet," I said. "Will I need anything else? How long will I be there?" I'm packing for camp, I thought.

"You'll just be there until we get you together with the judge," he said.

When I came back out of the house, I saw a sight I will never forget. It was Officer Richards standing by the right front fender of his police car holding out a set of handcuffs. I stopped and stared at him.

"You don't have to do that," I said.

"Yes I do," he said, walking toward me. And he snapped them on. Then he turned and, walking in front of me, led me to the police car. On the way, looking at his back, I imagined myself doing something awful. I imagined myself raising both hands, cuffed together as they were, over my head and then crashing them down on the top of his head. And then running away. I suppressed this urge.

He opened the back door of the police car, put his hand on my head, and ducked me down and in. There were bars between the back and the front, and when he closed the door I heard a click. The doors had locked.

Richards got in the front, started up the car, and drove out of my driveway and onto the street. I was full of questions from there in the back.

"Do you have to put the siren on?" I asked.

"No," he said.

"Are we going to the police station on Pantigo Road or the one on Newtown Lane?"

"Newtown Lane," he said. "You were ticketed in the village."

I gave this a lot of thought as we drove along. This was

right in the middle of downtown. We passed the bowling alley.

"Is there a way to drive up to the *back* door of the police station?"

"No."

"Everybody will see me come in the front. Everybody knows me."

"I have to drive up to the front."

"Could you take the handcuffs off in the car when we get there? I'd just walk in with you."

"Nope." There was a pause. "It's only just across the sidewalk. A couple of steps."

He turned left onto Newtown Lane, swung around, parked right in front next to the gas pumps, and turned off the ignition. Then he turned around, to make sure, apparently, I was still there.

I took a deep breath, and the officer came around to my side of the car, put his hand back on the top of my head, and helped me out, since it was awkward to do with the handcuffs on. The front door of the police station loomed ten feet across the sidewalk. And as I began to walk, out of the corner of my eye, I could see Speed King, in white apron, standing by his front door, looking out onto the street to see what was going on. He was without his spatula.

We stopped in the lobby, in front of another officer sitting behind the raised platform. Richards spoke to him for a moment. I was still handcuffed. Now a third police officer came out of the back, frisked me, and then they took off the handcuffs. This third officer had a manila envelope.

"Put everything in your pockets in here," he said.

I reached into my bathing suit pocket and pulled out my wallet and handed it to him. He showed me my name on the front of the envelope, then opened it wide, looked at me so I could see that the wallet was going inside, and then closed it up. It was a magic trick. No funny business.

"Anything else?"

"No."

"What about this?"

Richards was pointing to the pocket of my T-shirt. In the pocket was a pen. This was a German-made drawing pen called a Rapidograph that wrote with India ink. I handed it to the man with the envelope and he took the top off and stared at the tip of the pen for a moment. It had a sharp steel point.

"You think I'm going to stab myself?" I asked.

"We'll keep it here for you anyway," he said. And he re-opened the envelope and put that in.

The two men led me into a back room where there was a small steel jail cell. One of the men took out a set of keys and opened the iron bars that served as the door to this cell. This was a dream. Then they ushered me inside.

"Wait," one of the officers said at the entrance. He pointed to a small metal plate on the outside of the cell. It read IN-STRUCTIONS FOR PRISONERS. "Read this, please."

I read it, but I was so nervous that I had no idea what I was reading. When I was finished, I grunted and nodded and they motioned me inside, slamming the door behind me with a clang.

"What happens now?" I asked. I grasped the bars.

"You stay here and we get a judge to come and decide what happens next."

"Can I get anything to read? A magazine?"

"No. Sorry. You shouldn't be here long."

"How about a piece of paper and a pen, or pencil. I could draw something or write something."

"That would be all right."

I looked around. I was inside a steel room that later that day I paced off. It was six feet wide by eight feet long. It had a wooden bench along one wall and a toilet without a toilet seat. There was a roll of toilet paper. And that was it. No bed. A lockup.

As I looked more closely, it was apparent that this whole thing had been bolted together. It must have come as a kit. And they must have dragged the pieces there into the back room and assembled it. It did what it had to do.

They brought me a pencil and a piece of paper with the chief's letterhead on it. His personal stationery. What was I supposed to do with that? I put these items in the pocket of my bathing suit.

The only way to see out was to go to the bars of the steel door where I had come in. The bars were floor to ceiling, so you could see everything outside in the back room. I saw a clock, a row of metal lockers, some hooks to hang coats, a pay phone, and on the opposite wall some shelves. On the shelves were police helmets, billy clubs and belts, and what looked to me like crime evidence. There were boxes of things with names and dates on them, lamps, a baseball, a plaster cast of a tire track, and so forth. The things not in boxes had tags on them. I found myself looking out at this room for quite a long time.

Half an hour passed. There was some muffled talk in the front room but I couldn't make it out. Fifteen more minutes passed. The clock on the wall said eleven ten. It had been two hours since I had walked into my office. Nothing was happening.

I called out. The door to the front was open, and someone in a uniform came, looking at me quizzically.

"You want something?"

"I want to know when I get to see the judge," I said.

"We're trying," he said. "But we're having a hard time getting anybody. It's the weekend. Both judges are playing golf."

"Don't I get a phone call?"

"Yes."

"Nobody knows I'm here."

"You know a lawyer?"

"My dad uses Saul Wolf. His office is in Riverhead. I'm sure he's at work."

The officer got another officer and they asked me if I knew his number, which I said I didn't, and so they went away and came back with it. Then one officer put a nickel in the pay phone and called him. When he answered, the officer talked to him for a moment, then unlocked my door noisily and brought me over to talk to him.

"Hi, Saul."

"Where are you?" he asked. I told him. And I told him what was going on.

"They can't hold you like this. They have to find a judge right away."

"The judges are playing golf," I said.

"I'll call your mom and dad and tell them what is going on. I'll get you out."

"Don't call them," I said.

Half an hour later, I was still there. And I decided I should do something to pass the time. I'd write a letter. To a girl I knew named Ann.

VILLAGE OF EAST HAMPTON POLICE DEPARTMENT
17 Newtown Lane, East Hampton, NY 11937
Chief of Police Carl J. Dordelman, Tele. 516 324-0777

August 2, 1968

Dear Ann,

There is no way to get comfortable here. Jail is not what I expected at all. It is gray and depressing and Chief Justice Earl Warren wouldn't like it. I was brought in handcuffed, relieved of my wallet and my belt. My offense? Failure to stop for a blinking red light. I have no idea how long I will be here.

How are your folks?

Sincerely,
Dan Rattiner

Meanwhile, still nothing was happening. Around twelve thirty, the pay phone rang. And when an officer answered it, it was apparent it was Saul on the other end.

"We're trying, Mr. Wolf. They should be back soon."

I wrote another letter to Ann. A police officer came in and asked if I wanted anything from Speed's for lunch. I don't have any money, I told him. We'll pay for it, he said. I said I'd like a baloney sandwich with mustard, a Coke, and some Hydrox cookies, but could they please get it at Eddie's? In a short while he returned with these things and handed them in through the bars, and the food tasted very, very good.

Saul called again about two. And at three thirty there was another call. From inside the cell I could hear him shouting at the officer talking to him.

"Yes, Mr. Wolf. We'll do that. We'll look into it."

At twenty minutes to four, an officer appeared outside my cell with a set of keys and noisily unlocked the door.

"They found a judge," he said.

As I came out, I stopped to have another look at the jail instructions. I was really curious about them now. In fact, I had had a conversation with an officer who had come in to change his clothes about the fact that they were there on the outside and from the inside you couldn't read them and they ought to move them inside, and he said that's the way the kit came. It occurred to me that maybe they had put up that one panel backward. He shrugged.

I looked again at the instructions.

"No time," the officer said. "Come on."

Out front on the street, a police car had pulled up with two officers sitting in the front. Speed was not around. Nobody was around. But still, they took the time to handcuff me before we drove off.

"Where are we going?" I asked.

"Sag Harbor," one of the officers said. "We found a Sag Harbor Village judge for you. Judge Martin. You know Judge Martin? You know how to get to where he lives?"

"No."

"We'll have to stop in Sag Harbor and find out how to get to his house."

Fifteen minutes later, we pulled over in front of Village Hall on Main Street, Sag Harbor. There were a few people walking along. I tried not to make eye contact with any of them.

"See what you can find out," the man driving said to the officer in the passenger seat. He hopped out of the car and went inside. He was in there for quite a while.

And then, walking along the street, there was Barry Fleischman, someone I knew who owned a real estate office a block away. He had bought advertising. And he had seen me. He came over and looked in my window.

"What the hell is this all about?" he said cheerfully.

"Oh, it's complicated," I said.

At that moment, the other officer inside came out and Fleischman backed away.

"Nobody's in there," he said. "Do you believe it? People could walk right in."

Now Fleischman was gone.

"Get in," the driver said. "We'll try to raise somebody on the radio."

They barked a few unintelligible things over their police radio and they waited. There was no reply.

"What the?" the driver said. He tried again. Still no reply.

"Do you believe this? Who's running Sag Harbor?" And then, suddenly, a Sag Harbor Police car appeared, coming slowly up Main Street. And both officers jumped out and stood in the middle of the street waving their arms. Now I was alone in the backseat.

This is so ridiculous, I thought. I sighed, and put my head in my hands. Both police-car doors were open in the front. What a bunch of dopes.

They came back to the police car, breathless. "They know the way," one of them told me excitedly. "We're going to follow them."

And so we did.

We drove down Madison Street, past all the big Victorian mansions, and then, as the road narrowed into a newer suburban development, we came upon a small green ranch house on a well-mowed half acre.

"This is it," one of the officers said, noting the Sag Harbor police car pulling in. We got out. The officers led me up the lawn, still handcuffed, past a group of ten-year-olds throwing a ball around. They stopped when they saw us. One of them came over to me.

"What did you do, mister?"

"Didn't stop at a blinking light," I said.

Around the back of the house, there was a steel Bilco door that led from the lawn down into a small finished basement. The five of us went down there and just stood silently in the middle of this basement room, breathing hard, in front of an empty desk. The judge was not there yet, though from the sounds of the noises coming from upstairs, he would be soon.

This room had cedar-paneled walls, soundproof tiles on the low ceiling, and one high half basement window so the light could come in. Fluorescent ceiling lights lit the room. The small desk had a tiny American flag on a stand on it. Also a telephone.

Now I noticed that foot-square samples of different-colored bathroom tiles hung on the walls. Judge Martin apparently sold bathroom tiles.

Shortly, he appeared, coming down an inside set of stairs, adjusting his clothing. He walked over to his desk and sat down. A middle-aged man with slicked-back hair. He looked at us. Four officers and a man in handcuffs. And he cleared his throat.

"What have we here?" he asked the officers. They produced paperwork and gave it to him.

Judge Martin opened the proceedings by reciting a memorized speech about the court of law and his responsibilities to it and who he was and when his term expired, and then he took out a little gavel, banged it on the desk, and asked me to explain myself.

I had just started when the phone rang. He held up a palm. I stopped. And he picked it up. It was somebody calling about bathroom tile. He listened awhile. Then he spoke.

"Well, we can get it a little more pale blue if you want," he said. "But frankly, I think the darker blue will be just fine."

He talked and listened for several minutes. No hurry. We could wait. Finally he hung up. "Now where were we?" he said.

The rest of the proceedings lasted just five minutes. At the end, after hearing the officers' explanations and my explanations, he fined me fifteen dollars. And an East Hampton police officer, with a big smile on his face, took the handcuffs off me.

"You're a free man," he said. Then we went back up the stairs and out the Bilco door, and off to our police cars.

"Can you take me home?" I asked. "My car is home."

"Sure," the driver said.

It was six o'clock when I got home. I made myself a bowl of spaghetti, finished it off with some ice cream, sat down in front of the television, and instantly fell asleep. I slept for fourteen hours. The next morning, I wrote this entire story up on a typewriter just as it happened. It ran as the lead article in my newspaper the following week, entirely covering the first three pages.

Two weeks later, around noon on Sunday, I decided to go to the beach for a while. I'd take my sheepdog. At first I thought I'd just drive down there in my car, but then I thought I would go on my Lambretta motor scooter. I had devised a way to strap a big wooden box on the metal luggage rack in the back and had found that the dog enjoyed being in it, getting the breeze in his face as we went to new and fascinating places with new sights and smells and all.

We pulled right up to the wooden railing at the end of the road at the back of Main Beach, facing the ocean. There weren't many people there. I lifted the big dog out of the box and set him down. And then a police officer came over. It wasn't Richards. It was nobody I had ever seen before. He pointed up to a metal sign.

"You're in a no-parking zone," he said. "Can I see your driver's license and registration?"

My dog, Scampi, who had gone over to pee on a post, now came back and sat down. He cocked his head to await developments.

"I don't have it with me," I said, indicating the bathing suit and shirt I was wearing.

He went around the back of the motor scooter and looked at the license plate.

"It's expired," he said.

"It is?"

"Who are you?"

"I'm Dan Rattiner. I write *Dan's Papers*."

He missed a beat.

"You know there's a law that says when you drive a motor vehicle you're supposed to wear shoes."

"I didn't know that."

"Do you have a license for that dog?"

"No. His name's on the collar, though."

"What about a leash?"

"He's supposed to be on a leash?"

The officer missed a beat again. "Well, don't do any of this again, okay?" he finally said.

"Okay."

And he drove off. He could have issued me seven summonses, but he didn't. He must have read my story. Everyone had read my story. So this was the power of the press.

The following morning, Monday, I felt brave enough to stop at Speed's for breakfast. I went in, passed the stack of my newspaper on his cigarette machine, and sat down at the counter. Speed came over soon enough.

"Hi, kid," he said.

"I'd like an orange juice and a number seven, a stack of pancakes and some bacon. And coffee."

AN AD FOR SPEED'S IN *DAN'S PAPERS*.
(Courtesy of *Dan's Papers*)

"Coming up." But he didn't move. A smile spread across his face. I had never seen him do that. "Nobody ever wrote about me in a paper before," he said.

"Did you see me when they brought me in?"

"Couldn't miss it. Then it was all over town. People said since you were in a bathing suit, you must have done some awful thing on the beach. Maybe molested somebody." He looked me right in the eye. "I said no."

He served the breakfast and, when I had finished, refused to give me a check.

"On me." He grinned.

Two years later, I read a small article in a local newspaper about a police officer with the East Hampton Village Police Department by the name of Richards who had been suspended from the force for firing two shots from his revolver into the air after claiming that the Soviets were invading down at the beach. Other officers restrained him, separated him from his revolver, and an ambulance took him to Southampton Hospital for observation.

Nonie Self

I N the autumn of 1969, I flew in a small plane to Block Island, a place I had never been before. This potato-shaped island—about seven miles by three and a half—had long been a place of great mystery to me. It was nearby. You could see it from any high point in Montauk—a looming presence on the eastern horizon off in the Atlantic Ocean. But though it was just sixteen miles away, it might have been a thousand. It had no connection in any way with the mainland of Long Island—not by transportation or by communications or even by politics. It was part of Rhode Island, wherever that was. And it was not in the news as far as I was concerned. So I wasn't even curious about going there.

And so I was surprised to get a phone call from Bob King, a customer of mine who owned the Montauk Caribbean Airways. He was calling about Block Island.

"I've watched you grow your business," he said. "You've got newspapers in Montauk, the Hamptons, and the North Fork. And I get lots of business charters from your papers. But last spring, I wanted to put an ad in the newspaper on Block

Island. It's one of the places I go. So I flew over there to do that, but there *is* no newspaper on Block Island. If you put one there, I'll put an ad in it."

Personally, I had a lot of respect for Bob King. He had these twin-engine airplanes he ran out of Montauk in the summer, and then he'd fly them down south to run a charter business there for the winter. He had also started the first radio station on eastern Long Island, WLNG in Sag Harbor.

"You'll like Block Island," he concluded. "Let me fly you over there to look around. I'll drop you off in the morning, pick you up in the afternoon. No charge."

Three days later, first thing in the morning, I drove out to Montauk Airport, and Bob King took me to Block Island. It was astonishing to me just how short a journey it was. We went up in one of his planes, and as soon as we went up we were on our way back down. Fifteen minutes later, I was on the tarmac at Block Island Airport walking to the small cedar-shingle shack, just a little bit larger than the one in Montauk, in which there was a counter, a desk with some radio equipment on it for a traffic controller, and an old car seat in the corner for weary travelers. There was also a bulletin board, on which were several notes—for a lost dog, for roofing work, and for a taxicab, and even one for a charter plane. It wasn't for Montauk Caribbean. Well, he could have put something *there,* I thought. Outside, there was a woman leaning against an old stationwagon taxicab.

I spoke to the woman at the counter about my mission. She said I might want to call a woman who for a couple of years had published a mimeographed sheet for Block Islanders called

NONIE SELF AT THE RAILING OF HER
HOME ON BLOCK ISLAND, 1971.
(Courtesy of Dan Rattiner)

the *Hooter,* and she gave me the phone number, which consisted of just four digits. And she pointed me to the pay phone.

So, I got on the phone and, pushing in a nickel, spent some time trying to persuade this woman to run a newspaper for me on the island, but she said she had given up the *Hooter.* "Everybody's got their own opinion on the island," she said. "You get ten people, you get ten opinions. And if you write anything else they yell at you."

"How many people are on the island?" I asked.

"Maybe five hundred."

This woman on the phone said I might want to talk to one of these opinionated people, a woman by the name of Nonie

Self. An odd name. "She writes books," the woman said. "But she might do it."

I called Nonie Self and told her what I was about and that I was on the island for the day. And she said she might be interested and I should come over.

"I'll make you a cup of tea," she said.

"Where do you live?" I asked.

"The cabbie knows. She's right outside."

Block Island was like a fairyland. Narrow, curving roads went up through hills and down across valleys bordered by low stone walls, magnificent fields, tiny ponds, and classic New England cottages. There were almost no cars on the island and almost no trees, so from wherever you were, you could see beyond open pastures to the ocean in almost every direction. We drove through "downtown" Block Island, which consisted of a single street about a thousand yards long with stores on one side and some docks and boats on the other. I counted the stores. There were ten. Not nearly enough for a newspaper.

"Are there other places where there are stores and restaurants?" I asked the driver.

"A few. Mostly it's all residential. But there are four big old hotels. And maybe a few inns here and there."

We passed the Surf Hotel, high on a hill, a massive affair with rocking chairs on a wraparound porch. There were practically no people. Even downtown there were practically no people.

"The season's over," the cabbie said, apparently referring to July and August.

Eventually we got to Nonie Self's house, a big three-story

foursquare mansion with cedar shingles painted white, windows with black shutters, and a wraparound wooden deck on three sides, one of which, alongside a pasture with a pony in it, had a flight of stairs leading down to it. Everything overlooked the ocean. The cab stopped by the steps, I paid the driver and went up and pulled the brass knocker on the front door. A tall, slender older woman in her sixties answered the door. And that's how I came to meet Margaret Cabell Self, who asked me to call her Nonie, because everybody else did.

Nonie had, I could see at a glance, once been a great beauty. She held herself perfectly straight, was polite and well mannered, and spoke softly in a classic Virginia horsewoman accent, which is what she had been before she came to the island.

We sat in a dark living room over tea and talked. I liked her instantly. She was whimsical, delightful but restrained. I told her what I had in mind. A free newspaper for the tourists, with stories in it about shipwrecks and interesting characters and what to see and do.

"I might be interested if the newspaper would only be in the summertime," she finally said. "For next summer anyway. I just finished a novel. And I'm not planning on another until next fall. But it would have to be just in the summer. In the wintertime, I live in San Miguel de Allende, in Mexico."

I told her it would be just for the summer. "And, I'd love to see your new novel," I said.

"Oh, I doubt if you'd be interested," she said. "It's about a burro who lives in Mexico. And it's written for teenage girls."

"I'd like to see it anyway," I said.

"All right," she said. "Come with me."

We got up and went into the next room, which was a library. It was filled floor to ceiling on all four walls with hardcover books. Quite a collection.

"Let me see," she said. "Here it is."

She slid it out from between some others, and it was at that moment that I saw that the books on either side of it were by Margaret Cabell Self too.

"You've written these too," I said.

"Oh yes. I've done lots of books."

"How many?"

She motioned to the shelves all around. "All of them," she said.

I looked at the book she had handed me, which was called *The Shaggy Little Burro of San Miguel.* And I noticed that some of the others were about animals too—mostly horses.

"I used to have a riding school in Virginia," she said. "And then in Connecticut. I raised quarter horses. Most of these stories are about quarter horses."

Nonie asked me if she could give me a tour of the house, which she said had been built by an old whaling captain in the 1880s. And as we went through it, we came upon an elderly man out on the deck sitting at a table very absorbed in a game of solitaire. There was a small glass of scotch by his right hand.

"This is my husband, the Colonel," Nonie said. He stood up and I shook his hand. He made pleasant conversation for a few moments and then sat back down and continued with his game.

Nonie and I then went on a tour of the island. We drove out to Scotch Beach in the north, to the Mohegan Bluffs in the east, to New Harbor, where there were a few marinas and restaurants. (I was continuing to count.) And at each place we got out and walked around. There was a bright sun to warm you; a strong, steady, salty breeze to keep you cool; and a whole bunch of characters, all of whom knew Nonie. We talked about how one would do a newspaper.

"I write a lot of the articles in the newspapers myself," I said. "So you wouldn't have to write everything."

"Oh, that's not going to be a problem," she said.

I asked her what she thought we should call it. "How about the *Hooter*?" I said. "That's a great name." (*Hooter* referred to the sound made by ships and lighthouses at that time. There was no restaurant chain known as Hooters then.)

"I think we should have something new," she said. "But it's going to be your newspaper. So you think it up. Whatever it is, I'll like it."

As near as I could see, there were only forty-six possible businesses on the island, not nearly enough, even if you could sell ads to half of them, to support a newspaper. When I got back to the office, I gave that information over the telephone to Bob King.

"I don't think I can do this," I said. But, really, I was smitten with the island.

"Whatever you say," he said.

The next day, at my desk in the carriage house, Marge Miller, the secretary, said I had a phone call from a woman on Block Island. I took the call.

"I went to see the merchants yesterday to sell them the ads," she said.

I had left her with a copy of my Montauk newspaper and a total price for each space for the six issues of the summer. I had asked her to try to see if there would be any interest in buying any of the spaces for a paper that would be on the island.

"How many did you sell?" I asked.

"All of them," she said.

"There are forty-six merchant possibilities," I said.

"I sold all forty-six," she said.

Marge Miller turned to me. She was a beautiful young woman with a big smile who had taken a few days off to go to the hippie festival in Woodstock about three weeks earlier. It had been a national sensation, with about 600,000 people in attendance. I had been kicking myself for not going even though some friends had invited me. Too busy with the newspapers, I had told them.

"Was that who I think it was?" Marge asked, referring to the phone call.

"What do you mean?"

"She said her name was Margaret Cabell Self. There's a woman by that name who has written the bible on the care and training of quarter horses. She's famous."

"That's her," I said.

The *Block Island Times* newspaper appeared, full blown as a mature newspaper, in June 1970. The masthead—still in use today—had been designed by me using the unusual block lettering that spelled out the word WOODSTOCK on the cover of a 1969 edition of *Life* magazine. All the ads in it had been sold by Nonie Self and all the articles in it were by Nonie Self. For the next ten summers, this went on this way. Nonie writing all the articles in the summertime, some of them scathing and demanding, others complimentary and appreciative of something—I had no idea of what any of it was about—and never once did I have any of my own work in the paper.

I did send her things.

"There's no room this week," she'd say. "And you really have to understand the island to write about it." That made sense.

At least once a summer, I flew with my family to Block Island and stayed, at her insistence, at her house. Renting mopeds became a big deal during this time. Nonie vigorously opposed it in the paper. People were getting injured on mopeds.

Once, in about the fifth year, Nonie said that there would be a luncheon in my honor at the Manisses Hotel on Spring Street. Everybody on the island wanted to meet me. I should fly over. I did. There was Nonie, me and my wife, the owners of the Manisses Hotel, lots of food and drink, and maybe two other people. It was very embarrassing. But I took it well.

"They just aren't familiar with you," Nonie said to explain why almost nobody had shown up.

Every two weeks, Nonie would be flown over by Montauk Caribbean Airways, and after that by Bill Bendokas and his Block Island–based New England Airlines, which also offered to do it and which Nonie said she preferred. She'd come to the office in Bridgehampton for the day—I'd bought this private home on Bridgehampton's Main Street for our new offices by then—and bring with her all the latest articles all typed up and we'd retype everything and she'd edit and proofread, and then

I'd drive her back to the airport to meet Bendokas—but not before she went next door to the IGA Food Market to buy about five bags of groceries.

"You have no idea how expensive everything is on Block Island," she told me by way of explanation.

After the eighth year, it was apparent that Nonie was getting on. She was approaching eighty. And she couldn't get around as much as she used to, she said. She suggested that we hire a journalism student who came from a family that summered on the island to help her out. I agreed.

And that decision, within the year, resulted in a lawsuit. I learned about it, of course, when I got papers served on me. Something about a boat grounding on Block Island. We were being sued for half a million dollars. I called Nonie.

"You remember three weeks ago this article about a Chris-Craft coming up onto a sandbar during the night?"

I said I did. No one had been on deck and it had just roared up at full speed and got stuck. There had been two men, a twelve-year-old boy, and a woman on board. But when the Coast Guard had come by to inspect the boat, the captain refused to let them on, and when the Coast Guard had offered to take them off their boat so they could stay at a hotel, they decided they would stay on board until the morning high tide, then hire a private firm to tow them off, which they did. The article ended with a question—what had been going on aboard that Chris-Craft anyway? The implication was it had been running drugs. And what about that woman?

"I sent the young journalist," Nonie said. "He interviewed

the Coast Guard or said he did. I think he got it all wrong. Perhaps you should talk to him."

I did. And I also called the Coast Guard and the man who had filed the lawsuit, who owned a belt buckle manufacturing company in Providence, Rhode Island. He gave me an earful. They had stayed on the boat for the night because they feared looters might take the radio, sonar, and other valuables. The Coast Guard, contrary to what our bright-eyed and bushy-tailed reporter had written, had done a complete inspection of the ship and had found nothing—he'd send me the written report if I wanted to see it. And worst of all, there was no woman on board—there was none listed with the Coast Guard—but the twelve-year-old had been his son. And the report in the newspaper was a terrible thing to bring home to his wife.

I offered complete apologies and said I would write what did happen immediately, would describe our errors, and would publish the piece on the front page the following week. I did. And he dropped the suit.

One year, Nonie said she had reviewed the latest technology and found a way that we could send articles from Block Island to Bridgehampton electronically. It was a machine made by Xerox called a Telecopier. She would put a piece of paper onto a drum on her machine in Block Island and turn it on. The paper would spin around and electric charges would create a buzzing noise over a telephone which could then be instantly converted to words printed onto a blank Xerox machine in Bridgehampton. In minutes, I would have just what she had.

Neither of us knew it at the time, but this was the precursor of the fax, which was invented three years later. I bought two of these Xerox Telecopiers. One for her and one for me. Ours sat on a desktop in our office and when she would call to tell us she was sending us something, we'd load a blank sheet of paper, turn it on, and it would spin around and print what she wrote. It gave off a slightly pungent electrical smell as it did it. We used this method for three years until the fax machines arrived on the market.

In our last year with her as editor, she called to tell us she was using a desktop computer called a Radio Shack TRS-80.

"It's terrific," she said. "You should get one. Articles get saved on floppy disks. And I could mail them to you. I might even be able to figure out how to send them to you over something called an Internet."

I had no idea what she was talking about. So I decided not to take her up on her offer.

I could not let Nonie retire. She wanted to. But I told her if she wanted to retire she'd have to find somebody new to be editor. And she finally did for the summer of 1979, although she continued to write a column.

Nine years later, when she was still commuting between Block Island in the summertime and Mexico in the wintertime, Nonie's house on Block Island caught fire. Apparently, when she left for Mexico, she had left an electric blanket plugged in. Although the house was saved, there was much interior damage, Nonie told me over the telephone. And now she would have to paint the whole interior. She said this in a way that made it clear it would not be a workman painting it, but that she would paint it herself. She was now more than eighty-five years old.

I didn't hear from her after that. Once, I wanted to visit her, and I called her daughter, Lee Brotherhood, who lived with her family in the house behind her, and asked if Nonie was okay to visit and she said no. She said Nonie was lucid sometimes and not at other times, but she still lived there. She died a few years after that just days before her ninety-fourth birthday, and the whole island mourned. I mourned her too.

Today, the *Block Island Times* is one of the premier weekly year-round newspapers in New England. I sold it in 1988 to the man and woman whom Nonie had recommended take the paper over from her, Peter and Shirley Wood, and the paper got sold several times after that. Every week, since then and through to this day, on the masthead of the paper, under the names of the present publisher and editor, is the line "The *Block Island Times* was founded in 1970 by publisher Dan Rattiner and editor Nonie Self."

Ken Scanlon

I WAS very familiar with the interior of Scanlon's Liquor Store on Hampton Road in Southampton. I knew the arrangement of the bottles on the shelves. I knew the calendar on the wall behind the cash register. I knew the magazines that Mr. Scanlon liked to read when sitting on his stool at the register waiting for customers. It was *Hot Rod Magazine*. Mr. Scanlon liked cars, just like I did.

The reason I knew all of this about Mr. Scanlon was because of the etiquette involved in being a salesman and coming into a store to sell something. It became immediately clear to me as I went around town selling my summer newspaper ads in the springtime that I would have far better luck if, when a customer walked in, I stopped my sales pitch, looked at the customer and then at the merchant, and then, with a smile, stepped aside.

I learned this the hard way one day early on when a merchant told me in a very firm voice that he understood my enthusiasm, but that I had better step aside because a customer had walked in the door. The look on his face told me if I wanted an ad I ought to do that. So I did.

KEN SCANLON'S
LIQUOR STORE
IN 1963.
(Courtesy of Peggy
Scanlon)

Another lesson I learned was to make sure I was talking to the owner of the store, or at least a person who was in a position to make the decision about whether or not to buy an ad.

Once, I went into a store and began making my pitch to the only person in the place, a woman behind the counter who said, when I asked, that she was the manager. She listened to me patiently. I spread out the previous year's newspaper on her counter and went on and on about the giant circulation and how everybody read it and because of its readership, it was surely the most important medium in the town now. She listened patiently. I continued to talk with great enthusiasm and now showed her my sales dummy—the same blank newspaper with all the ad spaces set out with black Magic Marker. You bought one and it was yours for the eight issues of the summer. I was still coming out every other week. You could have upper right on page 3 or here at the bottom of the movie page. And here's the price. What do you say?

"I think I could show this to the owner, Mr. Barker, when he comes in," the woman said.

Then there was Bill Frankenbach, a tall, stern man who owned a garden center on County Road 39 in Southampton. He had been a marine in the Korean War and held himself ramrod straight. Behind him, as I waited for him to finish up with a customer, I saw the sign he had on the wall in plain sight. EVERY TENTH SALESMAN WHO COMES IN HERE WILL BE SHOT. THE NINTH JUST LEFT.

In any case, now I was standing, for the fourth time that spring, in front of the cash register at Scanlon's Liquor Store waiting for Mr. Scanlon. It was 1969, and it was the second year I was publishing my paper in the next town down the beach— Southampton. Now I had editions in six communities: Montauk, East Hampton, Westhampton Beach, the North Fork, Block Island, and Southampton.

Mr. Scanlon, the year before, had been a key to my plans for that town. I really thought, as I made my first Southampton selling dummy that year, that what worked in Montauk and East Hampton would surely work in Southampton. But then, I also thought Southampton (which includes Bridgehampton) might be a problem. It was the very centerpiece of the Hamptons and the richest community because of the very large number of wealthy WASP summer residents who had mansions down on the beach. And I wasn't one of them. There were so many of them, more than in any other community by far, that they had actually formed an association—the Southampton Association—through which they organized meetings and dinners where they discussed the events of the day.

The government of that village was controlled by the local people. They made the rules. But the members of the Southampton Association were the engine of the economy. They would make their opinions known.

One of the most active people in the local community that year, although he was not on the village board, was Ken Scanlon, the owner of the town liquor store. He was a trusted and likable man. If I could get him to advertise that first year, I thought many of the other merchants would do so too. And so I had gone there that first year, and I had sold him. I wanted him to take, and I got him to take, the very first ad on the right, when you opened the first page of the new Southampton edition of my newspaper. It was one-sixth of a page. It cost him $500 for the summer.

Now it was the second year, and I had been to his store early in April to get him to renew it. He had waffled. I was alarmed. I wound up my pitch and backed out, telling him I would come back in a week after he had had a chance to think about it. Since that first visit I had been back twice. So this was the fourth altogether.

Ken Scanlon was a handsome man, about forty at that time, with a nice smile and a pleasant manner.

His family was Irish, and although I did not know the genealogy, it was very likely that his grandparents had come to the community at the same time as the wealthy WASPs in the late 1800s aboard the same ocean liners, and as their trusted servants. By this time, several generations later, they were among the leaders in the community. But I did not know what Ken's problem was with the paper. I did ask. But he said he had no quarrel with it. It was just that he wasn't sure he wanted his ad again. Maybe he had family problems. I had already learned from him that he had eight kids.

As I had gone around town, I had sold all the other spaces on my blank newspaper by the time I had returned to Mr. Scanlon now for the fourth time. I even had turned down several requests for this page 3 spot. It was Mr. Scanlon's. And it would be his year after year, as far as I was concerned, until he said no.

"I am not saying no," he said, finally, when his customer had left. "I'm just not ready."

"But I go to the printer tonight," I said. "We are out of time. And I saved it for you."

"Then come out with the paper without me this issue. And see me after it is out."

And so I walked out of his store without the ad and in a state of complete confusion. In three hours I would head out to the printer in Sayville. And I still couldn't sell it to anybody else, even if there had been time. He still hadn't turned it down.

That night, at the printer, for the first time in the nine years I had been publishing this newspaper, I had no answer about what ought to go in this space. We stood in the print shop, me, Mike, Bob Sr., and Bob Jr., and we went over my blank newspaper for the first issue.

"I just don't know," I said.

"How can you not know?" Bob Sr. said. "You always know

every line and every square inch of what's in your paper. You've *never* not known."

"We'll worry about it later," I said.

And, of course, there was a later. It was two o'clock in the morning and there it was, this blank space at the top of page 3. Bob Sr. had made an ad square for the spot. He was ready.

"Here's what we'll do," I said. "Put this in the space: THIS SPACE IS RESERVED FOR KEN . . ."

"Write it down," Bob Sr. said.

I wrote it down.

This space is reserved for Ken Scanlon of Scanlon's Liquor Store on Hampton Road in Southampton. He had this space all last year. It's his. And I am not selling it to anybody else. But he hasn't said yes again. Show him that he can make money from this ad. Go into his store and buy as much J&B scotch as you can. He'll see.

And that's how the newspaper came out.

I was so shocked at myself that I had done this that I actually was afraid to go into Scanlon's Liquor Store. As I delivered the paper going from store to store down Hampton Road, I got to his store and stopped. I looked in the window. The clerk was in there, not Mr. Scanlon. So I went in and quickly put the papers in a stack on the cigarette machine, all the time looking around to make sure he wasn't there, and then I left.

I didn't see him the next day, or the next day after that. And I didn't see him even before the deadline for the next issue. His ad space went in blank, again. And this time I wrote this:

Readers: Unfortunately, I have been out of town for the past week so I do not know if our campaign is working yet. Keep going to Mr. Scanlon's liquor store and buy J&B for just a little while longer. In the end, he's just got to buy this space. I'll let you know what happens.

I got up my courage to go see him after that second issue had had time to have its effect. It was two days before the deadline for the third issue. We were now into July. He looked up from the magazine he was reading at the cash register—nobody else was in the store—and he said this to me.

"Keep doing what you're doing for the rest of the issues of the summer," he said. "And send me the bill."

L AST Saturday, thirty-nine years later, I went to an autumn harvest party at Channing Daughters Winery in Bridgehampton. It was a rainy day, but the rains had let up and we were now standing in a field with several hundred other partygoers when I saw one of my favorite people in the Hamptons—Isabel Sepulveda de Scanlon, a young Latino woman who is a leader of the growing Hispanic community here. We sit, among others, on the board of directors of the Bridgehampton Child Care and Recreation Center and frequently are in touch with each other about one issue or another.

"Hi," I said.

There was a man standing next to her.

"I want you to meet my husband," she said. "Ken Scanlon." I shook hands with him.

"Most people don't know I am married. Ken keeps a low profile. Honey, this is Dan Rattiner of *Dan's Papers*."

He looked exactly like him.

Ken Scanlon broke into a winning smile. "Remember those ads you wrote for my dad one summer?" he said.

Bobby Van

⎯⎯⎯⎯⎯⎯⎯⎯⎯⎯⎯⎯⎯⎯⎯⎯⎯⎯⎯⎯

I N 1969, Bobby Van opened what was to become the most famous bar in the Hamptons. It was on Main Street in Bridge-hampton, right across from the Candy Kitchen, an ice cream parlor and breakfast hangout where all the farmers and merchants in the town gathered early in the morning.

The year before it opened, it had been a banjo bar. I don't know what else to call it. You'd go in there in the evening and they'd have these big mugs of beer and pretzels on the counter, and around ten, after the dinner hour, a banjo band would come out. They wore red-and-white-striped suits, white straw hats, and shiny black shoes, and they'd play music very loud. I recall one night driving by there and hearing "Wait 'Til the Sun Shines, Nelly." And the crowd would join in. The place was always packed with some of the same local people who'd had breakfast at the Candy Kitchen that morning. It wasn't my kind of crowd at all.

The following spring there were new owners, and the place had a new name. Bobby Van's. What was that? I went inside.

The place had dark mahogany paneling, a hardwood floor, booths, and a grand Victorian bar with mirrors and wooden carvings and bar stools. And there were people inside, smoking and arguing. About books.

I had known that tucked away in the woods of the Hamptons were all sorts of novelists and playwrights and editors. But I sort of left them alone. Everybody left them alone. But here they were. I recognized them from their book jackets. As the days passed, I saw Truman Capote, Peter Maas, George Plimpton, James Jones, Irwin Shaw, John Knowles. I'd been an English major in college before going on to study architecture, and it felt like I had died and gone to heaven to be in the same room with these literary giants. They were all here. How could this be? I'd go in and sit at the bar. It would take me a while to get around to ordering a drink. I was not there to drink.

A lot has been written about Bobby Van's, the restaurant and Bobby Van, the man. In the evenings, he would sit at a black Steinway at the back of the bar, this small, quiet young man with a cherubic face, and he'd play show tunes, or jazz, or sometimes classical pieces. People would wander over and lean on the piano. Sometimes they'd sing the lyrics to the music while Bobby played.

As I sat there night after night—I would go there two or three nights a week and it became a welcome hangout for me—I would eavesdrop on these people. One night, with a few drinks in me, I happened to walk past James Jones sitting in a booth across from Irwin Shaw, the two of them leaning toward each other in close concentration, talking about character development and writing styles. I thought this was the most important, most earthshaking conversation that had ever taken place in the history of the world.

And sometimes, if I gained enough courage to do so, I would walk over and introduce myself to some of them.

"I run *Dan's Papers,* the free newspaper," I'd say.

"Oh yeah," James Jones might say. "I've read it."

James Jones, who had written *From Here to Eternity,* considered one of the three greatest novels ever written about World War II, was often there with some friends. He was a small, thin middle-aged man, and he always looked worried. He'd seen much action in World War II, and now he had a bad heart and other people worried about him too, especially his wife, Gloria, a beautiful blond woman, very funny and boisterous.

"We have another doctor's appointment tomorrow," she'd tell friends loudly. Then she'd ask him if he'd taken his pills.

For a while, James Jones had a bad back. He'd hurt himself lifting something. He complained about the chairs at Bobby Van's, but Bobby didn't do anything about it. Then one day, he came in with a chair from another bar in town called JG Melon, which was located one long block down the street. He himself didn't carry it. Gloria did, in deference to his back. "This is a chair I can sit in," James told Bobby, dramatically pointing toward Gloria. Bobby nodded and then went back to playing the piano. And so that is what happened for days until James's back got better. At four in the morning Gloria would walk James's chair back down the street and leave it under the awning at the front door to JG Melon, because it closed earlier.

Compared with these people, of course, I had no literary

credentials at all. So conversation would peter out and I'd go back to the bar, or back to the booth where I was having dinner with one of my advertisers. My newspaper was on the cigarette machine by the front door. So that was something.

The leader of the place, it seemed to me, was an editor I had personally never heard of before named Willie Morris. He had, at one time, been the editor of *Harper's* magazine, and during his tenure, he had transformed it from a dull literary read to a fiery advocate of anti–Vietnam War fervor. I could not understand how an editor could be held in such esteem in these circles. But he was.

"Willie's here," somebody would say as he came in the front door with some friends, and Willie Morris, a man with a southern drawl, would smile and say hello to those he knew and then settle at a booth or table somewhere. And then people would come over.

I remember a few fistfights. People would start shouting and they'd get up and start swinging, and then other people would get up and hold them back and after a while everybody would sit back down and there'd be a lot of cursing and very loud talking for a while. But I never saw anybody either injured or physically thrown out of the bar for breaking up the place.

I remember people getting into arguments and then getting up and walking over to the big map of the world that occupied the entire wall opposite the men's room. They would point to one country or another, perhaps British Honduras, and as a result prove who was right and who was wrong. That map is still there today, although the place is now a different restaurant.

BOBBY VAN AT
THE PIANO AT
BOBBY VAN'S,
1971.
(Photograph by
Marina Van)

I remember John Knowles, during the middle of the after-noon, watching soap operas on the small television at the corner of the bar day after day. I once asked him about that. "This is how I develop my characters," he said.

There were many others who spent time at Bobby Van's. Winston Groom, who wrote *Forrest Gump,* was a regular. Sportscaster Jack Whitaker was often there, as was Jim Jensen, the anchor for CBS News. (I avoided him studiously and hoped he didn't notice me. I still remembered the run-in I'd had with him over the phone years earlier about the sea-serpent story I'd made up.) Also there was classical composer Lukas Foss, and writer Peter Matthiessen. Charles Addams, the great *New Yorker* cartoonist, often stopped in there with his wife, Tee. Elaine Benson of the Benson Gallery came in, often accompanied by writer Shana Alexander. And then there were just the regulars, like me. And someone who actually came there every single night to listen to Bobby play and have his dinner, a guy named Johnny Angel.

Angel was a small man the size of a jockey who had no connection to the literary world whatsoever. I have no idea how he got his name. But many years later, in 1994 in Milan, I heard a young woman with a show on the radio who spoke both English and Italian and referred to herself as Johnny Angel. I called the station. Turned out she was the daughter of a man who owned an autobody shop in East Hampton, and when she grew up and moved to Milan, she took Johnny's name as her stage name.

Another of the well-known regulars there, often occupying the very first bar stool you came upon as you went into the bar, was the great figure of John "Bunky" Hearst, one of the heirs to the Hearst fortune. For a long time, Bunky had lunch and dinner at Bobby Van's every night. And he often suggested new items for the menu. Chicken Kiev. Mussels, Fried Chicken. If you asked the waiter about a new item, invariably he would reply "Bunky suggested it." Once, a Tuna Platter got on the menu and I asked Marina, Bobby's wife, about it. "Bunky called it in from California," she said. "He's at the Hearst Castle." One constant amusement to everyone, including Bunky, was that because of where he sat and because of his grand stature, he was often mistaken for the owner. Salespeople would come in the front door and they'd go right to him. Everyone would listen as Bunky let them go on and on until finally he would tell them they needed to talk to Bobby Van.

Big parties often took place at Bobby Van's whenever one or another of the major literary figures there had a book published. There was lots of food and drink and congratulations all around, and though I was pretty much on the sidelines, I watched it all go on. When John Lennon was shot on the night of December 8, 1980, everybody, without even thinking twice about it, went to Bobby's to mourn the loss. Bobby sat at the piano for hours playing Lennon's music.

One day in 1973, one of the great novelists of that era, Irwin Shaw, came over and sat next to me at the bar. Shaw was about sixty at that time.

He turned to me. He was a bit in his cups.

"You know," he said, "I think we all ought to be writing a column in your paper. You ought to have a different person write something every week. Something about the Hamptons and what it means to them."

"That would be great," I said. My heart was beating a mile a minute.

"Just ask people."

I couldn't ask people. I was terrified of asking these people.

"How about you ask them?" I said.

"I'll tell you what. I'll write the first one for you."

A week later, he invited me to come down to his house in Sagaponack the following Monday. He'd write something and I could pick it up. He told me eleven in the morning would be fine. He'd be up. And he gave me his address.

The day before I went, I stopped by Bobby's for a hamburger and asked some of the regulars about Irwin Shaw. I didn't know much about him. I knew he'd written many best sellers, including *The Young Lions, Rich Man, Poor Man,* and *Fire Down Below.* But if I was going over there, I should know more than just that. I learned he lived in a small house. And he had had a tumultuous life. He had lived in Klosters, Switzerland, after the war. He had gone to Hollywood and become a screenwriter. Perhaps the most interesting thing about him was that he had married the same woman, by the name of Marian, twice.

I asked Marina about Irwin Shaw, and she told me it was he, not Willie Morris, who actually ran the place.

"He'd come in and he'd tell me 'Call Gloria and Willie and tell them I'm here,' " Marina told me. "When he was at Bobby's, he held court."

Shaw's wife Marian was nowhere around when I showed up at their front door at the agreed-on time, however. Shaw answered my knock wearing a house robe and slippers, and we talked for a bit. He gave me something typed up and double-spaced on two pages.

"It's about farms and beaches," he said. He offered me a drink. I passed. It was 11:00 A.M. after all. But I couldn't help but notice that in the middle of the living room, all by itself, there was a small table entirely covered with half-full liquor bottles. It was his bar.

"Call some of the others," he said, as he led me back to the front door.

But I couldn't bring myself to talk to "the others" even though four years had passed since the place first opened.

Instead, I thought I would write them letters. Back at my office, I assembled the names and addresses of about thirty writers in the Hamptons and sent letters asking them to write short pieces about the Hamptons for the paper. I got three or four articles back. And I published them, doting over the names of the authors. One writer sent something that shocked me. It came from Jean Stafford, a woman who never went to Bobby Van's as far as I knew. But every day, going to work, I would drive past a small sign at the head of a gravel driveway on Wood's Lane in East Hampton that read LIEBLING/STAFFORD. Liebling was A. J. Liebling, the famous antiestablishment media writer. Stafford was Jean Stafford, the Pulitzer Prize–winning novelist. She wrote four words across the bottom of my letter and returned it to me, and I remember it to this day because I was so shocked by what she wrote.

"Go Peddle Your Papers," she had printed.

That was entirely unnecessary. Obviously she didn't read my paper. She would not have written that if she did. The paper was free. I could hardly peddle them.

And then one night at about ten I walked over to Bobby Van's and was immediately met by Bobby Van himself just inside the front door. This was quite unusual. He was always at the piano or in the back somewhere and never up front to greet anybody. The place was packed with people.

"You can't come in here," he said, barring my way.

"What?"

"You're out. Don't come in here anymore. I don't like what you wrote in the paper."

He glared at me. And I turned and, without another word,

went back out, closing the door behind me. I just stood there, facing the street. What would I do? Behind me, the front door opened. And it was Bobby again, holding my newspapers.

"And don't leave these here anymore."

This was about the worst thing imaginable. I held the stack of newspapers to my chest. What had I done? Had I written something bad about the restaurant? I hadn't. I thought about freedom of the press. He can't do this. I will go up against him. I will write an article about this eviction, challenging him. I have the right to write what I want. *Everybody* in there writes what they want. That's what being a writer is all about. But then I thought, It's more important to me to be allowed into Bobby Van's than it is defending the First Amendment. So I better *not* write about this. And then I thought, This is private property. A man's home is his castle. He can throw me out for any reason whatsoever.

And then I thought—and this was a sudden happy thought—This is in the great literary tradition. Any great writer at some point or another must get thrown out of a literary bar. I'm *in.* It should make me happy. It *did* make me happy. For about thirty seconds. Then I lapsed once again into woe. This was terrible.

I'm not *in.* I'm out.

I studiously avoided Bobby Van's for about a week. I'd sadly peer into the window, get just about ready to cry, and then move on. Then one day I was walking down the street past it and I looked in the window and there, inside, cleaning up, was Marina Van. I motioned to her, and she came out.

"Bobby threw me out of the bar."

"I'd wondered where you went."

"Look. Can you talk to him? I want to come back in. I don't understand this. I don't know what I did. How long am I thrown out of the bar *for*? Can you find out? Is there a time limit to this sentence? Is it, like, *never*?"

She put her hands on her hips. "I'll see what I can do."

A few days after that, she called. "The coast is clear," she said. And so I was back. Bobby Van never said another word about it, and I never said another word about it.

About a year after my eviction, Marina Van took up with the owner of a restaurant at the other end of town. It was a sensational thing. Where Bobby Van was quiet and thoughtful and rarely raised his voice—he hadn't even raised it with me when he threw me out—this guy she ran off with was a rough, loud, softhearted wiseass sort with a swarthy complexion, a thick mustache, thick black hair, and—people said—a heart of gold. Born and raised in Bridgehampton, he was a major town character. His name was Billy DePetris, and he too had opened a bar and restaurant—it featured Italian food and was about as unlike the one that Bobby owned as it could possibly be.

Billy's bar was an amazing thing. Billy had named it Billy's Triple Crown Bar, and inside it was a virtual museum and tribute to Billy's high school classmate Carl Yastrzemski who had gone on to become a major-league baseball star. For the son of a Bridgehampton potato farmer, Yastrzemski's fame and fortune were impressive.

Carl played for the Boston Red Sox for twenty-three years. In 1967, he was the best player in baseball, winning the Triple Crown, a feat that has not been achieved since. That year Carl hit the most home runs, batted in more runners, and had the highest batting average, the winner in all three categories, in the American League. Carl is now in the Hall of Fame.

As for Billy's Triple Crown, Billy DePetris filled it with all sorts of memorabilia about Carl's career. There were baseballs, programs, letters, news clippings, photographs (one showing Billy pitching to Carl, both of them in uniform, on the Bridge-hampton High School team of 1957), plaques, and even a letter to Carl from the Brooklyn Dodgers written in 1959 inviting him—this high school home run hitter—to tryouts at their winter camp.

"What she sees in him," I overheard Willie Morris say one day at Bobby Van's, referring to Marina, "I'll never know."

In the fall of 2006, I invited Marina Van (she had kept Bobby's name), now the longtime director of the East Hampton Chamber of Commerce, to have lunch with me at Bobby Van's.

Bobby Van's was now a very different place from what it had been all those years ago. After ten years across from the Candy Kitchen, it left its original location and moved across the street. Now it was bigger and grander and in a brand-new building just two doors down from the Candy Kitchen, and, thinking it was chic, Bobby deliberately failed to put the name of the restaurant above the front door for two years. So during that interval, if you drove into town, you'd never even know there was a Bobby Van's there. But it wasn't the same. Everyone said that about it. It wasn't the same. And a few years after the sign went back up, Bobby Van sold the place, although they kept his name.

Marina and I met out front. We went inside, under the EST. 1969 sign, and were shown to a table. After the usual pleasantries, I got down to the reason I had wanted to have lunch with her.

"Something has been bothering me for about thirty-five years," I told Marina. "Do you remember the time, years ago, when Bobby threw me out of his restaurant?"

"I remember it very well."

"You do?" I was quite surprised she remembered this. So I pressed on. "Why did he do that?"

"Something you wrote embarrassed him," she said.

"Like what?"

"You wrote an article about seceding from the United States. Forming a separate country. And he believed it."

Seceding from America? My God, I remember that story. "He believed *that*?"

The article about seceding from the United States, actually a series of articles, had come about because of the passage of the "One Man One Vote" law in Washington in 1964. Nobody could argue with the concept of one man one vote, but there were disastrous consequences in our local county that had to be dealt with as a result. Close to New York City, in the west end of Suffolk County, lived half a million people in four very suburban towns. On the east end, in an area five times bigger than the west end, there lived fifty thousand people in five very rural towns, mostly involved with tourism, fishing, and farming. These two areas were as different as night and day. Before one man one vote, a board of supervisors ruled the county. There were the five east-end town supervisors and the four west-end town supervisors. Then came one man one vote. Now the whole thing got turned upside down and the board of supervisors was replaced by a county legislature. One man one vote. There were fourteen west-enders dominating four east-enders. And these suburban types could do with us whatever they wanted.

Needless to say, our east-end supervisors were livid with this sudden turn of events. An attempt was made to create a new and separate county. We would handle our own affairs. The effort failed.

I had followed all this in my newspaper, and after it failed, I decided maybe we ought to think bigger. Why not have the east end, this unique place, totally secede from the United States and form its own *country*?

And there was something else about our new country that was unique. Much of the east end consisted of two islands— Shelter Island and the South Fork. The hallmark of these islands was their old colonial English windmills. They were all over the place. And then I realized that off our shores, on various other islands south of New England, such as Block Island, Gardiners Island, Martha's Vineyard, and Nantucket, there were more English windmills.

Why not bring them in too? In the Caribbean there are groups of islands called the Dutch Antilles. Our new country could be called the Windmill Antilles. Together we would have twenty-five windmills on seven islands, the greatest collection of windmills anywhere in the world outside of Holland. It seemed an absolutely absurd and wonderful idea.

I got some friends interested. We held a meeting. We

created a flag for the Windmill Antilles that had on it, of course, a windmill. And we created a T-shirt with a female version of the Uncle Sam Wants You logo where Uncle Sam asks you to join the army. Our recruiter was Windmill Aunt Tillie. She wanted you to join the navy. She looked just like that stern Uncle Sam, but with lipstick, eyeliner, and curls. And so I wrote about all of this in the newspaper. Week after week after week.

"And *this* is what Bobby fell for?" I asked Marina. "This man who ran the bar for the giants of literature on eastern Long Island? How could Bobby believe that?"

"You just had to know Bobby," she said. "He was, and still is, an extremely literal, an extremely stubborn, an extremely proud man. A classic Dutchman."

"Running a bar like that? A literary bar?"

"It had nothing to do with who came there. Bobby opened that bar because he wanted a gin mill where he could drink and play the piano. He grew up on Long Island, studied at Juilliard. Didn't finish. He was a Vietnam War vet. He came home and all he wanted was an ice cream cone. And people threw rocks at him. It was terrible for him. Then this opportunity came up for him to have a bar."

"Where did you meet him?" I was suddenly very curious about how these two had gotten together.

"I came out for the summer with a girlfriend and opened a hippie shop on Newtown Lane in East Hampton. Tie-dye. Beads. Et cetera. He came in."

"So how did you get me back in?"

"He knew I liked you. And he listened to me. Maybe he even knew I would plead your case. So he allowed you back.

But let me tell you, you weren't the only one. He threw people out all the time."

AFTER Bobby Van sold the place, he dropped out of sight. He'd turn up at private parties from time to time, playing the piano and smiling at everybody who came over to pay their respects to him. For each of the ten years that TV anchor Peter Jennings held his annual Christmas party in the 1990s, I'd come over to the Jennings house and find Bobby Van playing the piano.

I'd shake his hand and we'd smile at each other and I'd often wonder, when I'd come over to him at this or other events, whether he ever thought about that day he threw me out of his bar. But I never asked.

BOBBY VAN'S IN 1971.

(Photograph by Marina Van)

Stuyvesant Wainwright II

ON a warm summer afternoon in 1971, I drove my motor scooter north up Wainscott Harbor Road, and, following instructions, got to the place where the asphalt made a ninety-degree turn to the west. Instead of turning, however, I continued on straight across the railroad tracks and down the dirt road into the woods for fifty yards. Still on the road—I had been bumping along on my Vespa—I now stopped as I had been instructed to do, put the stand down to steady the scooter, with a twist of the wrist turned the engine down to a soft idle, and looked. And there it was. Just as I had been told it would be. I was looking at a huge mound of filing cabinets, desks and chairs, folders and papers that—if my information was correct—would contain top-secret military documents that I should never have been allowed to see. I stayed on top of that mound for the next two hours, alternately amazed, delighted, and frightened. It was a reporter's dream. But because I was running a weekly resort newspaper, I had no idea what to do with what I was finding.

This whole remarkable afternoon had come about because

of a crisis involving garbage. Before that summer, people just threw things "away." You put trash in one of the metal garbage cans in your yard. And when they got full, you put them in the back of your car and drove with them down to the dump. Now these piles of garbage down at the dump were turning into mountains of foul-smelling, seagull- and rat-infested mountains. The towns of the east end were beginning to grow uncontrollable mountains of plastic, Styrofoam, wrapping paper, and foodstuffs. And the authorities said something would have to be done. Nobody could believe it.

Garbage got to be a frequent topic in my newspaper. I wrote article after article about the problem, and since I had no idea where I stood on this subject, I often just reacted to some person who called me up, and then subsequently suffered through a whole string of letters to the editor.

The first indication I got that garbage would become an ongoing topic came from a phone call I got from a man who owned Dan's Antiques on Montauk Highway in Wainscott.

"You want to see somebody's tax return?" he asked. I had no idea what he was talking about. "Come on over. You'll see," he said.

It turned out that every Monday morning, Dan Harris would come to his antiques store to find several bags of foreign garbage in the trash cans behind the store.

He walked me around back and showed the cans to me. Three battered metal cans. The scene of the crime. We stared at them.

"They are empty now. But imagine them full. I have to lug them over to the dump, cursing all the way. Who could have done this? Sometimes I rummage through the bags, but I've never found anything. But it's high-class garbage, I can tell you, from some rich man's home. And this has gone on every single Monday morning for the last month."

"He must be on his way back to the city after a weekend here," I said. "Sunday night. But why doesn't he stop off at the dump on his way like everybody else?"

"It's easy. He just pulls in and puts the stuff in my garbage. Then he drives away."

"A mystery."

"Well, you know they've started charging every time you go to the dump, don't you?"

"I know they were talking about doing it. They've started doing it?"

This is often how I learned about new developments in the Hamptons.

Dan took me inside. And he opened a drawer to his desk. Inside was a New York State tax return with what appeared to be a big butter stain on it. He held it up.

"*This* is who it is," he said. "I found this in a bag in there this morning."

He handed it to me.

Joel Hannapane, 88 East 75th Street, New York, NY.

You could learn everything you ever wanted to know about this guy just by reading his tax return. He made a whopping sum for that year: $146,000, a lot of money then. He worked on Wall Street. He was married with three dependents. He had many deductions for entertainment and travel. He had deductions for his vacation home. It amazed me to see all this.

I thought, What am I doing publishing a weekly newspaper when I could be on Wall Street doing this? Then I thought, How could he have thrown such a document away? But then I thought, With what we are learning about the environment, there is no "away."

"What do you want to do about it?" Dan asked me, leaning across the counter in anticipation. He was waiting for me to tell him I would expose this person.

"I don't know," I said. "I think if I put all this information in the paper, he might sue. Or he might be ruined. This is awful."

"If you mention his name in the paper, I think he would stop leaving this stuff here," Dan said.

I told him I wouldn't do that. My mind was racing ahead. How was I going to get out of this? I got an idea.

"Tape the tax return to the top of a garbage can before you go home on Saturday night."

"That's it?"

"It'll work."

He said he would think about it. Monday, he called in triumph. There were no foreign garbage bags in his trash cans. And that, I thought, was the end of it. It wasn't.

Two weeks later, I was driving down Hedges Lane in Sagaponack. Today, that road, which is two miles long and straight as an arrow, is bordered along most of the way by green hedgerows blocking one's view of the big private summer mansions behind them. But back then, the vista along this entire road, from horizon to horizon in almost every direction, was just potato fields, with no fences or hedges anywhere. It was a wonderful, exhilarating drive. I had now opened an office on Main Street in Bridgehampton, a rented office, and often came to work on sunny days by riding my Vespa. I would take this breathtaking two-mile detour off Montauk Highway just for fun. I loved the great views over the potato fields almost all the way to the horizon. The ocean beach, which bordered all the farms along their southern end, ran parallel to Hedges Lane. I'd never seen anything like that. And buzzing along, I'd enjoy the wonderful, heavy smells of turned earth, potatoes, salt air. Once in a while, I'd see a country dog.

I even wrote about that experience once while up at grad school. I'd saved it until summer, and then published it in the paper. In Cambridge, where I had bought the Vespa, I wrote, city dogs would sometimes run stealthily alongside you, then slide over and out into the street to nip at your ankles. In Sagaponack, the dogs—country dogs—would see you coming from far off, walk out into the center of the road, sit down, and sound the alarm. Then you'd just whiz right past them, leaving them in your dust. This was Hedges Lane.

Halfway down Hedges Lane that day, I passed, as I always did, the reassuring buildings of the Dayton Potato Farm—a garage for the tractors, a barn, a farmhouse—all up by the road with four hundred acres stretched out behind. On this day, strung between trees in front of the barn, was this big bedsheet, with the following words painted on it.

**JOEL HANNAPANE, PLEASE COME
PICK UP YOUR GARBAGE.**

He was at it again. I buzzed past the sign, laughing out loud, went to the office, got my camera, returned, and took pictures of the sign. *That* I could put in the paper.

But it did puzzle me that a man in a position of wealth and good fortune such as Mr. Hannapane would risk humiliation in order to avoid paying a few dollars for a trash drop at the dump. Then, on that next Sunday afternoon, I saw something that made me realize that this wasn't about the money.

I was driving in my car past the Springs Dump on Springs-Fireplace Road on my way into downtown East Hampton when I came past the dump. I slowed. The dump was now closed on Sundays. A big sign on the chain-link fence right alongside a padlock announced that fact. And resting against this sign were bags and bags of trash that had been driven there by second-home owners on their way back to the city who were doing their duty by not leaving their trash out back of their homes where the deer and raccoons could get at it, but were taking it to the dump. This was bad. It seemed to me it was about the most stupid thing the town government could possibly do, closing the dump on Sundays.

The next day I called the head of the town highway department.

"We know there's a problem," he said. "We're going to deal with it beginning next Sunday by posting armed police officers out front of the dump."

"That's absolutely a crazy way to deal with garbage in my opinion," I said.

What was it with garbage? My whole paper was filled with

MR. AND MRS. STUYVESANT WAINWRIGHT II
AT EAST HAMPTON MAIN BEACH.
(Courtesy of Stuyvesant Wainwright II)

articles about garbage. But sure enough, by the following week, the dump was back open on Sundays.

And still the garbage problems continued. The fee for leaving stuff at the dump was going to be increased from $5 a load to $50. And people were simply rebelling at this increase. The dump employees, who were getting yelled at, didn't like it either. A few weeks after that, I found myself at the Sag Harbor Dump talking to an employee there named Pete Ross. He too had called. He said he had something interesting about garbage and would I come over? I went.

He led me to one side of the dump where he and two of the other workers there had erected, from discarded material, what appeared to be a sort of stage-set private home. There was a window frame with shutters nailed to some two-by-fours at about the height of where a window ought to be. There were tables with vases on them and silk flowers in the vases, beat-up old club chairs and sofas. There were rugs and broken TV sets, dressers and desks and broken swivel chairs. You would swear somebody lived there. This was hilarious.

"What do you think?" Pete asked me. He was tall and rangy, about thirty, wearing jeans and a workshirt. "Want to take our picture?"

"Absolutely."

He turned toward the small shack there where the men worked, put two fingers in his mouth, and whistled. Three other men came over on the double.

The following Thursday the paper went with that picture and an article about what they were doing. On Friday morning I got a call from Pete Ross thanking me for it. So many people had mentioned to him that they had read it. I told him I enjoyed writing the story, which I certainly did.

"Maybe it will at least delay them closing down the dump entirely," Pete said.

I was astonished to hear that. Here was something else about garbage. Every day there was something new about garbage.

"But you've earned a reward," Pete told me. "And so I am going to tell you where you will see something very extraordinary. It's off in the woods in Wainscott and it's a secret. Been there about a week. All you have to do to see it is follow directions."

And that's what got me scooting down Wainscott Harbor Road into the woods and to the top of this huge mound of stuff.

It took less than five minutes for me to realize that I had come upon the entire congressional papers of Stuyvesant Wainwright II, a man who had been elected to four terms from the First District of New York, serving from 1953 to 1961.

How had these papers gotten so far from Washington? I came upon an entire filing cabinet of letters from constituents hoping to have the congressman's help in getting their sons into West Point or the Naval Academy. There were letters of recommendation, forms filled out with pictures of the applicant glued in place. There was correspondence with mothers about drug problems, with campaign managers about strategy, with other senators and congressmen about bills that were being brought before the House. There were even letters from lobbyists.

This I could certainly write about, I said to myself. I was so happy. It was a warm, wonderful day, a beach day. I leaned back against a file drawer. Here I was basking in the sunshine on my own private mound.

And then I came upon an entire file drawer filled with folders marked SECRET FOR YOUR EYES ONLY consisting of reports, maps, photographs, and brochures of military facilities that contained atomic-bomb-making factories, laboratories, underground missile sites, even deep evaluations given to Representative Wainwright by the CIA about the estimates of the military strength of the USSR, including studies of the Soviets' missile facilities and submarine bases.

This frightened me. I could not write about this. Or could I? The Pentagon Papers had just come out. And like the Pentagon Papers, this stuff was not supposed to be read by anybody. What if anybody saw me? I could get shot.

And then, from out of nowhere, there came the unmistakable sound of a motorcycle crashing through the woods. They've got me! I thought. And before I could even get to my feet, to scramble off the mound, a ten-year-old boy on a motorbike came roaring through and into the clearing created by this pile, skidded sideways, and then, without so much as a word, drove off into the woods in the other direction. And that, I decided, was just about enough. I quickly grabbed some files, jumped on my motor scooter and fled.

Later that day, after calming down, I began to realize that this material was just too good to pass up. Wainwright had been out of office for a decade. This stuff could not be so sensitive anymore. Could it? And if it was, what could they do? It had passed into the public domain, quite emphatically.

So I wrote about it all in the paper.

It was only two days after the paper came out that I got the phone call. It came from Stuyvesant Wainwright III, the son of Stuyvesant Wainwright II. And much to my surprise, he was not angry. Nor was he apologetic. He was a thoroughbred. His people had been caught red-handed. He'd just get right to the point.

"That material you wrote about has already been removed," he said. "I sent some workmen over this morning."

"If you don't mind my asking, how did that stuff get put over there?"

"Dad went through a divorce two years ago," he said. "His wife got the house in the Georgica Association. He got the Manhattan apartment."

The Georgica Association, an exclusive private enclave of huge summer homes on Georgica Pond, was almost a straight line south of the woods where all this material had been dumped.

"From what I understand, his ex called him and told him she was renting out the house and wanted him to move all his files and papers from the basement. He didn't do it. And so she did it for him. She called a man with a truck and he came with some friends and moved everything out. Desks, filing cabinets, everything. And he dumped them in the woods."

"So he wouldn't have to pay the dump fees."

"Right."

"And where did your guy with the truck take everything this morning?"

"Um . . . to the right place."

I never did get to meet Stuyvesant Wainwright, either the II or the III. But I could imagine this fifty-year-old man, fighting with his young wife, probably his second wife, the trophy wife, and never dreaming that all his important papers would ever have to go somewhere else than where they safely were.

What an embarrassment.

MANY years after my foray into the woods, developers bought all the land to the north of the railroad tracks and simply continued Wainscott Harbor Road straight for about a mile to a dead end, paving it in asphalt and lining it with a curbing of expensive Belgian block. The woods were cleared, lots of two acres were surveyed out, and they were put up for sale. They didn't sell. Turned out the East Hampton Airport, which was rapidly increasing its flight activity, had its main flight path directly over this development. And there was nothing anybody could do.

The developers withdrew, and in about 2000, an imaginative developer named Harry "Coco" Brown, the man who built the Mulholland Drive development in Beverly Hills, bought it for a song.

And he had a marvelous idea. He would, on these 34 two-acre lots, assign each one to a world-class architect with instructions to design modest homes in his or her individual style. People wouldn't mind aircraft noise if they were looking at and living in important works of art, he surmised. Brown hired architect Richard Meier to supervise the project and, along with him, enlist some of the greatest architects of the day for the project. All thirty-four of them were assigned. And today, five of them, the works of Sir Richard Rogers, Michael Graves, Henry Smith-Miller, Thomas Phifer, and the late Philip Johnson, have been completed and sold. It is an extraordinary place. Anyone is welcome to drive through the development and see these wonderful architectural masterpieces.

And somewhere in there, in the deep woods that surround these five homes, you might, if you have a mind to, take a hike and find yourself tripping over a filing cabinet left behind containing papers about American or Soviet nuclear secrets.

If that happens, just keep it to yourself.

Saving the Bull's Head Inn

FROM the look of downtown Bridgehampton today, you would never know that in 1971, when I bought the house on the highway that became our office building there, it was a working farm town. Today, from one end to the other, this tiny hamlet is a chic high-end resort, with a French restaurant owned by Pierre at one end of Main Street, antique shops and fashionable clothing stores in the middle, and next door to the *Dan's Papers* office, at the far end of town, a shop called Urban Archaeology, which sells, among other things, the original statuary from the fountain at the l'Étoile end of the Champs-Élysées for just one and a half million dollars each. They have two.

In 1971, however, completely different businesses occupied the buildings in town. There was Danny's Luncheonette, where the farmers sat on bar stools and talked. (And once, while I was in there reading a magazine, I noticed Truman Capote walk over, plop down on a bar stool, and start reading a copy of the popular gossip magazine *Confidential* he had brought in with him. I knew he lived in Bridgehampton, on Daniel's Lane, in a small secluded house on a two-acre wooded compound surrounded by potato fields, but I had never been in it. I did drive by it as I came to work from East Hampton every day, imagining him in there, typing away. Now, in the café, I just thought I'd pretend he was not there. And did.) There was the J. L. Sandford Water Company, where Mr. Sandford, a taciturn man, did the paperwork and sent out the bills for the service his private water company provided in town. (Mr. Sandford himself drove around town in a pickup truck, wearing work boots, a railroad cap, and overalls, checking the water levels beneath the metal lids of the water pipes just under the surface of the shoulders of all the streets in town. Elaine Benson, the owner of the art gallery in Bridgehampton, once told me he charged her double for water every month. She had asked around and was told he charged whatever he wanted. If he liked you, it was less; if he didn't, it was more.) There was the butcher shop, where you could come in and inspect the hanging meat; a potato-packing plant, where black men worked ten hours a day putting potatoes in burlap sacks during the autumn harvest; and an Agway, where once a year the management held the biggest potato contest. Farmers would come in with their giant spuds and put them on a table in the middle of the store with their name taped onto them, and the winner would get a prize, and 50 percent off animal feed, fertilizer, and chemicals. Potato bugs, called nematodes, were a big problem at that time.

However, the most powerful impression about Bridgehampton as you drove or walked down the four blocks of Main Street was provided by gas stations. There were six of them, each with two repair bays and each managed by a friendly or ornery grease-covered auto mechanic. Much later when every one of them went out of business, a friend said it was because they didn't make cars like they used to. The cars that used to be made always broke down, but the carmakers said they'd provide the parts to fix them and they did. Now, the carmakers said their new cars wouldn't break down. So there was no need for mechanics.

From the second floor of the house I bought in 1971 as the new office of *Dan's Papers* at the western end of town, I could, at the beginning of that decade, see four of the six gas stations. There was the Chevron station across and down the hill to the west. There was a gas station directly across from me at the corner of Main Street and Butter Lane. There was the gas station owned by a handsome black man named Junior Brown right next door to me, and there was, two blocks down, across from where Bobby Van's Restaurant is today, a gas station at the corner of Main Street and Corwith Avenue that was owned by some very nasty people I never cared to get to know.

At the very center of town where the War Memorial Monument sits, however, were two more gas stations that were, as far as I was concerned, as a failed architect who had studied city planning, a terrible embarrassment to the community. The downtowns of both Southampton and East Hampton, to the west and east, were absolutely picturesque and beautiful, filled with historic mansions and windmills, grand elm trees and village greens. The center of Bridgehampton, by the monument, was, by contrast, a mess.

On the southeast corner in the center of town—looking

out to the monument at the only traffic light for six miles in any direction—was a historic three-story Greek Revival–style mansion built a hundred years earlier that featured four Doric pillars supporting a classic portico three stories up. But on the front lawn of that house was, incredibly, a gas station. The owner of the house, a man named Hopping, had leased out his front lawn to Gulf.

On the southwest corner of the center of town, there had once been, in Revolutionary times, the Village Green. The Bridgehampton Militia, which had marched off and up the Hudson to fight the British, had mustered here. Now the green was gone. It had been sold to a developer, and he had built a long, two-story retail building that now housed a liquor store, the butcher shop, and a fish store.

On the northwest corner of the center of town, there was a state historic monument, very sturdily built, announcing that on that site, two hundred years earlier, there had stood Wick's Tavern, where American spies had made plans during the Revolution. Now the site featured an Esso gas station run by the Damiecki Brothers.

That left the northeast corner. Here, there was another old nineteenth-century mansion called the Bull's Head Inn, built in the "Four Square style" in 1842 but now falling into disrepair. It had been owned by an aristocratic horsewoman named Carpenter for the ten years prior to my moving into town, and she had run it as a restaurant and inn. But the police had raided the place four years earlier and caught the cook selling dope out the back door. Now it was abandoned, and that summer the grass had grown tall in the front yard. What a mess.

THE BULL'S HEAD INN IN BRIDGEHAMPTON IN 1925.
(Courtesy of the Bridgehampton Historical Society)

And then I learned that the Sun Oil Company of Philadelphia had taken an option to buy the Bull's Head Inn. They
would tear it down to build—you guessed it—another gas station. What was happening to this town?

I was beside myself. I put the story on the front page. We
had a photograph of the Bull's Head Inn with the grass growing
high. And we had a story with a big headline: SAVE THE BULL'S
HEAD INN. Inspired, I also ran on the front page a coupon:
"To the President of Sun Oil. I enclose my Sunoco credit card,
cut in half in protest. Do not tear down our Bull's Head Inn."
There was an address you could send it to—1801 Market Street,

Philadelphia, Pennsylvania—and a place for you to write your name and address. There was also a place where you could fill out a form to join the "Save the Bull's Head Inn Society," which I had decided, on the spot, to create. By the end of the fourth week of running this coupon, I had the names of ninety people who declared themselves members of this "society," which, by default, I guessed, had me as "chairman."

And then came the phone call.

"Are you Mr. Rattiner, the chairman of the Save the Bull's Head Inn Society?" a male voice said.

"Who is this?"

"My name is Clinton Tibbetts. I'm a vice president of the Sun Oil Company in Philadelphia."

"Well, what about it?" I said. "You want to talk me into allowing you guys to build a gas station? Have you any idea how many gas stations we have in this town?"

"I am fully aware of it. I have been to Bridgehampton. We think the competitive situation is very advantageous in Bridge-hampton."

"Well, I don't."

"We want to meet with you."

"You want to come out here?"

"It's a long way. How about we meet halfway? We're ninety miles from New York. And so are you. Is that fair? You want to come to our New York office?"

I would not go to the Sun Oil Company's office. But I would meet with them. And so the meeting would take place six days later on the fourth, and top, floor of a brownstone at 136 West 11th Street. This was my girlfriend's apartment.

At the appointed hour of noon, on a windy day in late October, my girlfriend and I heard three people trudging up the stairs from the front entrance of the building. You could hear the feet. Just the sound of them coming up made me angry. I started pacing. What if people knew I was having this meeting? I was cavorting with the enemy. My girlfriend asked if I wanted to be alone with them.

"Yes," I said. She disappeared into a bedroom.

The men clattered up a final narrow set of stairs to our door—this apartment had been built as the servants' quarters of this home—and then came the knock. I let them in, three men in business suits and ties and shiny black shoes, and very out of breath from the climb. I did not offer them anything. It was very deliberate. One of them had some architect's plans.

"Well, let's get right to this," a heavyset man with a narrow black mustache said. "I'm who spoke to you on the phone. Clinton Tibbetts." He extended a hand. I hesitated but then shook it. They had come all the way from Philadelphia. "And these are my colleagues, Harold Zimmerman and Alfred Sey."

Sey and Zimmerman nodded grimly at me. They were taller. And they looked like bodyguards. Tibbetts unrolled the set of plans onto the small dining room table. And we all stood around staring at it.

"We understand that you don't want us to tear down the Bull's Head Inn," Tibbetts said, brightening, "and so we have an idea for a compromise."

I looked at the plans. "I don't get it," I said.

"Well, as you see, we have retained the Bull's Head Inn.

But we've moved it back on the property, and we've turned it ninety degrees so the front of it faces the turnpike on the side. On the *front* of the property, where the Bull's Head was," he was raising his voice dramatically, "we have our gas station. It is a very special gas station." We all peered down at an elevation of it. "It's our Colonial B style gas station, which reminds people of the colonial era. See? It has two false chimneys. And it has this little portico."

I could barely contain myself. "So you've come all this way," I said, "to suggest that the Bull's Head Inn be moved back and you put *this* in front?"

"And, I forgot to tell you, we will pay for the entire move. This will save your committee at least $30,000. And it will save the inn. Though of course, all the renovation costs and so forth will be yours."

"What about you leaving the Bull's Head where it is and putting the Sunoco Colonial B on the side facing the turnpike?"

Tibbetts stared coldly at me. "We can't do that," he said.

"So if we do this, there would then be *two* gas stations on the front lawns of two historic mansions on opposite sides of the street in the center of town, facing one another?"

"Yes. But the Bull's Head would be saved."

I didn't know what to do. I sat down in a chair. "I've got to think about this."

"Take your time."

"I mean, I have people to consult. It's a big committee. Hundreds of people. Thousands. I have to have a meeting, take it under advisement."

"What do you think?"

"Honestly? Not a chance."

There was a long silence. And then Tibbetts sighed. And he rolled up the plans.

"Well, thanks for meeting with us," he said.

"No problem."

"If there is any way you see this happening, let us know."

On their way down the stairs, I could hear the voice of one of the bodyguards. Sounds carry on those stairs. "Well, it was worth a try," the voice said.

"Anybody see a place you can have lunch around here?" asked the other.

The next morning, my girlfriend and I had breakfast and then said our good-byes. She had classes at NYU to go to. I had to head back out to the Hamptons.

A WEEK later, I got a letter from Sunoco saying they were withdrawing their offer. Three months after that, a rich man named Lynn St. John, who lived on Ocean Road in Bridge-hampton, bought the Bull's Head. The Sunoco idea was now dead. And St. John remained as the owner of the inn, keeping it up as an antique shop, surely at a loss, for the next forty years. It pleased me greatly that he had done that.

Today, Junior Brown's gas station is Urban Archaeology, the antique store. The gas station across from *Dan's Papers* is a small group of offices for a private investment company that has holdings mostly in Europe. The gas station across from Bobby Van's is a branch of the high-priced New York City toy store Penny Whistle; the gas station on the northwest corner in the center of town is a wholesale beverage barn; the Bull's Head Inn has reportedly been sold to Ralph Lauren; and the big mansion across the street with the columns out front has been bought by the town, the gas station on the front lawn bull-dozed and hauled off, and plans are in the works to restore the mansion as a museum with the grounds surrounding it a reproduction of a colonial farm.

Only the row of stores where the mustering grounds were remains standing. There's no hope of getting rid of that. But behind the stores, they have created a one-acre "Militia Park" with benches to sit on and a marble historic marker in the center.

I N 1990, at the annual Artists and Writers Softball Game, a traditional game held in East Hampton, I met Bianca Jagger and invited her to have lunch with me. She wanted to talk about the charity work she was doing in Nicaragua.

"I'm staying for the weekend at Ross Bleckner's house," she said. "Meet me there. Do you know where it is?"

Of course I knew where it was. Ross Bleckner, the painter, had bought the home of the late Truman Capote. I knew exactly where it was.

And so that Sunday afternoon, I drove down Daniel's Lane to the gravel driveway, turned in, but it wasn't the house. Strangers greeted me. And though they didn't know where Bleckner lived, or where the old Capote house was, they let me use their phone.

Turned out that Bleckner's house was two miles of potato fields down the road, in another small woods. For twenty years

I had been imagining the wrong person typing away in there. The right person, who might have been typing away, if he typed away, was just some ordinary person.

As for the Save the Bull's Head Inn Society, no meeting of it was ever held.

Robert David Lion Gardiner

N September 1972, I went to the gym in East Hampton High School to watch a debate between the two men running for Congress from our district.

Debates between candidates, whether on TV or in person, were a relatively new phenomenon at that time, and they were all the rage. Just twelve years earlier, the two candidates for president, Richard Nixon and Jack Kennedy, had held three televised debates that were broadcast around the country for the first time. In retrospect, there seemed little doubt those debates had swung the election from the sweaty, troubled Richard Nixon to the handsome, young JFK.

The high school auditorium held five hundred people, and on the evening of the debate, there were no empty seats. People talked excitedly among themselves. The candidates would come out in five minutes.

One candidate was Otis Pike. Lantern-jawed and austere, he was a Riverhead lawyer with a clear and authoritative voice. He was also the incumbent and very popular. For six terms he had won reelection by ever widening margins. This would be his seventh.

His opponent was a man named Robert David Lion Gardiner of East Hampton. A patrician millionaire from an old family, he had never run for public office before. And the reason he was about to come on the stage was that Otis Pike, three months earlier, had suggested at a press conference that the federal government purchase and preserve the crown jewel of the Gardiner family, a three-thousand-acre private island off the coast of Amagansett known as Gardiners Island. It had been settled in 1639 by the original Lion Gardiner, the first English settler in New York State. Now it had been handed down from father to son to grandson and great-grandson, on and on for fifteen generations, and the fact was that the present owner of the island, Robert David Lion Gardiner, was not getting any younger. (He was in his early sixties.) And he and his wife had not produced an heir. Up until now, it was true, there was just the Gardiner Manor House on the island. But there was nothing to prevent it from being subdivided into small building lots.

Gardiner flew into a rage when he heard of the plan. What did Otis Pike, this Johnny-come-lately, think his family had been doing for three hundred years? The next day he took it a step further. He said he would run against Otis Pike for his seat in the U.S. Congress, defeat him, and run him out of Washington.

Otis Pike was introduced first, and was told he would have fifteen minutes to make introductory remarks.

"I am Otis Pike," he said, smiling, "and I think you all know me. I am running for reelection on my record. And I think it is a considerable one. Let me tell you of a few things that I have done."

Pike talked briefly about the Long Island Expressway that was being built to connect the city to eastern Long Island. Fifteen years earlier, President Dwight David Eisenhower had approved a plan to build multilane expressways through every state in the Union. It was in the defense budget. If the nation was attacked, troops and tanks could get to where they were needed with great rapidity.

"I insisted an expressway be included down the center of Long Island," he said. "At the present time, this highway ends at Brookhaven. But now I am happy to report that largely due to my efforts, the new section to Riverhead will be open next month."

Pike talked about the potato harvest. His father had been a potato farmer. He talked about welfare and how it helped get many folks through the long, hard winter. He also talked about the fishing industry and the tourist industry in Montauk and all it had done. And he talked about the Soviet menace. During his tenure, an early-warning radar station had been built in Montauk. And Nike missiles were in place in silos in Wading River. Should the Soviets launch a nuclear attack, eastern Long Island would do its part.

Then he sat down.

"Mr. Gardiner is next," the moderator said. "He has asked me to introduce him by his full name, Robert David Lion Gardiner, the Sixteenth Lord of the Manor. Mr. Gardiner, you have fifteen minutes."

Fifteen minutes would not be nearly enough for Robert D. L. Gardiner.

He talked about how he had inherited the island from his aunt Sarah Diodati Gardiner, who had passed away in 1953 with a codicil in her will that her nephew and niece, who had grown up enjoying the family estate on Gardiners Island, should have, along with their heirs, the exclusive use of the place for now and forevermore.

He grasped the sides of his speaking podium, smiled, and leaned forward toward the audience. He would share a little secret.

"Many of you think I am just another of those rich men with old money who come out here in the summertime from New York City on the railroad in our parlor cars, then sit at our clubs drinking, clipping coupons, and wasting away our lives and the fortunes of our families.

"Nothing could be further from the truth. I have *made* our family's fortune. When I inherited Gardiners Island, which Lion Gardiner purchased from Montaukett chief Wyandanch, my family was going through considerably rough financial times. And so I took some of our land, a parcel in Bay Shore, and ordered that a shopping center be built there. I'm sure some of you know it. Gardiner Manor Mall. I hired an architect to design the mall, and when the buildings were being built, I acted as a salesman selling all the spaces. Our largest tenant would be Macy's.

"Let me tell you a story. At the meeting where the contracts were to be signed, the lawyer for Macy's said that they would need a title search done to prove that indeed the Gar-

MR. AND MRS. ROBERT
DAVID LION GARDINER
AT THE CORONATION
OF QUEEN ELIZABETH
IN 1953.
(From the Robert David Lion
Gardiner Collection)

diner family owned the land. I told him he had my word. But that wasn't good enough. So I said I would prove it to him. We would meet again in one week.

"At that second meeting, the lawyer asked did I have with me a title search? I am sure he expected I would produce a document of five hundred pages or more, attesting to all of the sales down through the years. Instead, I opened my bag and took out a single sheet of parchment paper. What I had done was go to the Morgan Bank in New York where they keep all our family papers, go down into the vault, and borrow the very piece of parchment that my ancestor had used to purchase the property from Chief Wyandanch. Here, I said. The land has been in my hands since the beginning. Here's the deed.

"I should point out that I was not selling the Bay Shore

property. That would be passed down by me to future Gardiners. I was offering it up, however, as a ninety-nine-year lease. They signed, and the shopping center is there today. I am told it is worth fifty-five million dollars."

At this point, I heard some rustling going on behind me. I turned. A couple in the audience were leaving the auditorium.

"This is *real* old money. The du Ponts and the Woolworths talk about old money, but they are just newcomers as far as I am concerned. Their money only goes back to the 1850s."

He grasped the podium again.

"Let me tell you another story. I am sure many of you are familiar with the expertise of the Dominy family of Southampton. For three generations in the eighteenth century, they made beautiful clocks, which are now antiques. Once, my chauffeur and I were unloading a grandfather clock from the back of the car in Southampton when Mrs. du Pont came strolling down the sidewalk. We were bringing the clock into Corwin's Jewelers. It was in need of a repair. 'Oh, Mr. Gardiner,' Mrs. du Pont said, 'isn't that a Dominy? Wherever did you get it?' I looked at her. 'We didn't *get* it,' I said. 'We had it *made*.' *That's* old money."

Gardiner told another story about one of his ancestors, John Gardiner, who owned Gardiners Island in the 1690s.

"One of the servants on the island was accused of murdering another man," he said. "John held a trial. He had the authority to do that. And he found the accused guilty, and had him hung from a hanging tree. That tree remains today, near the beach, on the island. When I invite people to the island, that is one of the things I show them."

Earlier that summer, Gardiner had invited me, as publisher

of the newspaper, to take a tour of the island with him. I had been writing about it, he noted. He told me I ought to see it for myself. "And I understand you have a young reporter working for you," he had said. "Bring him too."

That would be Jim Lytton.

Jim and I met Mr. Gardiner at Gardiner's Marina on Three Mile Harbor Road. There were about fifty boats in slips there, and the manager of the place was very deferential. Mr. Gardiner would be along. We should wait in the office.

Eventually, Mr. Gardiner appeared, wearing a blue blazer with brass buttons, a white captain's cap, and white trousers, and he led us to his yacht, a wooden affair painted all black, with a Jolly Roger flapping in the breeze above the flying bridge. It was called the *Laughing Lady.*

We got the full tour of the island, including the talk about the hanging tree, and about Mrs. du Pont and the Dominy clock. Also many others, which I expected, correctly, I would soon hear at this debate.

Gardiner talked about how John Gardiner had been paid a visit by Captain Kidd. *The* Captain Kidd. Kidd was turning himself in in Boston, but he wanted to bury his treasure somewhere ahead of time so he could bargain the treasure for his life. (He failed.) "He did bury it ahead of time, right there on our beach. And he threatened to kill John Gardiner and his family if anybody ever touched it."

"Mr. Gardiner, your time is up."

Gardiner raised his voice a notch and continued right on talking. The moderator again tried to interrupt. And failed.

"So Kidd was taken to London and hanged. And two years

went by. At that point, John Gardiner thought it safe to dig up the treasure. It would have to be returned to the Crown. He contacted the authorities at Boston and some merchant marines came and took it. They transported it to the governor in Boston and then the governor had it transported to England."

The moderator again tried to interrupt, but Gardiner raised his voice still another notch. Again I heard rustling in the audience. More people were getting up to leave.

"In 1953, when Eunice and I went to the coronation of Queen Elizabeth, I had an occasion to dance with the queen. During the dance, I told her I had with me the treasure receipt that had been in my family for two hundred and fifty years, and on it was this long list of rings and necklaces and diamond brooches and so forth that were in those treasure boxes. And I wondered if she had her receipt. It might be interesting to see if they matched. From East Hampton to Boston to London—perhaps there had been someone with light fingers along the way.

"She motioned for someone to come over. And she ordered him to find the receipt and bring it to her. The next day, we compared them. They did not match. Two hundred and fifty years later, we had uncovered a crime."

More people were leaving. In fact, the auditorium at this point was about half empty.

"You have to finish up, Mr. Gardiner," the narrator said. "We have to move on to the question period."

"I'll just be a few more minutes," Gardiner said.

Needless to say, in November, Robert David Lion Gardiner lost the election.

$\sim$

FOR many years after this debate, I would call Mr. Gardiner and he would agree to purchase a small ad for the marina that would appear every week in the paper. I would bill him monthly, he would pay promptly.

Occasionally, he would call me up to say that something in the paper I had written about him was entirely wrong. And he'd go on and on about it. And say that the *East Hampton Star* made a similar mistake.

"Thank you very much for pointing this out, Mr. Gardiner," I'd say.

"And let me tell you another thing," he would say.

And this would lead him to a story. I found myself, a young man who had grown up in the suburbs of New Jersey, trying to explain to one of the richest men on eastern Long Island, that I had another person in the room waiting to talk to me, and there was an appointment I had after that, but it would do no good. It was almost impossible to get Robert Gardiner to stop talking about his island.

One year, he ordered the ad stopped.

I called him up.

"I get a bill every month for six months," he says. "I have to write you six checks. It takes time."

"What if I bill you once a year for the whole amount?"

"If you could do that, put the ad back in."

On a warm August morning in 1981, I was having breakfast on the deck of my home on Three Mile Harbor in East

Hampton with my wife and two children, Maya, age nine, and Adam, age six. Our house overlooked the harbor, the boats, and several marinas, which is why I had bought it several years earlier. One of these marinas is Gardiner's Marina.

As we sat there talking, a black limousine drove up the street and parked in front of the entrance to Gardiner's Marina. The chauffeur got out, opened the rear door, and Robert David Lion Gardiner got out. He was holding some gardening tools. And I knew exactly what he was going to do because I had seen him do this before.

Right there at the entrance to the marina there is a sign announcing the name of the place, and there are three small flower gardens around it. There is also a weeping willow tree, or there was then—it got knocked down by a hurricane in about 1990—and in front of this tree and around his sign, Gardiner proceeded to garden.

He was wearing, as he always did, a dark blue blazer with brass buttons, and on this occasion he was also wearing a bright red and blue kerchief around his neck to catch the sweat.

It was a wonderful morning. On the deck, we talked and laughed and the kids ran around. At one point, Gardiner looked up and waved and I waved back. The chauffeur opened the trunk and Gardiner took out four small pots with little yellow and white flowers in them and set them on the ground. The chauffeur, other than open and close doors, did nothing. He just stood around.

After a while, it occurred to me to invite Gardiner up. I had never done that before. But I had fresh coffee. I whistled and he looked up. And I waved an arm, motioning for him to come. And he did. He left the chauffeur right there with the car, the flowerpots, and the gardening tools, and he crossed the street and came up our driveway to our deck.

I introduced him to my family. And I suggested he sit down. But instead he stood there for a moment and then stepped forward and squatted down in front of my daughter Maya, who at first gave the appearance of being afraid of him.

"What a beautiful name," he said to her, beaming. "And you are such a beautiful young lady." Maya was looking at a man of about seventy, very sweaty, with garden dirt all over his pants and heavy jacket—a jacket far too heavy for the heat of that morning—and she softened. After all, her parents were there.

"Hello."

"And hello to you," Gardiner beamed. "Do you have a boyfriend?"

"No," she said.

"Let me tell you something." He rolled up the sleeve of a very dirty right arm and held it out for her. On his pinky, he wore a heavy red-gold ring with a ruby in the center. And on his wrist he wore another piece of heavy gold jewelry, adorned, as it happened, with a skull head.

"You see the color of this gold? It is pirate gold. And it has been in my family for three hundred years. When you get a boyfriend, and he wants to give you gold, make sure he gives you pirate gold, like these pieces. Fiery. Red. Heavy. Only pirate gold is good enough for you."

He talked with Maya a bit further. He declined the coffee I offered. And then he left. For the next five minutes, Maya could not speak.

George Plimpton

I N September of 1991, I got this idea that we ought to have an article in the paper about all the activities going on in the wintertime. By that time, a huge transformation was taking place in our community. Up until then, all the wealthy summer people were out only from Memorial Day to Labor Day. But now crowds of people were coming out from April to Christmas. It was only in January, February, and March that things were reminiscent of earlier times. An article coming out in October, describing the goings-on in the winter, might be useful in helping people decide if they ought to be coming out then too.

And so, on a Friday in late September of 1991, I was sitting with seven people from the editorial staff around the big round table in the conference room of *Dan's Papers* in Bridgehampton, discussing upcoming stories. We did this every Friday. Still do.

"Anybody have any listings for things to do during the winter?" I asked.

Nobody made a sound.

"Anybody know of anything?"

People shook their heads no.

"Well, I'm writing the headline. PLENTY TO DO IN THE WINTER IN THE HAMPTONS. You guys take it from there."

When nothing came of this after a few days, I decided to just make events up. The next day, I wrote about the big annual Hamptons Eel Festival over the weekend of January 4–5, when teenage girls have an eel jump rope contest, and when we eat eel pie and crown Miss Eel of the Hamptons, and so forth and so on.

And I wrote about the doings on January 11–12, when we have the annual "Houses on the Outside House Tour." People trudge through the snow to stand on the sidewalk shivering and looking at boarded-up mansions.

I made up important weekend festivals for all thirteen of the weekends during January, February, and March of 1992, including one on March 7–8 called "Flight to Portugal." All our strong young local men drive their souped-up cars out to the Montauk Lighthouse, where they roar up a temporary wooden ramp one at a time to fly off into space, out over the cliff, and down into the sea eighty feet below with a big splash. The one who gets the farthest toward Portugal wins. First prize is a laurel wreath and a six-pack. Tommy "Burp" Arrington won last year.

The day after Christmas, which was about two months after this story appeared in the paper, I went off for a three-week holiday in southern California. When I got back, all tanned and warm, the first thing told to me by our general manager, Jolly Erickson, was about the "Flight to Portugal." At first I didn't even know what she was talking about.

"We started getting phone calls about it right after you

left," she said. "So far, two TV networks and three magazine editors have called wanting to get credentialed. We've had calls from the *Times of London, Newsday,* the *New York Times,* Channel 12 Long Island, and all sorts of people who just want to come. We've even gotten calls from an environmental group concerned about what the Flight to Portugal might do to the fish. And we've had this letter offering a first prize."

She handed me a two-page letter from the Portuguese National Tourist Office in Manhattan, written by the director, Carlos Lamieros. I read it silently.

"We have read about your upcoming Flight to Portugal contest and want very much to participate in it," he wrote. "We think this event is good publicity for Portugal. And so we offer this prize to the winner."

The prize would be a full week's vacation in Portugal for two, all expenses paid, including airfare.

"Is this true?" I asked Jolly, waving the letter. It occurred to me that perhaps I was being taken in.

"It's true," she said. "I called."

"What do you think we ought to do?" I asked. "This is a very big prize."

"I have no idea. But thousands of people are going to be coming to this. It's scheduled to happen in less than sixty days. I didn't want to bother you on vacation. You were only gone three weeks. So I've been waiting for you to come home."

I thought hard for a minute. "I think," I said, "I ought to talk to George Plimpton." And having said that, I felt the tensions all drop away. Everything would be fine. George would know what to do.

F the King of the Hamptons at that time was the Sixteenth Lord of the Manor Robert David Lion Gardiner, then Court Jester, Mad Scientist, and Chief Hoaxer was surely George Plimpton.

Plimpton was born and raised in aristocratic circumstances on Fifth Avenue in Manhattan. He went to St. Bernard's School and then Exeter and Harvard in anticipation of his joining his father's law firm, Debevoise & Plimpton.

But George would have none of it. Once, having coffee with him at the Harvard Club years later, he told me about it.

"One morning when I was about eleven, at breakfast, with the servants hovering over us, my father told me excitedly about the importance of mortgage indentures. Never forget, he said, mortgage indentures. One wrong word can cost millions. Accuracy and discipline are everything. I decided I hated mortgage indentures."

George graduated from Harvard with a degree in English literature and went to live in Paris. There—and this was just after World War II—he became the first editor in chief of the *Paris Review,* a new American-run literary journal published from the Left Bank. Plimpton interviewed Ernest Hemingway, Dorothy Parker, James Thurber, and others.

After a while, Plimpton came back to New York, and soon thereafter moved the editorial offices of the *Paris Review* with him. It occupied, and in 1991 when the Flight to Portugal announcement ran, still occupied, the first floor of a beautiful brownstone he purchased on 72nd Street right where it overlooks the East River. The *Paris Review* was on the first floor. Floors two through four were the Plimpton residence.

He wrote a best seller called *Paper Lion,* about his experience playing quarterback for one play of a preseason NFL game with the Detroit Lions. He got the ball and he ran with it, but a very short way. He wrote another best seller called *Out of My League,* about his experience pitching one inning at the All-Star Game (during the pregame festivities). He founded participatory journalism, which consisted of his joining a professional team, usually a sports team; playing with them once very badly; and then writing about it. He played a tennis match with Pancho Gonzales, got it in his head he could beat him, and as a result got seriously trounced. He went three rounds with light heavyweight champion Archie Moore. He joined the circus and they taught him the trapeze. He played the triangle with the New York Philharmonic Orchestra at Carnegie Hall. Many of his books became best sellers.

He kept popping up, Zelig-like, everywhere. He was on TV. He had parts in movies. He was with Sadat in Egypt, Muhammad Ali in Zaire, Bobby Kennedy at that hotel in Los Angeles when he was shot. (Plimpton, along with former decathlete Rafer Johnson, wrestled down the killer, Sirhan Sirhan.) He became the constant companion of presidents and prime ministers, kings and queens. With his tall, lanky good looks, fine manners, and the great shock of hair that always fell over his forehead, he was a great overgrown prep school boy and a great presence in this culture in the 1980s and 1990s.

He also became interested in fireworks, probably, as he

later told me, because he had been trained as a demolitions expert when he was in the army. He arranged for great fireworks displays in New York City—the Fourth of July, the Bicentennial, fireworks over the Statue of Liberty, the 100th anniversary of the Brooklyn Bridge—and was regarded as New York's unofficial fireworks commissioner.

Here in the Hamptons, that was how I met him. Or tried to meet him.

One morning in January 1977, at seven, a huge explosion somewhere far off rattled the windows of my home, waking me. And then I remembered. I'd read in a publicity release that George had arranged with the Grucci fireworks company to build and then set off the world's largest firework. The goal was the *Guinness Book of World Records*. To that end, he'd arranged for the attempt to be made at a garbage dump in town just before dawn. I wanted to write about the experience for the paper, but my alarm had failed to go off. Now it was too late to go down there. I rolled over and went back to sleep.

Finally, I did meet him, but it went very badly. It was in 1986 and now he was holding, ten days after the Fourth of July fireworks display in the town, his own fireworks to celebrate Bastille Day, the French independence day on July 14. He would have it at his estate facing the ocean in Wainscott for friends and invited guests. I was not an invited guest or friend, but I wanted to be. So I crashed the party, getting myself and my girlfriend in with our press credentials.

It was awkward meeting him under these circumstances, with people such as Jackie Kennedy Onassis, Norman Mailer, and others sitting on blankets on the lawn, or walking around mingling with jugglers and dancers who had been hired for the occasion, but I did meet him and his wife Freddy and I shook hands with them, just before the beginning of a big disaster.

Off in the distance, on the dunes, the firemen (and George, who could not resist going down there) were setting up the fireworks as a great fog rolled in. Soon the fireworks went up, seemed to disappear into the fog, and then in cometlike streaks began coming down on the heads of the guests.

Over the PA system, Freddy started shouting as loudly as she could, "George, stop the fireworks! George, stop the fireworks!" And he did, but not before at least several people got either frightened or mildly injured from burned-out fireworks sizzling through the trees down upon them.

The party went on, without the fireworks. Great food. Several entertainments. I actually had a conversation with Jackie Kennedy Onassis by the food buffet, returning excitedly with this information to my girlfriend. Now, however, huge crowds of people were beginning to appear at the party and seemed to be getting out of control. Finally, we began to see people with earpieces walking around talking to people, asking them if they had been invited to the party and if not, to please leave, as it was private. Before they could get to us, we quickly packed up and, apologizing to some people who were sitting with us by this time, left the party before it was over. Very embarrassing.

The next day, my girlfriend asked if I was going to write about the fireworks coming down in the crowd. I said that because we had crashed the party I really shouldn't. It wouldn't be right.

"It's news," she said. "You have a newspaper. I would write about it if I were you."

And so I took her advice. The result was that when one particular man filed a lawsuit against the Plimptons for a minor injury suffered as a result of the raining-down fireworks, my newspaper report was presented at trial as evidence.

This truly upset George Plimpton, people later told me. He was polite to a fault, usually, but this got to him. I was not on the party list. And now *this*. Well, it took about five years, but he got over it, and pretty soon we were on speaking terms.

Also as a result of this debacle, George decided he could no longer hold a fireworks display at his home. And so, the following year, the event was held on the grounds of the Boys Harbor camp overlooking Three Mile Harbor in East Hampton. The fireworks would be set off from a barge in the harbor. He did this every year for the next sixteen years, narrating the fireworks and raising millions for the camp.

I wrote about these events and George would call me about this and others. At one point, he called to ask if I could find employment for his son, Taylor, at the paper as a staff writer and I did.

On another occasion, he interviewed me for an article he was writing for the program celebrating the 35th anniversary of *Dan's Papers*. This was in 1995. In the article, he referred to me as "avuncular."

"What kind of word is that to describe somebody?" I asked him. "Nobody is going to know what that means." We were at a party being held for the staff of the *Paris Review* at the end of

the summer at the home of Ben Bradlee and Sally Quinn in East Hampton.

"It's a word," he said. "Look it up."

I really did admire George Plimpton, even wonder if someday I could be appreciated the way he was appreciated. We were, it seemed to me, in the same business. But he was so well mannered, well connected, and well bred, and everybody liked him. I was from New Jersey. I could *never* be as good as him. He'd cornered the market.

From far left to right:
GEORGE PLIMPTON,
DUSTIN HOFFMAN,
ADOLPH GREEN,
AND GWEN VERDON
AT THE 1972
ARTISTS AND
WRITERS GAME.
(Courtesy of *Dan's Papers*)

THE taxi rumbled down East 72nd Street, crossed First Avenue, then York Avenue, and then suddenly hit the washboard of the fairytale cobblestone road that was the eastern tip of 72nd Street leading to George's town house, overlooking the river. We stopped in front. It was quiet. Not a sound. I paid the cabbie and went up to the front of the brownstone and rang the bell. In moments, the door opened. And there stood a very pretty girl who could not have been more than nineteen.

"George Plimpton?" I asked.

"Oh yes," she said. "Are you Dan Rattiner? He's expecting you. Please follow me."

We walked through what had been a former living room, now crowded with young editors, the oldest no more than twenty-five I thought, sitting at desks and writing on computers or talking on telephones.

"We're on deadline," the pretty girl said to me happily as we went up a staircase to a second floor.

The whole place was filled with the memorabilia of George's trips to faraway places. There were skeletons, moose heads, African spears, pictures of dictators, musical instruments, a boxer's punching bag, Turkish rugs, Victorian lounging sofas, baseball bats, lacrosse sticks, a chess table, and then, on a third floor, a pool table, at which George stood holding a cue. We shook hands and smiled, and he handed the cue to me and indicated that I should take a shot. We played silently for a while.

I wondered if the story about the Flight to Portugal might surprise George, but really I knew nothing surprised George. He'd seen it all—and been part of most of it. I opened the copy of the paper from the autumn when PLENTY TO DO IN THE WINTER IN THE HAMPTONS had appeared and he read the article, and then I told him how the proverbial roof had fallen in. He wasn't surprised.

"What do you think?" I asked him.

"It's interesting that out of those thirteen festivals you wrote about, this was the one that got everybody's attention."

"I've wondered at that," I said, turning to it. There it was, occupying just a few inches of space on page 58.

George grinned. "I think people are attracted to life-and-death situations. None of your other festivals are in that category."

"That's true."

"In late December, they got their appointment diaries for the new year. And this was one date they didn't want to miss. So they penciled it in. And then made a call just to make sure that it was on. You have to hold the Flight to Portugal," he said finally. "No way around it."

"OK," I said. "How do I do that?"

Outside the window a big barge was slowly drifting by on the East River. We looked at it for a while. A big tanker was gliding by.

"What's the most interesting thing you've seen on the river since you began living here?" I asked.

"Floaters."

"Floaters?"

"We've had our share," he said.

A floater is someone who got shot and dumped in the river upstream, he told me.

A ND so we held the Flight to Portugal. Looking back on it, I have to say that this was about the most fun I've ever had with the newspaper.

First of all, two weeks before the event was supposed to happen in March, we published an item noting that this year, the event was being postponed until August, when the water was warmer and "there was a greater chance of survival." The new date would be Saturday, August 22, 1992. That gave me some breathing room.

I got an enthusiastic thumbs-up from the Montauk Historical Society to hold the event on the lighthouse grounds. They were in charge of the property at this time.

I went to a meeting of the Montauk Boatman's Association and talked them into donating a $100 bond to create a college scholarship fund for the winner in the under-twelve category. They also promised to have fishing boats bobbing in the water just off the lighthouse.

We sent out press releases to all the media, inviting them to send reporters, cameramen, or photographers to the "Media Area" of the event from which they could cover it. I included an aerial-view map of the lighthouse grounds, with the Media Area noted.

I went to see Grumman Aerospace, the manufacturer of the Apollo Lunar Module and warplanes for the navy, at their main office in Bethpage, Long Island, and after getting a security visitor's badge, visited their labs and asked them if they could provide us with a GPS system—this had just been invented— so we could have great accuracy in judging where the entries splashed into the sea. They said the GPS fit on the back of a big truck and they'd try, but they couldn't guarantee it. In the end, they came without it. But they did serve as judges.

We hired a caterer for the day of the event, and the staff set up a barbecue grill and sold out of food in the first hour. We had a four-piece band, the Jim Turner Band, playing sets all afternoon by a pumphouse on the lighthouse lawn, and we had a grandstand for the spectators and a "pit" area where entrants could fine-tune their entries. And then we had the "launch runway." Everybody would have five minutes to get ready and then go down the runway. We broadcast the final countdown, backwards from ten, over the public-address system.

Down on the beach, we had the members of the Eastern Long Island Surfing Association with their surfboards, ready to either pick up debris from the ocean or rescue entrants. And we had the biggest ship from the Montauk Coast Guard Station, the fifty-five-foot *Point Wells,* which anchored off the lighthouse at the beginning of the event—all its men in dress whites—but then after just one hour had to run off to handle another maritime rescue in the heavy surf of that day.

Of course, we did not have cars driving off the cliff. Our event, which drew fifty-five entries, including one from TV personality and Montauk resident Dick Cavett, consisted of lighter-than-air model aircraft, many of them homemade, launched by hand over the edge of the cliff. And the one that went the farthest won the trip to Portugal. About a thousand people watched this three-hour-long event, though not George Plimpton, who, though invited, had to be in London. He did send me a metal toy car with wings, however.

The winner of this event was a couple from Port Washington, New York. At the awards ceremony, where the director of the Portuguese National Tourist Office, Carlos Lamieros, presented the first prize, we learned that the wife was afraid of flying. I don't know what happened after that. But somebody went to Portugal.

As the years passed, I had other encounters with George. Every August, he played first base for the writers in the annual celebrity baseball game that has been contested every year for fifty years on the sandlot baseball diamond in the park behind the East Hampton A&P.

For some reason that is lost in the mists of time, around 1980, I began to be the official umpire calling balls and strikes behind the mound year after year, which from a journalist's position is a dream. I'd call Christie Brinkley out on strikes. Then I'd write how she got called out on strikes.

In the summer of 2002, I heard that George was ill. He suited up for the game anyway but didn't start. However, he did come slowly to the plate as a pinch hitter in the top of the ninth, took two strikes, then a ball, and then hit a clean single to left. In the paper the following week, I wrote, hoping it would help him rally from his illness, that "George lashed a single to left," and when I saw him at a party several weeks later he told me he liked that word. Lashed.

In the summer of 2003, George came in to pinch-hit in the ninth. And again he hit a single to left, though this time it was just a slow roller that the third baseman had trouble fielding. Then they put in a pinch runner to run the bases for him. He looked very ill.

Again, in the paper, I wrote that George Plimpton lashed a single to left, but this time there was no response. A month later, George died in his sleep in his apartment in Manhattan.

Here in the Hamptons, George was widely mourned. At a party, someone told me a story about George that took place before I even came on the scene. It was in 1955 and he was a member of the Devon Yacht Club in Amagansett on the Fourth of July, and that evening it was he, of course, who was setting off fireworks at the club to celebrate the occasion.

One of them, a Roman candle, shot off sideways, landed in the cabin of a yacht that was occupied by an older female member of the club, scared the daylights out of her fizzing around, and then finally bumped off the stern and into the water, where, inexplicably, it exploded, scaring her even further.

The next day, at lunch at the club, George, who would have been twenty-eight at the time, walked over to her and presented her with the French military honor called the Croix de Guerre, a large bronze medal on a ribbon that got awarded for bravery above and beyond the call of duty. He placed it carefully over her head and down around her neck.

He had gotten it in the war, he told her. Not personally, perhaps, but gotten it nevertheless. Now it was hers. A medal for bravery. And everyone applauded.

Billy Joel

I N 1992, I wrote what I considered just about the best headline for an article that ever ran in the paper: BILLY JOEL WALKS INTO A POLE.

A week earlier, my girlfriend and I had gone to the movies at the East Hampton Cinema. The movie ended. Everyone got up and went out the exit onto Main Street, and there, under the streetlights, we saw the delightful sight of Billy Joel and model Christie Brinkley skipping along, clearly in love, laughing and talking. Christie was a shimmering blonde. Billy looked like the frog you kiss who turns into a prince.

It seemed to me, at the time, that other people coming out of the theater had noticed them too. And so basically, we were all enjoying watching them, but we were also ignoring them. You don't bother lovers. And here in the Hamptons, at that time anyway, we tried not to pay much attention to celebrities. They came here for privacy after all.

Billy Joel and Christie Brinkley had been living in town for about three years by this time. They'd bought a house in Amagansett on the ocean. They'd had a daughter. The media dubbed

Billy and Christie the Crown Prince and Princess of the Hamptons, and they were often seen at fund-raising events and parties.

As we watched the two of them that evening after the movie, a startling thing happened. Billy broke away from Christie at a store window and skipped on ahead a bit and BAM! walked right into a metal traffic pole. He fell down. And Christie came running over and helped him up. He staggered a bit, checked himself to see if he was bleeding, which he wasn't, and then they continued on.

What struck me at the time, and what this headline and story I wrote was all about, was how local people in these parts will go to great lengths to leave well-known people alone, and from that perspective, if Christie Brinkley had not been there, Billy Joel would just have lain there on the sidewalk, with the crowds of people stepping over him. He would have been in greater physical danger than an ordinary person, if you think about it. He might even have died.

It was a short piece. BILLY JOEL WALKS INTO A POLE. To this day, I enjoy this headline. I pride myself on this headline.

Just two years later, Billy Joel and Christie Brinkley got a divorce. It was sudden and not amicable. Billy Joel stayed in town. Christie Brinkley moved away.

And it was shortly after that that Billy Joel showed up at *Dan's Papers* unannounced. He was looking for me. The office contacted me by cell phone—I was not far away—and I came in the front door to be met by my office manager, who seemed a bit in a dither about having him there.

"He's upstairs in your office," she said. "He was waiting in the lobby for a while, but people kept looking at him."

I walked into my office to see him contemplating the various photographs—mainly of family—I had on my office walls.

He turned and held out a box of cookies.

"I brought you some Mallomars," he said. "I was told you like them."

I took them. "I do," I said. We sat down. I opened the box and we had a few.

"The Mallomars are a bribe," he said. "I want you to do something for me."

"What?"

"I have a girlfriend who is a painter. I know you reproduce paintings on the cover of your newspaper. I want to ask if you would consider putting one of hers there."

This made me smile. "I might look at this possibility favorably," I said.

"Well, what if I come back tomorrow morning with my girlfriend Carolyn and some of her paintings?"

"I'll be here," I told him.

That night, I considered that there was something quite remarkable about Billy Joel. It had nothing to do with celebrity. He had a girlfriend. It would be hard to imagine anyone as pretty as his ex-wife Christie, but I was sure she would be fine. And here he was going out of his way to help her like this. There were not many men, I thought, who would personally seek out a total stranger for this purpose the way he did.

Then I thought of the Mallomars. Very remarkable indeed.

If Christie Brinkley was the all-American girl, Carolyn Beegan was this edgy redhead sophisticate. Billy was only about five seven and Christie was taller than he was. Carolyn came in

about five eleven. She was quiet and serious. Billy was talkative and funny.

As for the paintings, they were good enough, but painters were clamoring for covers. I had only one to give away a week. I had thousands of slides to choose from. I would use hers.

Somehow, as a result of this bargain we had made, Mallo-mars for a cover, Billy and I struck up a friendship that lasted many years.

We had dinner from time to time. Once, at the American Hotel—we'd sit way in the back where nobody would see him or bother him—I discovered that he too had liked the headline I had written all those years ago.

"BILLY JOEL WALKS INTO A POLE," he sang to me across the table. He'd been working on it, he said. But it hadn't yet grown into a full-blown song.

Besides the obvious, which is that it is always nice to know a celebrity, I really came to love this man very much. When he had first approached me with the Mallomars, he had talked a bit about his career and where it had taken him.

"Beginning last year, I broke the record for having the most albums go platinum of any songwriter ever," he said. Then he smiled this little smile. "I am going to hold this record for about one more month," he continued. "And then I am going to be passed by Garth Brooks. So that will be that."

Even when you're on top of the world, he was saying, there is always somebody who will beat you out.

At the American Hotel one evening, he told me why he had come to move out to the Hamptons.

"I'm a Long Island boy, born and raised," he said. "But I'm from the workingman's Long Island. Levittown. Hicksville. I grew up admiring people who worked with their hands. Clammers. Farmers. Fishermen. Those people have been forced out from where I used to live. Now it's all suburbia and shopping malls in Hicksville and Levittown. The workingmen and women live out east. And I want to be among them."

Billy had ordered a fishing boat built that looked like a lobsterman's boat. It was probably the most expensive lobsterman's boat ever built. He called it the *Alexa,* named for his daughter, whom he was raising out here. He kept it in a slip in Sag Harbor. But he often spent time with the Bonackers, a name that described a group of baymen and clammers, many of whom we both knew.

"But do you really think this is going to last out here?" I

asked him. The celebrities were closing in. He was among them, like it or not. The glitterati were following.

"I want it to last out here. This is the real Long Island. It's what Long Island means to me."

One day, when we met, he was very upset.

"Somebody came on the boat last night and stole all the life jackets," he said.

"Why would anybody do that?" I asked.

"Because they say 'Alexa' on them. Souvenir hunters. This is very upsetting to me."

I said that I didn't understand.

"This is our safety equipment. What if we had been out there on the water and we needed it and didn't know it was gone? The jackets were out of sight, stowed away. It could happen. This is terrible."

I said I did understand. But there was nothing I could do. Except tell him he ought to replace them with life preservers that did not say anything on them. He shook his head.

Another day, a law was passed limiting the way the Bonackers caught fish on the beach. Netting stripers by an ancient method called haul seining was now illegal, and without haul seining, their ability to earn a living was severely compromised.

A few days after that, Billy was down at the beach with the Bonackers, getting himself arrested by participating in an illegal haul seine. I arrived as the police, who were escorting him back up the beach to a police car, allowed him to stop and talk over a microphone.

"We have to save these people, allow them to earn a living," he told the assembled crowd. Then the police took him further on and he walked right by me without even noticing I was there.

He wrote a song called "The Downeaster Alexa." It became the most popular song in the country at the time. It was an ode to the loss of the commercial fisheries on Long Island.

One day, with a few glasses of red wine in us, we got to talking about divorce. I'd already been divorced twice. His with Christie was his second too.

"How did you and Christie meet?" I asked.

"I've always thought I wasn't good-looking enough to get girls," he said. "So I took up playing the piano and composing songs. I just wanted to meet girls. One day I was down in the Caribbean at a bar in Saint Jean in Saint Bart's and I came across three of the most beautiful women I had ever seen. So I sat down and began to play piano there and sure enough they came over. They were Christie, Whitney Houston, and Elle MacPherson. I took a liking to Elle. And so that's who I started up with. When we were over, months later back in New York, I remembered Christie."

"What brought you to Saint Bart's?"

"I had a gig there. Not at the bar where we met but at another bar. And they were on a gig too. They were doing a *Sports Illustrated* bathing suit shoot. I could play and sing my songs. I was a songbird. I figured that would level the playing field."

"It sure did," I told him.

Billy invited me to his house for lunch. We went from room to room. It was an enormous estate, formerly owned by a member of the Social Set. One of the rooms had a black-and-white-checked marble floor with a beautiful black grand piano at one end and absolutely nothing anywhere else in the room.

"This is my composing room," he said. "I used to keep my motorcycle here, right by the door. But Christie said it got the floor dirty. So I had to leave it out. Now I can have it here again."

We both stared rather happily at this imaginary motorcycle. A win for us guys. One, anyway.

I ran several covers of *Dan's Papers* for Carolyn. And I went to a gallery opening on the second floor of a building overlooking the docks at Sag Harbor where she and Billy were holding forth. Carolyn was carrying around a little dog with her. It was the kind you can keep in a canvas bag. Somebody told me Carolyn had wanted to get married to Billy but he wasn't up for it yet.

"So that's why she got this dog," this person said.

For a long time during my relationship with Billy, there was something I wanted to talk to him about that I just could not get myself to bring up. About ten years earlier, he had come out with an album that had on it an old '50s rock 'n' roll song called "For the Longest Time." Or at least I thought it was an old '50s rock 'n' roll song. When I had bought the album, back then, I saw that Billy was credited with having written this song. He would have been just a kid in the 1950s.

I *know* I've heard this song, I thought to myself. I looked through my records but couldn't find it. Someday it will turn up that I have it among all my old records. It bothered me that I thought he had really stolen this song.

But now, after several years of friendship, I decided, one day while we were walking down Main Street in Sag Harbor, to bring this matter up with him.

"You know that song you wrote called 'For the Longest Time'?"

"Yeah."

"Did you *really* write it?"

"Yes, I did."

"I could *swear* that song was written before you put it out."

"No, I really wrote it," he said. "I wrote it as a rock 'n' roll song. It does have that sound. But it's mine."

Well, I thought, if you put it that way. And so I dropped the subject. He really did write it.

Billy went out on a world tour for a while in 1994, something he had to do, he told me, because his finances were not in order. He had had a manager who had stolen millions of dollars from him. And he had spent it, and so even though his lawyers sued the manager, it was never coming back.

"I'm also going into the boat-designing business," he said. He was up in my office again and he drew a rough sketch of what it would look like. It looked sort of like a gentle wooden touring boat from the 1930s.

"I'm going to have these built right here on Long Island, on Shelter Island, at the Coecles Harbor Boatyard."

"I didn't know they had a boatbuilding business on Shelter Island," I said.

"They don't. But they did. It closed down. I'm reopening it."

"Are you sure this is going to work out?"

"I have to do something to make a living when all the rock-star stuff wears out. I talked to my accountant about this. And he said it would be okay. I just have to build one at a time or maybe two at a time, and then sell those two and then build two more and then keep going with that. I can afford to do that."

"What's it like going out on a tour?" I asked. "I mean, they have groupies that follow you around? Women that will do anything that you want?"

He thought about this. "You get kind of used to it after a while," he said. "I mean, you know in advance how it is going to turn out."

"Could I go with you sometime?" I asked hopefully.

"You wouldn't like it. Also, you aren't a rock star."

"I could play the tambourine."

The next year, when the first boat got built, Billy took me for a ride in it in Gardiner's Bay. There were two ladies along. One was his daughter, Alexa, who was nine at that time. The other was my new wife.

The boat was about thirty-eight feet long and looked exactly as the plans did—an old-fashioned wooden touring boat, which Billy called a "picnic boat." You could toodle along in it and find a beach on a bay somewhere to drop anchor and have a picnic.

Except this "picnic boat" was packed with twin 350-horsepower engines and, if challenged by any other boat from a standing start, could leave the other boat in the dust, so to speak. And it had a top speed of 40 knots. Billy demonstrated. We held on.

It also had every electronic device imaginable on board. "It almost drives itself," Billy said. "You just punch in your starting point and your destination and it goes around anything nearby and any underwater reefs or anything that might be in your way."

What a boat. The price to own one would be about half a million dollars. I wrote about all of this and put it in the paper. I never did learn whether it helped him sell one, but on the other hand, he was certainly going to sell them with me or without me.

In July of 1999, something happened that, in my opinion, ended my friendship with Billy Joel. In the course of my day at the paper, I had had a meeting with the owner of the Windmill Restaurant in East Hampton, a man named Eric Haberman. Eric was a charming man, and in the past I had sometimes done some fund-raising promotions that took place both in the paper and at his restaurant. However, sometimes they had not worked out. His advertising would not get paid for. His promised celebrities had not shown up. But as I said, he was very charming. He could talk you right out of your socks.

What Eric Haberman did get me to agree to do was to invite my "friend" Billy Joel to come to a children's fair he was holding on the restaurant property that would benefit the local chapter of the Children's Diabetes Foundation.

"You *have* to do this," he said. "We are going to have clowns, pony rides, games, and even a raffle, where the winner will get a weekend at Disney World, all expenses paid for himself and his family. All we want to do is ask Billy to make an appearance. He will love it."

I asked him, and he said he would, but we would come in separate cars, because he had to go someplace else soon afterward.

I arrived first and parked by the side of the road. And boy, did I know this was trouble. There was this big crowd on the lawn all waiting excitedly for the great man. I got out of the car and walked over. There was a loudspeaker, there were indeed rides and games, there was even a ducking stool where you could throw a ball at a metal circle just above the head of who was in the ducking stool and it would release a latch and send him or her flying into the water. Frightened, I went back out to the street to sit in my car.

"There he is," somebody shrieked.

And indeed, there was Billy Joel, pulling up in his antique 1967 Deux Chevaux automobile and getting out just in front of me. In a second, people had surrounded the car. Oh God, I thought. I put my head in my hands.

Billy was doing his best to fend people off. He was signing autographs, smiling, and shaking hands. He walked through the crowd. And then I struggled through the crowd over to him.

"I had no idea," I said.

He shrugged. "We'll get through this."

"Let's get him on the ducking stool!" somebody shouted. And the crowd began to slowly march him over in that direction.

Somehow, Billy and I, separately, got through this afternoon. We didn't speak. My lingering memory of that day was of the raffle where Eric picked a name out of a bowl in front of a crowd of a hundred and fifty people.

"And the winner is . . ." Haberman said. And he named somebody, who, as it happened, was right there in the front row waiting for their name to be called. It was a woman. And her lack of enthusiasm about it was so apparent that people commented on it. As for me, knowing Haberman, it made me think that the fix had been on. It was one of his relatives. Nobody would be going to Disney World. But I was never able to prove that.

What I could prove was that a total of no money arrived in any reasonable amount of time into the pockets of the Children's Diabetes Foundation. There was an item about it in the *East Hampton Star*. The director said it was two months later now and Haberman was still giving them the brush-off. How it ended up, however, I do not know.

Another thing that I know, however, is that that was the last time I spoke to Billy Joel for quite some time. After a fashion, I called him. There was no returned phone call.

And then I learned that Billy Joel had sold his oceanfront home to Jerry Seinfeld for $32 million and that he had bought an enormous 32-room mansion fifty miles away on the North Shore of Long Island in the very heart of the estate section where wealthy WASPs were still holding forth. It was a secluded mansion, but the New York daily papers were able to send planes to fly over and take pictures of it. It looked like Windsor Castle. And so he was gone.

E IGHT years later I was in a restaurant in Water Mill with my girlfriend and another couple when, right at the table next to us, Billy Joel and his new young wife, along with another couple, sat down. They made no indication that they knew we were there.

Eric Haberman, is what I thought.

"Don't you *know* him?" one of the guests at our table asked.

"Yes and no," I said.

"Why don't you go over and say hello?"

"I don't wanna," I said.

"Why don't you ask him to write the introduction to the book you are writing?"

"I don't wanna."

As we got halfway through our meal and had filled ourselves with some wine, however, I thought better of it. And I had an idea. I called over the waiter.

"I would like to buy a round of drinks for everybody at that table," I said.

The drinks arrived. They drank. And then Billy's new wife, Katie Lee, caught my eye, mouthed "Thank you," and waved me over.

I stood behind Billy and put my hands on his shoulders. He turned and looked up at me.

"Where have you been?" I asked.

"I'm moving back. I've bought a house in Sag Harbor with a dock. And I'm buying Roy Scheider's house in Sagaponack on the ocean."

"I've written a memoir," I said. "It will be out next spring. And it's about a lot of people I knew and know and all the changes that have taken place in this community. I have a chapter about you in it."

"Send me the manuscript. I'm going to Europe next week. I'll read it on the plane."

A month later, we were having lunch at the Dockside Restaurant on Bay Street in Sag Harbor.

"How come you left the North Shore?"

"The house I bought was waterfront and had a dock.

I thought I could put one of my boats there and speedboat to Manhattan in twenty minutes when I needed to go. But the dock was in disrepair and hadn't been used in years. And then the village gave me a hard time. In the end, they wouldn't let me do it. So I just gave up on it. The house is for sale."

"Why *two* houses out here?"

"During the week, we're right here in busy downtown Sag Harbor. I can walk around. I have a World War II German motorized bike I can use. It's a great town. On the weekends, we can go to our vacation home on the ocean. And there's nobody around."

"I have a question I'm sort of afraid to ask you," I said.

At that moment, his wife, with another woman, came in the restaurant. They said hi. Then they indicated they would not be joining us.

"You two boys talk about what you want to talk about. We'll talk about what we want to talk about."

They sat down two tables away.

"Here's the thing," I said. "Are you mad at me? We had that terrible time at the Windmill Restaurant. Then I never spoke to you again. I felt so guilty to have involved you in that."

"I was mad at *him,* not at you," he said. "I just lost touch with a lot of my friends when I moved away. Now, I'm *back.*"

Spalding Gray

A⊤ noon on June 3, 2000, I was supposed to meet up with Spalding Gray at his house in Sag Harbor to talk to him about a party that would be held to raise money to shut down the Millstone Nuclear Power Station.

I really looked forward to meeting him. Several years before, I had seen him perform "Swimming to Cambodia," a two-hour-long monologue where this slight, curly-haired New England WASP person simply sat at a table facing the audience and, with only a glass of water to interrupt his discourse from time to time, wove the most fascinating stories about his experiences as an extra in the making of Roland Joffé's movie *The Killing Fields.* And then in 1999, I saw him again, this time as a new resident of the Hamptons, performing his monologue "Monster in a Box" under a big tent on the lawn of the Parrish Art Museum in Southampton. He sat on a chair at a desk for an hour and a half, talking continuously, with the audience laughing uproariously from time to time, and he patted this white cardboard box on his desk, the only other object on the

SPALDING GRAY
HOLDING FORTH.

desk other than the glass of water, which he said contained the
novel he was writing. It was the Monster in a Box.

It was a hot, sweaty night under that tent. But it was a riv-
eting performance. Everybody stayed to the end and gave him
a standing ovation and then two encores.

Spalding and his wife, Kathy Russo, and their little kids
had moved from upstate New York to a little house with a
white picket fence in Sag Harbor in 1996. During his monologue, he had talked about this house, about Sag Harbor and
what a cute place it was, about his wife, his anxieties, and his
hopes and dreams.

He was a phenomenon. He had been on television and in

movies and Broadway shows and had developed a national reputation telling his wild and analytical stories. And he was here with us now.

I called him up at home about ten to confirm the appointment.

"The roofers are here," he said. "They're Mexican and they're throwing shingles off the roof. It's chaos. I can't stand it. We can't stay here. We're all going to the beach."

I really wanted to talk to him about STAR. Protests about nuclear plants were not a dime a dozen in 2000. It was news.

"Could we do it later back at the house?" I asked. "I'm on a deadline."

"I don't know when we'll be back. Look. I know Christie Brinkley really wants me to do this with you. So just come to the beach. We'll be bringing a picnic basket for lunch. Sagg Main Beach. We'll be over on the left."

"Noon okay?"

"Yeah."

He didn't sound very pleased about this. As a matter of fact, neither was I very pleased about this Millstone thing, except that now I'd get to know Spalding Gray a little better. I had spoken to him on the phone once. I'd been at his house once for a party. That had been it.

Driving down there that sunny, windy late-spring morning, I reflected on how Christie Brinkley had pretty much roped everybody into this. After getting divorced from Billy Joel, she had moved to Manhattan for a while but then married a handsome local Southampton architect named Peter Cook. And she now had two little kids and had moved back here to raise them. As a matter of fact, she had bought a small stone castle on a hill in Bridgehampton that some rich man had decided would look pretty neat back in the 1920s. It even had turrets. Turrets for the Princess.

In any case, apparently Christie had noticed something I had noticed twenty-five years earlier when thousands of us were demonstrating to stop the construction of a nuclear plant. Back then, in 1970, the lighting company was building a nuclear plant at Shoreham, about forty miles to the west of the Hamptons. And we had stopped it. The police had used tear gas on us as we climbed chain-link fences to try to storm it. Buses had carried us off. Those were the sorts of things that happened back then. Eventually the governor stepped in and stopped this nuclear plant. It never opened.

But though I had joined in that protest, I did ask some of the protest organizers at that time, rather meekly I thought, about the fact that the Millstone plant across Long Island Sound in Connecticut, just thirty miles from the Hamptons as the crow flies, was an even bigger threat. It was ten miles closer than Shoreham would be. And Millstone was already up and running.

The organizers sort of glazed over when I talked about Millstone then. Shoreham was right here on Long Island. Millstone was Connecticut's problem. Someone even told me that with the prevailing winds from the southwest, the people who had to worry about Millstone were in Massachusetts. We were perfectly fine here on Long Island.

Well, that was before Christie. Prior to my scheduled meeting with Spalding Gray, she had been all over the news talking about the dangers of Millstone. Had she only known, she said, she wouldn't have moved here to raise her children. She would have gone with them elsewhere. But who knew about the nuclear plant across the water? The real estate people hadn't told her. So now she wanted to close Millstone. She had taken the reins of a small organization called STAR founded by another concerned woman. STAR. Straight Talk About Radiation. And she would be having a fund-raiser. Her ex Billy Joel said he'd be on the board. Spalding Gray was on the board. And when I had called her to ask about all of this, and told her I had a deadline, she said she was headed off to the West Coast just then but would get one of the other board members to talk to me. An assistant called me back later in the day to say I would be meeting with Spalding.

I parked in the lot and, getting out of the car beneath the seagulls that were circling around there, immediately realized I was not properly dressed for the beach. It was a hot day and everyone was in bathing suits. I was wearing a white dress shirt, shorts, and sandals. Nevertheless, I padded out onto the sand and down toward the sea. In my breast pocket I had a small tape recorder.

I found the Spalding Grays pretty easily. He and his family were sitting on a blanket right where Spalding had said they would be, right up near the water. There were the three kids alternately running around and fighting over a sand castle, there was his wife Kathy reading a book, there were beach toys, a Styrofoam cooler, and several towels. As I was dressed, and everybody else was in bathing suits, I felt very out of place.

"Hi," I said. I stood there.

"Hi," Spalding said, lifting up his sunglasses. He didn't say anything further than that, no hello, this is my wife Kathy and so forth and so on, and so feeling even more out of place, I walked around the blanket to the corner where he was sitting and beyond the blanket I squatted down in the sand.

"So," I said.

"You wanted to talk about STAR and Millstone?" he asked.

"Yeah."

Here was his reply, from the tape, which I still have. This is how his mind works.

"Well, there's two events. I think that Priscilla Star is doing one. I don't know where she's going to do it. Is it finally at the Star Ranch?

"But also, Billy Joel is doing an event. What's happened, there's a lot of disintegration and disharmony of egos in the STAR board because there's a lot of strong-headed celebrities that have opinions about what should be done when, and I think that the powers that be at STAR felt that Priscilla was wrong in trying to have a benefit that would be confusing and somehow be kind of unproductive to the Billy Joel event. So STAR is doing something with Billy Joel in July and Priscilla is doing something with jazz musicians in August, and I won't be here for either of them."

Gray then launched into the reason why he wouldn't be here, which was because Gore Vidal was remounting his play *The Best Man* on Broadway—he had first done it there in 1960—and Vidal had cast Spalding as one of the leads, so he would be going in for rehearsals beginning in late June.

"I suppose my character is modeled on Adlai Stevenson

and the other is more of a Tricky Dick person, you know, a Machiavellian politician, and we're both running for president. We're also both in the same party but you're not told what the party is. The Machiavellian gets my psychiatric records to prove that I've had a nervous breakdown, and he's gonna release them.

"It's a lovely day here. I'll have very few days like this. I'm leaving this territory, you know we're renting our house out, we're going to Greece for eight days in July, then we're coming back and we will be up in Putnam Valley for the rest of the summer, where Kathy is taking on a Fresh Air kid to hang out with Forrest. But I'll miss it all, I'll be in New York in rehearsals."

By this time, I realized that I would not be staying for whatever the picnic lunch was they had brought. Kathy Russo was the boss, I guessed, and he hadn't consulted her, so I moved to quickly wrap things up.

I thought of something I thought was witty. "Do you think it's confusing for Priscilla Star to be connected with this organization?" I asked.

"I think it is confusing for Priscilla Star because her name is Star. When I first went to her ranch in Montauk, I thought the foundation was named after her, but it turned out to be just one of those wonderful coincidences."

I stood up to leave. Indeed, I felt I should not have come.

"I want to tell you I really like your paper," Spalding said suddenly. "I love that piece you just wrote about, what was it, lions in North Haven? About how this guy from Holland had brought in lions to thin the herd of deer there? Brilliant. How do you find these stories out when no other newspaper gets them?"

I drove home, and when I got there, I listened to this last part of the tape again and again. Yup. He believed this made-up story I wrote about them bringing in lions to eat up all the deer in North Haven. And one that any normal person would, in my opinion, conclude had been a made-up fantasy story. For example, there was the part about the neighbor's German shepherd confronting the herd and having gotten eaten.

How embarrassing.

The dueling STAR events were never held. And soon afterward, the STAR organization collapsed for lack of funds. Christie soldiered on, but Millstone is still huffing and puffing on the shores of Connecticut today.

Gray costarred in the revival of the play *The Best Man.* But the next June, while driving on a narrow road in Ireland, he was in a car crash and suffered severe injuries, some of them head injuries. And much to the dismay of those who knew him and loved him, he was never the same.

Gray killed himself in early 2004 by slipping over the side of the Staten Island Ferry into the freezing cold waters of the Narrows.

Between the time of his accident and his death, he tried to kill himself at least two other times, one of which had resulted in his having to be talked down from the bridge that connects Sag Harbor and North Haven. This bridge rises to a height of about twenty feet above the water. But it was a suicide attempt anyway, in the cold of winter.

One day in 2002, I walked past Spalding Gray in the hallway of the Ross School in East Hampton, a private school where his children went, as did one of mine. The children were doing some sort of theatrical performance in the theater at the school at that time, and this was the intermission. He sat on a cushion in a bay window, his hair disheveled, his face unshaven, and his shirttail out, and he was looking at the floor. He never even raised his head to say anything when I stopped to greet him. I walked on.

Bill Clinton

I N the spring of 1988, the Village of East Hampton closed the park behind all the stores in the center of town in order to fix it up. They tore out the softball field that was there and in its place they put sandboxes, slides, seesaws, swings, and a wooden jungle gym. I worried about it and so one day I called the village clerk.

"That's a very famous softball field," I said.

"We know," was the reply. "Don't worry. We're just moving it to the back end of the park. And it will be ready by August 13."

"Are you sure?"

"Count on it."

This park was famous for only one thing. Every year, on the second Saturday afternoon in August, two baseball teams would assemble on the park's field at three in the afternoon to play nine innings of softball. One of the teams consisted of "The Artists." The other consisted of "The Writers." Since some of the most famous artists and writers in the world lived in the Hamptons, this annual event was a very big deal. Hundreds would come to watch the game, and reporters covered it for the national media.

The first of the games, which had featured Franz Kline, Jackson Pollock, Willem de Kooning, and Harold Rosenberg, the art critic for *The New Yorker*, was held in 1948.

Another year, Eugene McCarthy, who ran for president in 1968, played second base for the Writers. This was in 1969. He was much revered by Democrats by that time and was then working as an editor at Harcourt Brace Jovanovich. And if anybody told him after the third inning that, after he slid into second, the back of his shorts had split open to confirm he was wearing white underwear, he didn't care.

Also in 1969, hippie Abbie Hoffman had taken one pitch low and then had raced off to steal first base. He got called back. The soccer star Pelé played in the game in the 1990s. Boxer Gerry Cooney played during that decade too.

In any case, if the field might not be ready for the game in 1988, it would have been two years in a row that there had been a problem.

In 1987, the year before, there had been a Frisbee game going on at the ball field when the artists and writers arrived at 2:00 P.M. Among those scheduled that year for the game were artists Larry Rivers and Roy Lichtenstein, photographer Peter Beard, actress Dina Merrill, and singer Paul Simon. And for the writers, Kurt Vonnegut, George Plimpton, Carl Bernstein, and Jim Salter. Some of these luminaries—watched by about a thousand spectators, umpires and coaches, and TV and magazine reporters—arrived with bats and balls and mitts and just came to a halt. It's a public park.

"We were here first," said one of the Frisbee players, a fifteen-year-old with a baseball cap on backward. "It's first come, first served."

And that was true. And so all these powerful people hung around and waited until the kids got tired, which was about three thirty. And then the game began.

In any case, here in 1988, the town construction crews were still working on the field up until the very day before the game. And so, on game day, Saturday, there it was—the metal backstop up, the foul lines painted, and the eight rows of wooden stands in place along the first- and third-base lines all ready to go.

I arrived around two with some of the others, noticed the lack of Frisbee players, walked around the infield kicking the dust for a while, and then took a turn at batting practice, which was just getting started. Batting practice for me, though, was just a formality. I would not be playing. As I had done for each of the prior eight years, I would be standing out behind the pitcher's mound calling balls and strikes. Artist Leif Hope, who had been designated the official organizer of the game—against his will, since it involved all the politics and bruised egos of who would be allowed in and who would be left out—had decided that that was my job.

Leif Hope was a burly blond man who had been a member of the merchant marine in the Swedish navy before coming to America to take up his paintbrushes. He arrived for the game about ten minutes after I did. He was carrying a clipboard, and looking very distracted for having come a bit late for practice. But it was all just fine. The food table was set up. The T-shirt table was set up. All the players were out there in their sneakers and shorts, tossing balls around. It was a magnificent day.

This particular year, the proceeds from the game—it cost $15 to get into the park, although you could go around the back if you really wanted to—would benefit East Hampton Head Start. In addition, Leif had asked some of his fellow artists to each paint a "letter" on a canvas two feet by three. The canvases, done in the inimitable style of the artists invited, hung on a clothesline and, looking like somebody's wash, collectively spelled out the word ARTISTS. They'd be individually auctioned off after the game. Some of the artists who had painted them were in attendance. They included Chuck Close, Eric Fischl, Hedy Klineman, and Christophe de Menil. Also on hand was Bianca Jagger, in her signature sunglasses and black slacks. And in the stands, flamboyantly dressed in red tights, spangles, and a leotard, was writer Suzanne O'Malley. With pom-poms and a baton, she had arrived to invigorate the crowd by leading them in cheers and would, shortly after the game began, be coming down front to do so.

At ten of three, Leif came over to see me at the back of the pitcher's mound.

"We've got another celebrity umpire for you this year," Leif said, handing me the game ball.

"Okay."

The year before it had been Congressman Charlie Rangel from Harlem. The year before that it had been New York mayor Ed Koch. And the year before that, model Christie Brinkley. This was a new thing, putting in celebrity umpires to call balls and strikes for a few innings. I didn't mind it, so long as I started the game and ended the game.

"Who is it?"

"He's not here yet," Leif said mysteriously. "It's sort of a surprise."

Now it was almost three o'clock: game time. I stood out there on the mound behind Mort Zuckerman, the billionaire real estate man (and owner of the weekly magazine *U.S. News and World Report*), who was the starting pitcher for the Writers that year and who was throwing a few warm-up pitches. I raised both my arms.

"Play ball," I said.

And all talk stopped. Playing center field for the Writers was Ken Auletta, in left was *Washington Post* editor Ben Bradlee, on first was George Plimpton, and behind the plate was Ed Tivnan.

"Batter up!" I shouted. And out walked the leadoff hitter for the Artists, superagent Sam Cohn.

I have to say that it was a very heady feeling to be some normal person out there in the center of everything, deciding the fates of the luminaries who were playing that day.

Sam Cohn grounded out. Next up was Christopher Reeve, the late actor who portrayed Superman in the movies. And he hit a long drive that Ken Auletta caught right in front of the snow fence at the back of center field. Two outs.

Suzanne O'Malley, a real knockout, now appeared at the sidelines to do a cartwheel and a handstand, then did a little dance and rattled her pom-poms as she led the crowd in the following cheer, which she herself had written.

Manet, Monet
Rembrandt, Vermeer
All for the Artists
Stand up and cheer!

If early on this had been a game just between the artists and writers living in this community, in more recent times there came to be a strong push to allow Hollywood types to play. Steven Spielberg had moved out to East Hampton. Marisa Tomei was here. So was Kathleen Turner. And who were we to stop them? They came as "artists," and who was to say that they were not?

Behind the backstop, a microphone was set up on a table where a person noted for his wit would narrate the game. In 1987, the year of the Frisbees, the honor had fallen to Howard Stringer, who has since gone on to become the CEO of Sony. In 1988, the honors were done by the late John Scanlon, a noted public relations man from New York.

"Now coming up for the artists is Eric Ernst, an actual painter," said Scanlon. "A man who paints canvases with paintbrushes from paint on a palette. A dying breed."

At the end of the first inning—the Writers had scored five runs in their half of the first—Leif walked out to the mound to talk to me.

"Our celebrity is here," he said.

"You want me to let him start umpiring the second?" I asked.

"Yeah."

"Who is he?"

"Bill Clinton."

"Bill Clinton?"

"He's the governor of Arkansas."

What has he got to do with the Hamptons? is what I thought. But I didn't say that.

"Think he can do the job?" is what I did say.

"We'll see."

The governor of Arkansas was making his way to the mound behind Hope. He was, at that time, forty-two years old. He looked nice enough. I handed him the ball.

"If you need any help, I'll be behind third base," I said.

"Thanks," he said.

And so I trotted off the mound and over to the umpire's spot on the third-base line—I'd have this lesser spot—still wondering what a governor from Arkansas would be doing in East Hampton. Who's idea was this?

Clinton took to umpiring this game with both enthusiasm and accuracy. He did not make a single mistake that I could see calling balls and strikes. He also accurately called a man out on a close play at third in the bottom of that inning. As I was third-base umpire, this should have been my call. I saw the man as safe and was about to call him that when Clinton, who was suddenly right there, beat me to it and called him out. Nobody objected. So I kept my hands at my sides.

It had not always been the case that a celebrity umpire was good at this job. When Congressman Charles Rangel tried it, he could not even remember how many outs there were, much less what the balls and strikes were. We had a member of the Supreme Court who didn't even know what a foul ball was. He

BILL CLINTON UMPIRING BEHIND SAM COHN.
(Photograph by Julie Gervais; courtesy of *Dan's Papers*)

started laughing when people started complaining. Leif pulled him and brought me back in.

At the end of the second inning, I walked out to the governor to talk with him. I particularly wanted to talk to him about the call at third base.

"Do you overrule my decisions at third because you are the main umpire or because you are the governor?" I asked.

"Because I'm the governor," he said.

"You're doing fine," I told him. "Keep it up."

"You want to come back in?" he asked me, holding up the ball.

"Leif will let us know," I said. Then I walked back to third.

Clinton continued to call this game with great enthusiasm.

And as the second inning segued into the third, I began to wonder if I was ever going to be called back in. He was fun to watch, doing his job like some big kid. In the bottom of the third, I started to feel jealous. Nobody had ever stayed in as celebrity umpire for more than two innings. Now Leif was indicating from the first-base sidelines, where he worked his second job at the game—coach of the Artists—that I should stay where I was for the top of the fourth. I looked coldly at him. The governor of Arkansas?

Between the top and bottom of the fourth inning, Leif indicated that enough was enough and I should come back in and call balls and strikes.

"So there goes Bill Clinton," Scanlon said, "shuffling off to Buffalo or wherever the hell he came from. Good job, Governor. Let's give that man a hand."

And we all did.

At the beginning of the fourth inning, a group of thirty older men, all with red T-shirts and some sort of signs on sticks, wandered up into the stands. I had no idea who they were. There were white letters on the red T-shirts that read JUSTICE FOR JANITORS. The signs they held up—the fans made them take them down after a minute or two because they blocked their view of the game—read LOCAL 925. ZUCKERMAN UNFAIR.

Mort Zuckerman had been laboring away at the mound for the Writers, and had not yet let in a single run. The Writers were running away with the game and now were ahead 10–0.

"They don't like your pitching?" I asked Zuckerman, leaning over his shoulder.

Zuckerman did not reply. Instead, he pitched a perfect

strike to Sam Cohn. John Scanlon, who had now been joined by Howard Stringer, the announcer from the year before, explained things.

"We've got hecklers," he said. "These are janitors from a building Mort owns in the city. Strikers."

Sam Cohn struck out to end the top of the inning. In the bottom of the inning, this exchange occurred between Scanlon and Stringer as writer Walter Isaacson came up to the plate.

SCANLON: Isaacson is much taller than he looks.
STRINGER: Winner of four Pulitzer Prizes.
SCANLON: Author of Spinoza's *Ethics*.
STRINGER: His works will be read long after
    Shakespeare's are forgotten.
SCANLON: But not before.

O'Malley, on the Writers' side of the field at this point, offered up this cheer.

Dostoyevsky, Dickens
Shakespeare and Poe
Writers usually win
Keep the status quo!

In the top of the eighth inning, I had to make a ruling on a play that simply baffled me and just about everybody else. A huge melee occurred as people who wanted the batter called out stormed the field to argue against people who wanted the batter called safe. The Writers were well ahead by that time, but it didn't matter.

The bases were loaded. "Artist" Paul Simon was up, and with two strikes on him, he hit a pitch high in the air above the first-base line. George Plimpton, the first baseman for the Writers, drifted over and, looking up, edged into foul territory, where he began to step into a part of the crowd that was sitting on blankets between the stands and the foul line. They were not supposed to be sitting there. He'd look up, then down to see he wasn't stepping on anybody, then up again, and then he leaned farther into foul territory and at that moment the film actress Lori Singer, who was suited up to play for the Artists but was sitting on a blanket there, leaped to her feet and shoved George just enough so that when the ball landed in his mitt for the final out, it popped back out and into the crowd.

I saw this all very clearly, but I didn't know how to call it. She had interfered. Intentionally. And the choice was to call the batter at the plate either still at bat with the count one and two, or out of there, as in out, inning over. Change sides.

I ruled that it was an out. And the inning was over. And that's when all the ballplayers tumbled out onto the field to let me know what they thought of me.

I wavered. "So it's just a foul ball?"

Bill Clinton was nowhere in sight. I stood my ground. And we moved on into the bottom of the eighth.

After the game ended and the auction had been held, all the players went over to the Laundry Restaurant at the far end of the park to share a few beers and talk about the game. The Laundry was owned, at that time, by Leif Hope, and he sort of held court there, out on the restaurant patio where there was an outdoor bar and plenty of room to move around and mingle.

Everyone was hot and sweaty and covered with dust from the infield. People who had hit home runs were congratulated. At this game, as at every annual game, the "Player of the Game" was selected, and this particular year it was Mort Zuckerman.

On that patio, a remnant of times past and a reminder of why they called the place the Laundry, there was a six-foot-tall metal commercial washing machine, a relic of the time before the place was converted to its present use. And it was halfway up that, on a narrow metal ledge of this contraption, that Leif stood to make the award.

"A hard-fought game," he said. "Mort? A complete game. And you batted in three runs yourself. This one's for you." And everyone applauded as Leif presented him with a jeroboam of champagne. Then Leif proceeded to announce that a record amount had been raised at the game for East Hampton Head Start.

"Largely because of the art auction and Bianca Jagger's generosity in buying many of the letters," he said, "the total this year is $18,500."

Everybody waved their beer bottles in the air and cheered for a few moments.

"Where'd you get this governor of Arkansas?" somebody shouted up at Leif. There was general laughter.

The governor had not come to the after-game party.

"Now calm down, calm down," Leif said. "He did a pretty good job."

I n the summer of 2007, Bill Clinton was at a fund-raiser in East Hampton for his wife, Hillary, just five houses down from where I live on Three Mile Harbor Road. I was there too. A whole lot of water had gone under the bridge since the day twenty years before when he had umpired our famous game. But I wondered if perhaps he had remembered it. So I asked him.

"Of course I remember it," he said. "It's in my book."

Then he looked me up and down. It seemed he was trying to remember where I fit into things on the day of that game, but soon he gave up. Then he extended his hand. As I shook it, he said, "Nice hat."

He turned to talk to someone else.

The next day, in the BookHampton bookstore, passing some time, I picked up a copy of his book *My Life* and went looking for the reference to the game. It's on page 343.

ACKNOWLEDGMENTS

THE author would like to acknowledge:

Radio personality Jean Shepherd, whose description on WOR radio of armed sanitation workers in canoes paddling through New York City's underground sewer system hunting ferocious grown alligators flushed down the toilet by Manhattan parents after six months as cute little baby alligator house pets taught me that in the media, sometimes anything is possible.

Newspaperman Harry Golden, who in 1955 founded the *Carolina Israelite,* a one-man newspaper in Charlotte, North Carolina, with the premise that Jews, North Carolina, and America should be praised, admonished, and celebrated all at the same time. He once admonished state officials for embracing a route for the proposed national highway system through the state by telling them the state would be better off if things were just left alone, because if they built this thing, motorists would not pull over to get gas, eat, spend the night, and otherwise support the North Carolina economy. He coined the phrase "Only in America."

Newspaperman I. F. Stone, who felt the federal government in Washington should be praised, admonished, and celebrated all at the same time and did so in the pages of his one-man *I. F. Stone's Weekly* between 1953 and 1971.

Public relations expert James Moran, who in the 1930s was hired by a tuna fish company that produced brown tuna fish at a time when pink tuna fish was what America thought tuna fish should look like. His job was to reverse sagging sales. Moran thought of a single line of type, which when written on the outside of the cans of the company that hired him revolutionized the entire tuna fish industry. The single line that he wrote was THIS TUNA FISH GUARANTEED NOT TO TURN PINK IN THE CAN.

Moran also, on one occasion, famously hired all sorts of people with eye maladies, rented Bunker Hill, put the people into uniforms, put the patriots at the top of the hill and the redcoats at the bottom, and yelled "Don't fire until you see the whites of their eyes!" And on another occasion he organized—for no particular reason—a party and food fight at the Waldorf-Astoria Hotel in Manhattan for any persons named either Herbert or Dominick to celebrate two popular songs of the time: "Shoot the Sherbert to Me, Herbert" and "Shoot the Meatballs to Me, Dominick Boy!" These events had a great impression on me.

High school journalism teacher Harry Friedlander, who told the class in 1956 that journalists always told the truth, that the facts belonged on the news pages and the opinions on the editorial pages—something I violently disagreed with—and once said, "If you see a big front-page headline on the *Daily*

News it doesn't mean anything, but if you see one with the same size type on the front page of the *New York Times,* don't even read it, just run."

English professor Richard Gollin at the University of Rochester, who told me that he had spoken to Dean of Students Cole and no matter what I did to hijack all the copies of the college newspaper and replace them with fake ones written and produced by the humor magazine staff that week, unless somebody got hurt, they would see to it I was not thrown out of school.

The New York Press Association, for spending twenty years before finally changing their policy, which at first was that a free newspaper did not qualify for membership in their organization because if people didn't pay for it, it wouldn't get read. Now it's okay to join, but we have to have our own special category.

The Pulitzer Prize Board for not even going that far.

T HIS book could not have happened without the help of my girlfriend, Chris Wasserstein; my agent, Scott Miller; my assistant, Joan Gray; Kelly Merritt; Joel Rodney; Jessica Murray; Alexandra Storch; Joan Zandell; my kids, Maya, Adam, David, and Gabriel; Dan King; Ingrid Lemme; Peggy Scanlon; Stuyvesant Wainwright II; Marina Van; Terri Greene; Tom Ratcliffe III; Frank Borth; Lee Brotherhood; Tom Swinimer; Emily Weitz; Roger Rosenblatt; John Reed Jr.; Robin Strong; Lyle Smith; Janet Dayton; Julie Gruen; Mary Gardiner; Susan Smyth; Eric Cohen; my editor, Julia Pastore; and Kathy Rae, who has assumed the title of publisher of *Dan's Papers* so I can step back from the business end of the paper to focus my attention on my writing, not only for future editions of the paper but for books such as these.

This book is written in remembrance of Nick Monte and my parents, Jen and Al Rattiner.

ABOUT THE AUTHOR

Dan Rattiner is best known for having created what has become the largest circulating newspaper in the Hamptons, *Dan's Papers*. He founded it in Montauk in 1960. Today, a quirky, irreverent, and informative publication, it sometimes runs more than three hundred pages a week, distributed free in more than fifteen hundred locations in Montauk, the Hamptons, the North Fork of Long Island, and Manhattan. Mr. Rattiner usually writes between three and five articles on a wide variety of topics every issue. He's been called the "Unofficial Mayor of the Hamptons."

Mr. Rattiner was born in New York City but raised in New Jersey. He moved to the eastern end of Long Island in 1956 when he was sixteen, brought there when his father bought a local drugstore, and he has been there since. He started *Dan's Papers* as a summer newspaper while in college. It is believed to be the first free newspaper in America.

He studied at the University of Rochester where he received a B.A. in English, then studied architecture at the Harvard University Graduate School of Design, but he left after three years without receiving a degree.

He has been married three times, has four children and two grandchildren, and currently lives with his significant other, Christine, in East Hampton and Manhattan.

For eight years in the 1990s, he broadcast "Dan's Hampton Report" on WQXR, the radio station of the *New York Times*.

He's written several books, has received numerous awards for his writing, and continues his work at the paper to this day. Visit his Web site www.danrattiner.com.